TREASON & BETRAYAL

How the Military Is Poisoning Its Veterans

JOHN P. LYONS
Navy SWCC

Ballast Books, LLC
www.ballastbooks.com

Copyright © 2023 by John P. Lyons

ISBN: 978-1-955026-22-2

Printed in Hong Kong

Published by Ballast Books
www.ballastbooks.com

For more information, bulk orders, appearances or speaking requests,
please email info@ballastbooks.com

Standard Disclaimer

The author is not a doctor or medical professional and does not assume any liability for any opinions expressed.

The content is not intended to be a substitute for professional medical advice, diagnosis, or treatment. Always seek the advice of your physician or other qualified health provider with any questions you may have regarding a medical condition. Never disregard professional medical advice or delay in seeking it because of something you have read in this book!

All information used in this book was collected from interviews, publicly available information, and documents available through the Freedom of Information Act (FOIA) 5 U.S.C. § 552.

Redactions have already been made by issuing government organizations to protect classified or sensitive material.

Some names have been changed to protect their identities.

All have agreed to provide evidence and testimony validating the content of this book.

As always, should you be contemplating suicide or harm to others, **dial 911** to receive professional help and assistance.

Thank you for purchasing my book. Your purchase will fund free copies to veterans and their families so that they may understand why they are getting sick; why they have experienced miscarriage, stillborn births, and post-partum; why their children have been born with birth defects; and most importantly, why they or their loved one is experiencing mental unrest or is contemplating or has already committed suicide. As you will see, it isn't their fault. It is the fault of the Department of Defense, Department of Veterans Affairs, and more.

John P. Lyons

This book has been submitted to and approved for publication by the Department of Defense and United States Navy.

Redactions have been made with the following statements added to satisfy the changes they have required:

"The views expressed in this publication are those of the author and do not necessarily reflect the official policy or position of the Department of Defense or the U.S. government."

and

"The public release clearance of this publication by the Department of Defense does not imply Department of Defense endorsement or factual accuracy of the material."

To view the redactions required by the Department of Defense, request a copy of this publication via Freedom of Information Act Request to:

DEPARTMENT OF DEFENSE
DEFENSE OFFICE OF PREPUBLICATION
AND SECURITY REVIEW
1155 DEFENSE PENTAGON
WASHINGTON, DC 20301-1155

Reference Document: February 14, 2022 Ref: 22-SB-0023

This book is dedicated to my wife, my children, and my fellow US Navy SWCCs, SEALs, Sailors, and their family members whom my actions have poisoned. They concealed this from us. I didn't know. They did not tell me. I am sorry for the miscarriages, stillborn babies, premature births, and birth defects. I am sorry for the sickness, disease, and death I may have caused you, your spouse, and children, on behalf of the United States Navy and Naval Special Warfare Command.

GMC (SWCC/SW) John Patrick Lyons
United States Navy, Retired

CONTENTS

16 September 2020

From: John P. Lyons
To: Collin Green, Commander Naval Special Warfare Command

Subj: MALICIOUS RETRIBUTION AND RETALIATION ICO JOHN P. LYONS

Admiral Green, on the enclosed disc, you will find a copy of the book I have promised you for the past few years. Still being edited, it will be published in the very near future.

The first of two books, you will find your actions, and those of your predecessors, exposed for the world to see. Volume One, *The Science,* chronicles the consequences of those actions to your fellow Navy SEALs and their families that you have betrayed. Volume Two, *Treason and Betrayal,* lays out step by step the malicious retribution, retaliation, and betrayal executed by Admiral Brian Losey, his staff, you, and others up to President Donald Trump himself to conceal it. Actions you continue to engage in requiring my photo on BOLO posters taped to the walls of your buildings calling for my arrest.

For years, I have sent you and everyone in my chain of command evidence documenting those you continue to employ have lied, falsified reports and documents, made false statements to federal investigators, and committed perjury during a federal hearing. John Bacon, Barry Francis, Jeff Fishel, Walter French, Navy SEAL Warrant Officer Joseph Fischer, and more. Evidence that they knew all along that they were poisoning me, every Navy SEAL, SWCC, and our families. Evidence of malicious retribution and retaliation against me to conceal their actions to maintain pay and position. Instead of firing them and fixing your programs, you keep them and allow the poisoning to continue.

Despite my offers to settle the wrongful termination lawsuit we are engaged in and assist you in stopping this poisoning, you persist in committing fraud against the government and relying on the illegal activities of your employees to cover it up. Felonies, Admiral, you are responsible for as well. Haven't you, your attorneys, NCIS, and the Navy Inspector General learned your lesson from the recent Eddie Gallagher case?

After reading this book, your attorney will confirm the window of opportunity for you to take decisive action to right the wrongs committed by your predecessors, you, and your staff is quickly closing. One way or the other, those under your command will be made safe and those responsible for our poisoning will be held accountable. It is my sincere hope you make the right choice and take action now.

I suppose I, your Navy SEALs and SWCCs, every Veteran, their families, and the citizens of this great nation owe you and the Navy our gratitude. It was your actions that allowed me the opportunity to make the discoveries that will make the world a better place.

John P. Lyons
GMC(SWCC/SW)
USN Retired

BOLO
<u>B</u>e <u>O</u>n the <u>L</u>ook<u>O</u>ut

JOHN P. LYONS

Retired Navy Chief John P. Lyons has been deemed
a hazard to Naval personnel and facilities and is barred
from all Naval property and installations in the
Southwest United States. These include military housing,
gas stations, stores, medical facilities and within
100 yards of docks, piers and shoreline.
If seen, immediately call 911 and report.

I would have given my life in service to my country.
What I did not know was that they have taken it anyway.

John P. Lyons
August 18, 2016

CHAPTER 1
Living with Lead

May 30, 2019

I awoke to the sound of muffled coughing and the smell of bile and feces permeating my room. As I lay in the early morning darkness, half-asleep, I listened to the quiet murmurings of a nurse telling the patient at the far end of the room that it would be an hour or more before fresh bedding could be arranged. The window shade to the left of my bed was open, revealing the lights of a city still asleep. Through the darkness and curtains that separated us, I could hear the soft voice of a wife quietly attempting to calm and console her husband.

I lay in a four-man room with three other veterans in the Veterans Affairs Medical Center in La Jolla, California. The day before, I'd had surgery for a total hip replacement, one of almost a dozen surgeries I have received as a result of a very active military career. I was recovering in a room, staying overnight, and would be discharged later that morning.

Dozing in and out, I listened as the hospital slowly came alive. Later, my surgical team stopped by to check on my progress. They informed me that I would be going home as soon as the discharge paperwork was processed. This was not so for the older veteran next to me on the other side of the curtain. He was dying.

Disturbed, I listened curiously as hospital staff told him that they were discharging him. He replied that he "lived alone" and had "no one to care for him." They persisted, providing options for twenty-four-hour care and in-home hospice services. I asked myself, "Aren't they listening? He wants to stay. He doesn't want to go home to an empty house, alone, to await the end."

After breakfast, I overheard conversations identifying my other two roommates, who were dying as well. Two beds down, one of the veterans and a chaplain were discussing the end. In a one-sided conversation, the chaplain was telling the vet how to come to peace with and prepare for his death. At the far end of the room, I listened as a doctor apologized to the other man in the room and his wife, the ones who had awoken me before dawn.

The doctor told him he was sorry, but he wasn't on the medical team that had been working with him before. "Instead," he told the patient and his wife, "I'm here now and can work with you on how to proceed in the coming months." I listened as he continued, "You need to concentrate on how to proceed now, instead of focusing on why you weren't diagnosed earlier."

I learned the patient was a retired Navy captain. He and his wife were attempting to cope with the fact that the VA had failed to identify and treat his cancer earlier. The doctor told him, "By the time we caught it, the cancer had spread to a point that treatment will have little effect," and explained, "I've had other similar cases where people have lived for up to four months, or not."

"God," I thought, "I can't wait to get the hell out of this room and away from this hospital."

Later, as my wife wheeled me out after lunch, I recognized the retired Navy captain as an officer I'd worked with at some point during my naval career. As I passed by, I couldn't see his name, but our eyes locked.

I instantly recognized his and his wife's sense of lost hope, anger, confusion; the frustration on their faces; and the beginnings of the forlorn acceptance of their fate. "At least," I thought, "they get to prepare for the end, see his family a few more times, and have those last conversations." My last thought as I left the building was, "My God, he's only in his late fifties too."

Three days earlier, I had received a phone call from my good friend and brother Navy Special Warfare Combatant-Craft Crewman (SWCC). A man I'll call Joker, he still works for Naval Special Warfare Command, still serves our country today. You'll note that I use nicknames throughout the book for those whose identity needs to remain classified.

Joker and I had served together and have been good friends for over twenty-five years. Joker has the rare talent of finding humor in even the most absolute worst situations, putting those around him at ease. Joker was calling to notify me that another coworker, friend, and Navy SWCC brother of ours had died.

He went on to tell me that Master Chief Pat Battles had collapsed on the floor of the locker room of the Naval Special Warfare Command headquarters building on Coronado Island in California. He had been changing his clothes after working out, preparing to start a new day.

I was shocked. I told Joker, "My God, the last time I saw Pat, we were in our pickup trucks, stopped at a red light in Dam Neck, Virginia. We had nodded our heads in acknowledgment, and then he waved and smiled at me as he pulled away."

Pat had served in the Navy for thirty years only to die alone on the floor, without his family, from massive heart failure. He was a good friend and mentor. Pat was fifty-seven years old. I will always remember his smile.

Joker and I briefly discussed the deaths of other coworkers and friends. "Bohica," Master Chief SWCC Kelly Webb, too, had died from massive heart failure. Kelly was fifty-nine. We spoke of Navy SWCC Cleatus Doyle Jr., who died at forty-one years of age—again, from massive heart failure.[Photo 1.1]

Navy Chief Marley Jones had also died from massive heart failure. She died right in front of Joker at Naval Special Warfare Unit FOUR in Puerto Rico. Marley had simply stood up from the table she was seated at to give a speech during a Christmas party in 2001. Her last words, as she collapsed to the floor in the Commanding

Officer's arms, were "oh my." Joker guessed that she was in her early forties too. We went on to discuss the death of Diamond Dave Shields. A great Navy SEAL we both worked with and liked very much. Always joking and smiling, Diamond had also died of massive heart failure at fifty.

We discussed Joker's own heart attack when he was forty-seven. We went on to describe the high blood pressure, hypertension, and other illnesses, disease, and injuries a career spent serving our country had bestowed upon us.

When I got off the phone with Joker, I called another good friend and coworker of ours, Wilson W. Wilson. Named after the *Tool Time* character whose face you never saw, Wilson is one of the smartest people I have ever met. I relayed the news about Pat Battles. Wilson replied that he had just found out. Word of Pat's death had spread like wildfire throughout Naval Special Warfare Command, where he and Wilson worked. He was just as disturbed as Joker and me at the circumstances surrounding Pat Battles's death. It was all too familiar.

We discussed Wilson's call on Thanksgiving Day in 2013. He had called to tell me that my coworker, retired Navy SEAL Dennis Gilbert, had passed away. Wilson said that Dennis had just dropped dead on a mountain trail while running with his son-in-law, preparing for yet another cross-country marathon. Dennis died from massive heart failure. Wilson and I thought Dennis had been fifty-six. Wilson also said another friend and coworker, Navy Master Chief Gunners Mate Foy Harris, had died.

Wilson knew that I had served with Foy since 1987. Despite being in phenomenal shape his entire career and establishing competitive body building as a sport within the Navy, Foy had died of heart failure after completing thirty years in the Navy at the age of fifty-four. Wilson knew Diamond Dave Fields, and we discussed his death as well.

Then there was a retired Navy SWCC Master Chief I had known and served with for over twenty years. Big Dawg had recently collapsed in Wilson's arms from a massive heart attack while at work.

If he had not gone into work that morning or if Wilson hadn't been there to assist him and call 911, he, too, would have been just another casualty found dead on the floor in the Naval Special Warfare Command building or on the boat where he lived without ever being heard from again. He was fifty-four. There are many, many more.

What do Joker, Wilson, Pat, Kelly, Cleatus, Marley, Diamond Dave, Dennis, Foy, Big Dawg, the others, and I have in common? We were all Navy SWCCs, SEALs, Special Forces, and veterans who had dedicated and sacrificed the best years of our health and youth in service to our country.

For decades, we'd kept our bodies in top fighting form. We began each day with a minimum two-hour workout, three- to seven-mile runs, and two thousand–meter swims performed five days a week, seven days a week when deployed. On weekends and during vacations, we could not get away from the need to work out—our bodies demanding the exercise.

We maintained our health and fitness, even after retirement, out of habit and concern for our futures. More importantly, we were all weapons technicians, experts, and warriors. We used, carried, ate, slept, lived with, and were exposed to all manner of weapons and ordnance during our decades of service. What we did not know—what the military did not tell us and what was concealed from us—was that we and our families were being poisoned, day in and day out, throughout our entire military careers. Poisoning that our government knew about and that would continue for at least forty years after we had retired and were no longer exposed.

Poisoning that would kill us, robbing us and our families of the retirement years we had worked so hard to achieve. Surviving war and riding ships "through thunder shattered hurricanes,"[1] we were poisoned by 146 hazardous and toxic compounds identified by the Department of Defense (DoD) over twenty years ago.[2]

Toxic compounds recognized by the Department of Defense, US Army, US Navy, US Air Force, US Marine Corps, Veterans Affairs (VA), Centers for Disease Control and Prevention (CDC), the National Institute for Occupational Safety and Health (NIOSH), the US Environmental Protection Agency (EPA), the Department of Labor, the Occupational Safety and Health Administration (OSHA), the Department of Health and Human Services, and multiple other federal, state, and local departments and government agencies for up to fifty years or more.[3]

Poisoning that caused the deaths of my friends and coworkers. Poisoning that caused my wife, my friends, coworkers, and their families premature births, miscarriages, birth defects, and other illnesses and disease. Poisoning that caused violence, suicide, and death. Poisoning that is slowly killing me.

I am retired Navy Chief John P. Lyons. More correctly, I am Retired Special Warfare Combatant-Craft Crewman and Surface Warfare designated Gunners Mate Chief Petty Officer John Patrick Lyons of Pearland, Texas. I am an accredited Navy and special operations boat, weapons, ordnance, LASER, and gun-firing range expert and instructor with more than thirty years of experience.

I had spent roughly half of my twenty-four-year active-duty career in Special Operations Command as a Navy SWCC working for Naval Special Warfare Command. The other half, I rode big gray ships as a weapons and ordnance specialist, instructor, and ship driver. SWCCs or Navy Special Warfare Combat Crewman are the little-known brothers of the infamous Navy SEALs. We drive high speed boats.

SWCCs employ light, fast, heavily armed boats and other craft conducting special operations on and around rivers and the coastal regions of the world. [Photos 1.2-1.3] We specialize in clandestine and (Redacted[101]), over the horizon, insert or extract of special operations and (Redacted[101]). We perform reconnaissance missions gathering intelligence on military installations, shipping and other targets of interest. We conduct direct action interdiction missions and joint operations and training with both foreign and domestic military and law enforcement personnel. What pisses off most Navy SEALs is that when they get in trouble, they call us to bail them out.

Commonly referred to as the "taxi drivers" of the SEALs by the jealous and ignorant, we perform the vast majority of our missions at night, in inclement weather, and the only Navy SEALs onboard may be the occasional officer. Hah! In fact, when you see the Navy SEAL infomercials and videos featuring fast boats leaping across the water, it is all a lie! Those are Navy SWCCs like me. The SEALs are just the seasick passengers along for the ride and, as usual, talk shit and try to hog all the glory!

The only boats SEALs drive are the little black rubber blow up boats you see in videos as they paddle through the waves at the beach. Funny thing is, if their little 25 horsepower outboard motor breaks down, more often than not, the SEALs will just sit around waiting to be rescued by us SWCCs because they lack the skills to fix and keep their boat running.

SWCCs drive 5000 horsepower high-speed boats! From 24-foot Guardians and Hurricanes up through 65-, 68-, 82- and 171-foot Mk 3 and 4 Sea Specters, Mk V Special Operations Craft and Typhoon Class Patrol Coastals. We don't just drive them; experts in weapons, communications, navigation, and engineering, we maintain them as well.

I had begun my Navy SWCC career assigned to Special Boat Unit 26 in Central America. That is where today's SWCCs were born. The progeny of the Vietnam era brown water Navy, Special Boat Unit 26 was established in 1987 at Rodman Naval Station, Panama. Officially, its mission was the defense of the Panama Canal Zone and to provide Mobile Training Teams to Central and South American Countries.

Unofficially, Dirty Boat Guys like me trained and served alongside the Navy SEALs at Naval Special Warfare Unit Eight. We worked all of Central and South America, from Bolivia to El Salvador, conducting counter narcotic operations.

Definitely not a standard Navy Harbor Patrol Unit or SEAL taxi service, SBU-26 had a unique relationship with (Redacted[101]   ) back in the states. We were trained by and operated with many of the SEALs (Redacted[101]   ). If you have ever read Richard Marcinko's books, *Rogue Warrior*, *Red Cell*, etc., then you will recognize names like Horseface and Indian Jew. The SEALs that trained us were Vietnam Vets and the real deal. At the time, if you were a Navy SEAL or riverine-based boat guy that trained to operate in the jungle, you came down to Panama to do it.

Before I continue, let me set the record straight. SWCCs and SEALs may seem to get along like oil and water, but the reality is we are brothers. Family. We may tear into each other, occasionally breaking a nose or finger in a fight, choking each other out or playing Friday morning jungle rules water polo in the Combat Training Tank on Coronado Island, and that's ok. Life on the edge is brutal, and it takes brutal men to get the job done. Sweat, blood, and bruises are the glue that binds us together.

When push comes to shove, at 2:30 a.m., when a couple of Navy SEALs leave the beach of a hostile country, swim two miles through reefs and shark-infested waters, battling the current and five-foot swells, on a dark, rainy, overcast night when night vision goggles are useless, they know they can depend upon us to be there for them.

We will travel hundreds of miles, in bad weather, avoiding all maritime traffic and our adversaries, conducting precision navigation, taking into account the wind, tides, and current, to arrive precisely at the time and point we need to be, to pick them out of the water, shove a thermos full of hot soup into their hands, and get them home safely. They know that when the shit hits the fan and they need a hot extract, after being discovered and taking fire, we will not hesitate to come barreling in laying down massive amounts of firepower to get them to safety.

Today, for my troubles, after a twenty-nine-year Navy career working with weapons and at shooting ranges, at age fifty-nine, I suffer from lead and firearms poisoning. The symptoms, sickness, and disease will eventually kill me—kill me long before my wife, family, and I get a chance at a full retirement—as it has the other men and women listed here.

The day before my surgery in May of 2019, I received a letter from the VA notifying me that I had yet another symptom of poisoning: "borderline dilation of the aortic arch contour, which can be seen with hypertension." My high blood pressure had been caught and diagnosed by the Navy in 1999, upgraded to hypertension by the VA in 2009, and then finally culminated in hypertensive heart disease in 2019.

The hypertension had been caused by decades of continued exposure to lead and firearms poisoning, chronic long-term stress, and the many other hazards and comorbidities experienced throughout my entire military career. After exposure ceased six years ago in 2014, blood tests have revealed that I am still being poisoned by lead. Today at 5.3 mcg/dL of blood, my blood lead level remains more than twice that of the average adult.

Navy and government reports, which I will reveal here, document that I am destined to live with lead leaching out of my bones while it will continue to poison me for the next thirty-four or more years.

As a former combat medic and EMT, I had to look it up to understand what had caused not only my heart problems but also those of my friends and their deaths. It is simple, really.

The aorta is adjacent to the heart. It is the largest blood vessel in the body. Decades of service to my country resulted in damage of the aorta and circulatory system by high blood pressure and hypertension. Conditions induced by chronic long-term stress, firearms and lead poisoning, and the 145 other toxic and hazardous compounds produced when firing guns and expending ordnance eventually results in the weakening of the walls of the aorta.

Unable to maintain its integrity, the aorta swells and, like a balloon, can pop at any time. This results in an immediate loss of blood flow, causing instant heart failure, stroke, or death. The entire body quickly dies due to lack of oxygen. Remember Navy Chief Marley Jones? It happened so quickly that the only words she could utter before dropping to the floor, dead, were "Oh my!" Dennis Gilbert died instantly in front of his son-in-law. Foy Harris died in front of his wife after getting into the passenger seat of their car as they were leaving for the emergency room. Pat Battles and others died alone, in silence, with no one to catch them as they fell.

In 2009, after retiring from the Navy on active duty, I continued to train Navy SWCCs, SEALs, and Special Forces. I was employed by Naval Special Warfare Command as a Department of Defense firing range employee. SEAL Teams ONE, THREE, FIVE and SEVEN were my primary customers. My fellow SWCCs at Special Boat Team TWELVE and other local naval commands used the range as well.

Day in and day out, I opened the Naval Special Warfare Group ONE Indoor Shooting Range at 6 a.m. As the Primary Range Safety Officer, weapons, and LASER instructor, I ran pistol, rifle, and LASER firing evolutions Monday through Friday until 4 p.m. I worked nights and weekends too covering SEAL and SEAL Reserve Team training.

Five years later, in June of 2014, it was discovered that I had been horribly poisoned with lead. A Navy blood test revealed I had a blood lead level (BLL) of 66 mcg/dL (micrograms per deciliter of blood). That blood test began a journey that would explain the sickness and disease I had suffered for over two decades as well as reveal the cause of so much suicide, death, and tragedy experienced by our veterans, their families, law enforcement, first responders, and many others in our country.

After I found out how seriously poisoned I was by lead, I was then fired for whistleblowing. Whistleblowing about how my supervisors and the safety department personnel within Naval Special Warfare Command had poisoned me. Not just me but every Navy SWCC, SEAL, and person who had been exposed to the weapons and ordnance they were responsible for. Poisoning that Naval Special Warfare Command, the Department of the Navy, and the Department of Defense had concealed from all of us for over twenty years.

Naval Special Warfare didn't just fire me; they went out of their way to maliciously attack my career and reputation. They removed my security clearance, barred me from all naval property in the

Southwest United States, hung BOLO posters in buildings in the region calling for my arrest if spotted on base, and even called friends and coworkers telling them I was dangerous and might try to enter the facilities they worked at to do them harm.

I was barred from naval commissaries, exchanges, gas stations, the naval housing both my niece and son lived in, and even the naval hospital and medical clinics in the region. I could not take advantage of the benefits I had earned through three decades of honorable service nor even see my doctor to get medical care.

They did this in an effort to ensure I was no longer employable and to drive my family and me into submission and bankruptcy. In 2016, after filing a wrongful termination lawsuit, the Navy offered to settle during mitigation. Their offer? If I signed a nondisclosure agreement to never discuss my poisoning and Naval Special Warfare Command's actions again, they would officially change my termination to "resigned," remove my Barment from naval property, reinstate my security clearance, and pay my attorney and court costs to date. That's it. Nothing else. I laughed.

Never a quitter, I declined.

As I investigated further, via Freedom of Information Act (FOIA) requests, I discovered years of emails, official reports, statements, and documents they had falsified to cover it up. To cover up their actions, I learned that my supervisors had begun attacking me as early as 2010, four years prior to my termination.

This included personal attacks that labeled me as prejudiced, racist, and mentally unfit in an effort to prevent my being promoted to Naval Special Warfare Group ONE Safety Manager, a position that would have revealed what I later discovered after being fired for whistleblowing. My supervisor and safety personnel had concealed the official Navy reports that documented my poisoning and dismantled the lead safety programs in 2010 that would have prevented it. Not just me, every other person that used the 105 ranges they were responsible for.

Malicious allegations concealed from me for five years, used behind my back by my supervisors to defame my character and career to conceal their violations of Navy, Department of Defense, and federal laws and regulations. Laws and regulations that would have prevented my poisoning, as well as that of my fellow SWCCs, SEALs, and our families. Allegations that, once revealed, were proven false by all of my annual performance appraisals, multiple official reports, emails, personal awards, and medals—they were simply lies to cover up their laziness, incompetence, and willingness to break the law.

In 2015, I had whistle blown my findings to Admiral Brian Losey, Commander Naval Special Warfare Command. I presented him evidence of criminal activity and retribution and retaliation conducted by his employees. I presented evidence that his Safety and Occupational Health Department employees had failed to do their jobs, had no functioning programs, dismantled existing programs, and were not in compliance with mandatory Navy, DoD, and federal laws and regulations. This included evidence that they had falsified and concealed official reports and were poisoning every Navy SWCC, SEAL, affected employee, and their families. He did nothing. He was under investigation and later found guilty of retribution and retaliation himself. He was forced to retire by Congress in 2016, because of his dishonorable, illegal activities.

I then whistle blew the information to Brian Losey's boss, Chief of Naval Operations Admiral John Richardson. John would reveal during his speech at Brian Losey's retirement that they had been good friends since being stationed together in Hawaii years earlier. He did nothing.

In 2016, after filing a wrongful termination lawsuit with the Merit Systems Protection Board, the case, and subsequent hearing, revealed that the Navy had terminated me using evidence and statements it knew to be false and untrue. The hearing revealed the Navy had presented falsified official statements, documents, and reports and that Navy personnel had colluded on and presented false statements to the federal judge, under oath, known untrue. Fraud and perjury.

The judge's initial decision? The Navy had committed retribution and retaliation in firing me.

The judge then ruled that they would have fired me anyway. The judge based her decision on the falsified documents and testimony presented by the Navy at the hearing ignoring that I had never been counseled or received a negative performance appraisal. Ever.

Continuing to investigate, I discovered more evidence corroborating false statements made by my supervisors to senior naval officers and officials, federal investigators and during the federal hearing. I would receive documents through Freedom of Information Act responses that the Navy had recognized that my supervisors and safety personnel had colluded to conceal and falsify statements and testimony that the Navy relied upon for my termination. Still, they did nothing; it is a cover-up.

I would go on to expose that they were poisoning not just me, but every Navy SWCC, SEAL, sailor, employee, and family member exposed to the weapons, ordnance, and ranges that my supervisors and the Navy were/are responsible for. Not just the Navy, I would expose the entire Department of Defense doing the same. Poisoning that had occurred over my entire career.

As I continued whistleblowing my findings up the chain of command through the secretaries of Labor, the Navy, and the Department of Defense, I was met with further denial and inaction. At every step, I asked myself, "What are they hiding? Why aren't they taking action to stop this poisoning and hold those who are responsible accountable?"

I reported my findings to OSHA only to learn that OSHA had failed to file violations for crimes committed by the Navy. I learned that my supervisors had lied to the OSHA compliance inspector for my case and that she had resigned after the official report had been filed.

I then presented seven years of official Navy reports to the director of OSHA San Diego Area Western Region, containing dozens of federal law violations chronicling how I and every Navy SWCC and

SEAL and their family members were being poisoned. Andrea J. Reid, OSHA San Diego Area Director, ignored my submissions.

At a meeting at the Naval Criminal Investigative Service (NCIS) offices on the San Diego 32nd Street Naval Station, Ms. Reid confirmed for the NCIS that my supervisors had presented falsified information to her and the OSHA compliance inspector during their investigation of my place of employment. Her comments, actions, and failure to investigate make her complicit in the cover-up of our poisoning as well. Poisoning that she continues to allow to this day.

I reported this to both Naval and Department of Defense criminal investigative services. I handed them evidence of falsified official documents and the proof of falsifying statements to federal investigators and perjury under oath during a federal hearing. I learned that David Salazar, the NCIS agent who assured me they had the necessary evidence to proceed and convict, was no longer employed and the case had been closed. The agent I spoke with refused to tell me if he had resigned or been fired.

I reported this to the Office of Special Counsel and the Navy and Department of Labor Inspector Generals. I uncovered evidence that Navy Deputy Inspector General Catherine Donovan was complicit in the cover-up as well. I continued to dig until I found out why.

I had discovered Admiral Brian Losey, Admiral John Richardson, and the Office of the Navy Inspector General all responsible for our poisoning and complicit in the cover-up. Per mandatory naval regulations found in the Navy Safety and Occupational Health Program Manual OPNAVINST 5100.23G, they, as well as every Navy SEAL admiral I have reported my findings to (including Admiral Collin Green), are personally responsible to ensure the Navy and their commands have functioning safety programs in full compliance with Navy, Department of Defense, and OSHA regulations. They do not.

They were/are responsible to conduct the daily, monthly, semiannual, annual, and three-year inspections and program reviews necessary to ensure compliance. The evidence I uncovered documents they failed to do their jobs. They were/are also responsible per naval and OSHA regulations to notify their employees when they are being poisoned. Instead, they conceal reports and lie, telling us we are not being poisoned and *there is no source of poison* in our place of employment.

Even now in 2021, Naval Special Warfare Command continues to ignore FOIA requests concealing reports documenting their employees' poisoning. Reports requested by the doctors of those poisoned vital for their successful treatment and recovery.

I sent this information to both parties of the Senate and House of Representatives. Only goose eggs, nada, nothing but crickets, and no action taken to hold anyone accountable or address my findings. No action to stop or address our poisoning.

I discovered that Congress had been briefed on our poisoning in 2012[26] and were made aware of the consequences to veterans and our families. Made aware that Department of Defense (Army, Navy, Airforce, Marine Corps), Veterans Affairs, and OSHA regulations were dated and did not protect us from lead poisoning. It was making us sick and killing us. They did nothing.

I whistle blew this information to their boss, the chief executive officer of the United States government and commander in chief of all US Armed Forces, President Donald Trump. After receiving a nice memo thanking me for my submission, he did nothing, took no action. The people responsible are still employed, and the poisoning continues.

In November 2019, I sent a whistleblower complaint to Attorney General William Barr and made every senator and member of Congress aware of it. No one has contacted me.

I continued to ask myself, "What are they hiding? Why aren't they doing something about this?"

During the second week of March 2020, I received a text from a close family friend. Sal was a Navy sailor I had known and worked with since 2005. After retirement, we remained good friends. Sal had written:

John,

How are you doing? Did you move to Texas yet? If you need another idea for the book, research the effects that burn pits in Iraq and Afghanistan are having on vets. It's the new Agent Orange, and I am experiencing some of the side effects.

Hope all is well,

Sal

I called Sal that evening and found out he suffers from symptoms of poisoning as well, symptoms experienced by the victims of both military burn pits and firearms poisoning. Exposures he, too, had experienced throughout his twenty-year career. I told Sal about what I'd uncovered and apologized for my role in his poisoning. I hadn't known.

I promised to look into it deeper, and as you will see, it led to unimaginable discoveries and further betrayal by our government. At Sal's urging, I had found what our senior government officials had been concealing from us all along, the reason why they were reluctant to address our poisoning and its consequences. Finally, I had the answer.

What began as simple sloth, incompetence, and a cover-up by my supervisors Shaun Marriott, Barry Francis, Jeff Fishel, and Warrant Officer Joseph Fischer; Naval Special Warfare Group ONE Safety Department Director John Bacon and Safety Manager Walter "Skip" French; Naval Special Warfare Command's Admirals Brian Losey, Collin Green, and more; Chief of Naval Operations Admiral John Richardson; Navy Deputy Inspector General Catherine Donovan; and all the Navy, Department of Defense, and OSHA personnel responsible, was kept hidden by multiple admirals and personnel within the highest levels of government and resulted in the revelation of an epidemic of poisoning that affects not just veterans, but also the rest of the nation and world in general.

This willful negligence, conspiracy, and cover-up occurred at the highest levels of a government that knowingly exploited its veterans, law enforcement, first responders, and their families. The government ignored the evidence and allowed its citizens, communities, and environment to be poisoned while taking no action to mitigate or stop it.

But that is not what this book is about; that will be addressed in detail in the near future in Volume 2. This book reveals what they are hiding and the science behind it. Here, you will discover and review the existing research that validates my findings.

Using government reports and documents, I will reveal the source of this poisoning and how it spreads throughout our lives. Together, we will look at the cause of the sickness and disease it is responsible for and discuss the consequences of this poisoning to our loved ones, surrounding communities, and society. I will identify who knew what and when, including what they did or did not do to stop it.

Most importantly, I will reveal the cause of the increase in veteran, law enforcement, and first responder suicide. I will link the source, sickness, disease, and death to firearms, Agent Orange, Gulf War Syndrome, military burn pits, World Trade Center, and other poisoning.

You will discover the VA and government's utter failure to treat and address our poisoning. I will document gross—if not criminal—negligence, fraud, conspiracy to cover up, and malpractice in misdiagnosing and mistreating veterans and their family members. This malpractice is driving veterans to suicide and their families into poverty. Veterans and their survivors who were denied treatment and benefits because of it.

Although much of the information revealed here concerns military exposures and testing, this book is not just for the military and their families. It is simple, really. Military personnel and their families comprise the single largest demographic of those who were chronically exposed to this poisoning over long periods of time, many who were and are firing weapons, working on and in contaminated machinations of war and facilities, and wearing contaminated clothing while eating and sleeping with weapons and gear. This demographic is being poisoned daily and spreading it by secondhand contact throughout their environment, their surrounding communities, and in their homes—poisoning their friends, families, and loved ones.

The government, Department of Defense, and their subordinate departments all have extensive medical, safety, and occupational health departments that have produced a large body of published works as well as reports that are subject to the Freedom of Information Act. After nearly thirty years as a government weapons expert, I know where to look and how to get them.

Investigations and official reports that were falsified and concealed. Documents and research that Congress, the US government, and the military have ignored. Federal laws passed by Congress that have been blatantly disregarded. Actions taken by Congress to hinder enforcement and programs that would have prevented the poisoning of our veterans, our nation, its people, and the environment that continues today.

After the military, the one million or so law enforcement officers in this country and their families comprise the second largest demographic. Wearing contaminated weapons, gear, and clothing daily, this demographic is being poisoned and spreading these hazardous and toxic compounds throughout their workplaces, vehicles, and homes. They poison themselves and their families without ever knowing it. As law enforcement agencies are spread out among federal, state, and local agencies nationwide, no coordination of effort exists to examine this problem.

Next are the firing range employees, those who work in ammunition and weapons sales, reloading, refurbishment, and repair. This includes those who handle the contaminated items that permeate our society and environment. These people generally do not fire weapons daily but work in contaminated facilities with contaminated equipment and are poisoning themselves and their families daily through secondhand exposure via the "Toxic Hand-Off."[4]

Then there are the fifty million shooting-sport participants[5] and their families who are being poisoned by the exposure their hobby bestows upon them. On one end of this spectrum are the competitive shooters who avidly participate in paramilitary-style competitions, exposing themselves and their families to tremendous poison and contamination levels. At the other, the hunter or home defense shooter who fires less than a box of ammo per year, harvesting game to fill the freezer, or occasionally practicing to maintain weapons proficiency for home defense.

Arguably, the largest demographic is the surrounding communities and environment. This demographic does not even realize the danger of poisoning by the spread of toxic particles down to smaller than 2.5 microns[6] through secondhand exposure, toxic particles that range in size from visible dust to smaller than a red blood cell.[7] The secondhand exposure they encounter is being spread to every aspect of our daily lives by those in our communities.

I am not an author. I cannot even type due to injuries suffered during my military career. Writing this is hard for me, and as the clock winds down on my health, I do not have the time necessary to produce a best-selling work of art. This information has to get out so that those like me can keep from getting sick and poisoning our families, coworkers, surrounding communities, and the environment. This has to be revealed to prevent further violence, birth defects, sickness, disease, and death by these hazardous and toxic compounds.

This has to be disclosed to educate the public on the cause of increases in veteran, law enforcement, and first responder suicide and the sickness, disease, and death caused daily by Agent Orange, Gulf War Syndrome, and military burn pits. As you will come to realize, all are connected. I have to divulge these truths before this poisoning takes my life, like it has for those I have lost already. At fifty-nine, my time is running out.

How's my investigation into the Naval Special Warfare Command cover-up and whistleblowing going? In 2020 and 2021, I have received FOIA responses from NCIS and Naval Special Warfare Command confirming they have conducted internal investigations recognizing my supervisors' illegal activities. Internal documents recognizing the falsified information used for my termination and in the Merit Systems Protection Board Wrongful Termination Case we are still engaged in.

Despite this, the Navy continues to employ these individuals in violation of multiple Navy and Department of Defense regulations and federal law. They refuse to withdraw my termination, reinstate me, and settle the case. Instead, Naval Special Warfare Command and the Department of the Navy continue to engage in retribution and retaliation against a whistleblower in an attempt to cover up our poisoning. In short, they know what I know and cannot afford to let me get the information out. As you will find in the upcoming book, it gets much worse.

CHAPTER 2
What Is Firearms Poisoning?

Before we get started, you will note that official United States government reports are presented almost exclusively to document this poisoning. This is done to clearly establish full culpability for taking no action to stop the continued poisoning of our military and law enforcement, as well as the fifty million people who participate in shooting sports per year, their families, surrounding communities, and the environment.

Full culpability for the failure to act is established by the United States government, the president and chief executive officer of our government, Congress, and various department heads from the Department of Labor (OSHA), Veterans Affairs, Departments of Defense, Army, Navy, Air Force, and so on.

Full culpability is established by the US government and every other government organization, business, or entity who failed to comply with federal law and regulations, beginning with the OSHA General Duty Clause of the United States Occupational Safety and Health Act of 1970[8] 29 U.S.C. § 654 5(a)1:

*Each employer shall furnish to each of his employees employment and a place of employment which are free from **recognized hazards** that are causing or are likely to cause death or serious physical harm to his employees.*

The term *recognized hazard* is used repeatedly throughout this book to establish that the United States government, as an employer, is fully culpable for poisoning its employees and responsible for providing treatment, benefits, and damages to those it failed to protect.

First, let me present a brief history of legislation enacted by Congress and the government that recognizes the hazards of this poisoning and its sources as it spreads throughout our communities.

The early 1970s saw a brief proliferation of legislation enacted to protect Americans from lead and other toxic and hazardous compounds. President Richard M. Nixon signed into law the United States Occupational Safety and Health Act of 1970,[3] the Clean Air Act,[9] the Lead-Based Paint Poisoning Prevention Act of 1971,[10] and the Clean Water Act of 1972.[11] The next significant legislation did not occur until twenty years later. In 1990, amendments to the Clean Air Act were passed that recognized and banned the use of lead in gasoline.

Despite what you will discover here, no new significant legislation has been enacted by Congress to address lead and firearms poisoning in our country over the last thirty years. To the contrary, as I will reveal later, Congress has continued to pass legislation ensuring this poisoning continues to spread unchecked throughout our society, while protecting the government, its employees, and special interests from accountability.

Worse, despite new discoveries made by multiple government agencies over twenty years ago recognizing the source, route, and cause of this poisoning, Congress and our government have turned a deaf ear to the plight of our country in dealing with its consequences. As you will see, this mass negligence has had severe implications on our veterans, our nation, and our children.

US Army Environmental Center (USAEC) Contract No. GS-10F-0131K, Order No. DAKF11-01-F-0072, and the Environmental Protection Agency's AP 42, Fifth Edition, Volume I, Chapter 15: Ordnance Detonation

In 2000: *Due to the lack of credible data concerning emissions from training ordnance when used in their tactical configurations, the*

U.S. Army Environmental Center (USAEC) established a program to quantify emissions from the detonation of ordnance.[6]

Perusing the historical documents on the Environmental Protection Agency's (EPA) Air Emissions Factors and Quantification Compilation of Air Emissions Factors (AP 42) website[6] establishes that the EPA first published its AP 42 in 1968 under the US Department of Health, Education, and Welfare. The AP 42 was issued for use by local, state, and federal agencies to provide accurate data on the quantity and characteristics of emissions from sources that contribute to air pollution.

In 1971, the AP 42 was transferred to the US Environmental Protection Agency.

In 2004, the US Environmental Protection Agency published Chapter 15 of the AP 42. Chapter 15 consists of test results of ordnance detonations compiled by the Department of Defense and the US Army via USAEC Contract No. GS-10F-0131K. Further updates were published by the EPA in 2006 and 2007. Chapter 15 states:

> *The information in this document has been funded by the U.S. Army Environmental Center (USAEC) and prepared by MACTEC Federal Programs, Inc., under Contract No. GS-10F-0131K, Order No. DAKF11-01-F-0072. It has been reviewed by the U.S. Environmental Protection Agency (EPA) Office of Air Quality Planning and Standards (OAQPS) and has been approved for publication.*

Beginning in 2000, the US Army conducted tests on ordnance used throughout the Department of Defense at its Aberdeen and Dugway Proving Grounds. The tests were conducted to determine what compounds were produced when detonating ordnance and firing guns.

The army tested everything from .22 caliber long rifle bullets through 120 mm tank and 155 mm artillery-propelling charges. They tested grenades, rocket motors, demolitions, illumination, and signaling and pyrotechnic devices. The army test results identified and *recognized hazards that are causing or are likely to cause death or serious physical harm to his employees,*[8] listing 146 hazardous and toxic compounds produced by ordnance.[6] Test results document that not all ordnance in use by the Department of Defense was tested. The tests listed in today's AP 42 Chapter 15 chronicle only the ordnance used by the army from 2000 to 2006.

Despite recognizing the hazardous and toxic compounds that our military and civilian government personnel and the environment are exposed to, the Department of Defense and government has not added any other ordnance to this list since 2006. Ordnance in use by civilians, the Air Force, Navy, Marine Corps, and other government employees is conspicuously missing. What has prevented the EPA from undertaking further testing to add to and update its Chapter 15? I will explain later.

Since the first test results were recorded in 2000, the government has recognized this ordnance is poisoning us—all of us—and yet has made no attempt to test the remainder of the ordnance used by the military, law enforcement, or civilian communities.

The Army, Navy, Air Force, Marine Corps, and even the Coast Guard all use the same rifle, pistol, shotgun, and machine gun bullets documented in AP 42 Chapter 15. These weapons were not just used by the military—the 2000 tests revealed civilian law enforcement and the public use the same ammunition as well.

One example that I will examine in detail is Chapter 15.1.4 A059.[6] A059 is 5.56 mm (caliber .223) M16 and civilian AR15 assault rifle ball ammunition. Look it up online.[6 Appendix A Table A1] Table A1's *Hazardous Air Pollutants and Toxic Chemicals* lists fifty-one hazardous and toxic compounds produced by this cartridge. Sixty-two combined hazardous and toxic compounds when you add 9 mm and .45 Cal pistol, 5.56 (.223) and 7.62 (.308) rifle ammunition and 12GA shotgun shells.[Photo 2.2]

Test results for each are documented and available online in the EPA's AP 42[6] Chapter 15.1. Sixty-two hazardous and toxic compounds found on every firing range across the nation, both civilian and military alike (see Table 2.1).

Table 2.1 Hazardous and Toxic Compounds Produced by Small Arms

Note: This table contains only the sixty-two hazardous and toxic compounds listed in the EPA's AP 42 Chapter 15 for handguns, rifles, and shotguns. It does not include all of the compounds listed for these weapons nor the remaining hazardous and toxic compounds listed throughout the AP 42 Chapter 15. As of June 2021, the AP 42 did not contain all ordnance in use by civilians, the US Military, and the US government. Missing too are the compounds released into the environment from the projectiles and payloads that are present on firing ranges throughout the United States today. Compounds spread by wind, water, and secondhand contact.

Acenaphthene

Acenaphthylene

Acetaldehyde

Acetonitrile

Acetophenone

Acrylonitrile

Aluminum

Ammonia

Anthracene

Antimony

Arsenic

Barium

Benzene

Benzo[a]anthracene

Benzo[a]pyrene

Benzo[b]fluoranthene

Benzo[g,h,i]perylene

Benzo[k]fluoranthene

Benzo[a]pyrene

Benzo[e]pyrene

Cadmium

Hexavalent Chromium

Chlorobenzene

Chloromethane

Chrysene

Copper

Particulate Cyanide

Total Dioxin/Furan Compounds

Ethylbenzene

Ethylene

bis(2-Ethylhexyl)phthalate

Fluoranthene

Fluorene

Formaldehyde

1,2,3,4,6,7,8-Heptachlorodibenzo-p-dioxin

1,2,3,4,6,7,8-Heptachlorodibenzofuran

1,2,3,6,7,8-Hexachlorodibenzo-p-dioxin

1,2,3,7,8,9-Hexachlorodibenzo-p-dioxin

1,2,3,4,7,8-Hexachlorodibenzofuran

1,2,3,6,7,8-Hexachlorodibenzofuran

Hydrogen Cyanide

Indeno[1,2,3-cd]pyrene

Lead

Manganese

Methylene Chloride

Methyl t-Butyl Ether

Naphthalene

Nickel

Nitric Acid

Nitroglycerin

1,2,3,7,8-Pentachlorodibenzo-p-dioxin

1,2,3,7,8- Pentachlorodibenzofuran

2,3,4,7,8- Pentachlorodibenzofuran

Propylene

Selenium

Styrene

Sulfuric Acid

2,3,7,8-Tetrachlorodibenzo-p-dioxin

2,3,7,8-Tetrachlorodibenzofuran

Thallium

Toluene

Zinc

Sourced from US Army Environmental Center (USAEC) Contract No. GS-10F-0131K, Order No. W911S0-04-F-001, test results published in the US Environmental Protection Agency (EPA) Office of Air Quality Planning and Standards "Air Emissions Factors and Quantification" report in Chapter 15, "AP 42 Section 15"[6] sections below:

12 ga shotgun	15.1.2, 15.1.3
9 mm pistol	15.1.21
.38 cal pistol	15.1.23, 15.1.24
.45 cal pistol	15.1.25
5.56 mm rifle and machine gun	15.1.4, 15.1.5, 15.1.6, 15.1.7, 15.1.8, 15.1.9
7.62 mm rifle and machine gun	15.1.12, 15.1.13, 15.1.14, 15.1.15, 15.1.16

Table 2.1

A059 is the Department of Defense Identification Code (DOD-IC) assigned to M16 assault rifle ball ammunition. It is also one of the most available and widely used ammunitions in use today by civilian shooters in their beloved AR15 assault rifles and its variants. Likely more dangerous is the wide availability of cheap, foreign AR15 5.56 ball ammunition imported from countries with no environmental regulations whatsoever.

Worse, as I will examine later, the AR15 and M16 are the weapons responsible for directly poisoning more Americans than any other gun in use today.

"Ball" ammunition consists of a simple, inexpensive lead bullet covered, or "gilded," in a shiny copper-zinc alloy coating. This alloy protects the soft lead core of the bullet from friction and the high heat that is generated as it accelerates through the rifle barrel. Otherwise, under extreme use, the soft lead would melt and "slide" off the bullet. Picture the chocolate from a candy bar sliding onto your fingers on a hot day. Without the gilding (or the hard candy coating covering the chocolate), that soft lead would eventually foul or plug up the barrel during rapid fire with catastrophic results. Note that lead, copper, and zinc are three of the sixty-two hazardous and toxic compounds listed in Table 2.1 above.

If you look up Section 15.1.4[6] and select the "Summary Page" of the army's M16A1 spreadsheet, you will note that on March 23, 2000, at the Aberdeen Proving Grounds, two tests of twenty rounds each were conducted. The "Final EF" spreadsheet identifies compounds produced that include all of the above, plus benzene, hexavalent chromium, particulate cyanide, sulfuric acid, toluene, and numerous other toxic and hazardous compounds that poison the shooter when firing a gun. In fact, there are all but ten or so of the compounds listed in Table 2.1 above.

Hazardous and toxic compounds clearly identified, defined, and regulated by the Clean Air Act of 1971[9] (CAA), Resource and Recovery Act of 1976[15] (RCRA), and Emergency Planning and Community Right-to-Know Act of 1986[12] (EPCRA). Laws and regulations ignored by the military, Department of Defense, and every civilian range I have contacted.

It also identifies the total suspended particulates (TSP) in sizes from visible dust (gun smoke) down to smaller than 2.5 micrometers (microns). On their website, the EPA recognizes[13]:

> *PM stands for particulate matter (also called particle pollution): the term for a mixture of solid particles and liquid droplets found in the air. Some particles, such as dust, dirt, soot, or smoke, are large or dark enough to be seen with the naked eye. Others are so small they can only be detected using an electron microscope.*
> *Particle pollution includes:*
> - PM_{10}: Inhalable particles, with diameters that are generally 10 micrometers and smaller; and
> - $PM_{2.5}$: Fine inhalable particles, with diameters that are generally 2.5 micrometers and smaller.
> - *How small is 2.5 micrometers? Think about a single hair from your head. The average human hair is about 70 micrometers*

in diameter—making it 30 times larger than the largest fine particle.

For a better perspective, a human red blood cell is 7.5 to 8.7 microns across.[7] Bacteria are as large as 3 microns. The army tests recorded toxic particulate matter smaller than 2.5 microns ($PM_{2.5}$). Particulate matter clearly visible in photo 2.3.

Take a look at illustration 2.4. The EPA included it on its Particulate Matter (PM) Basics web page.[13] It successfully illustrates the size of the 146 hazardous and toxic compounds floating around in the air to settle on, and coat, everything in the vicinity. The shooter will then breathe it in and absorb it straight through the skin to be poisoned.

Jump on the internet and take a look at Herra Kuulapaa High Speed Ballistics Photography at kuulapaa.com.[98] I wish I could have afforded to include these photos in the book. Spend some time looking at the photographs illustrating the minute particles identified here and you will understand. Sixty-two hazardous and toxic compounds are on display issuing forth as particles, smoke, and vapor to settle on and poison everything in the vicinity with every bullet fired.

What else do these army test results document? The following statement, included in each Chapter 15 Background Document, states:

> *It should be noted that the air emission factors documented herein are only representative of emissions associated with the use of the propelling cartridge. Emissions associated with the impact of the propelled projectile are addressed elsewhere.*

The results document that these tests were only conducted to identify what hazardous and toxic compounds were emitted when expending ordnance at the firing point (the location that the weapon or ordnance was fired or detonated). The results do not include the bullet or projectile debris at the point of impact. Why is this important?

This forms the basis for plausible deniability for range owners and employers when it comes to firing range maintenance and hazardous waste cleanup and decontamination—cleanup and removal that only include the debris at the point of impact. Little attention is paid to the source of the dust that contaminates everything this fine particulate matter covers at the firing point and its immediate vicinity: the toxic particulates (smaller than a red blood cell) that permeate the air to settle on the shooter and those in the immediate vicinity, including their clothing, equipment, floor, walls, tables, and stands. Everyone, and everything, is coated by the TSP that is deposited on them. We will examine this next.

Each background document in the army's report also includes the statement:

> *The USAEC Firing Point . . . testing was conducted in the Emission Characterization Chamber (ECC) . . . The ECC is a 3/8-inch-thick steel cylinder with parabolic caps welded to each end. The chamber is approximately 7 feet in diameter and 15 feet long . . .*

Why is this significant? The first fifteen to thirty feet of any range, whether indoors or outdoors, is contaminated primarily with the particulate debris produced from the weapon-firing process. It can be seen accumulating as an orange or yellowish-brown dust on the floor in front of the shooter.

In simple terms, this visible dust is comprised of the unexploded gun powder, lead, and other toxic and hazardous compounds blown out of a gun barrel as the total suspended particulates identified in the AP 42 Chapter 15.

Once the trigger is pulled on a firearm, the hazardous and toxic compounds produced or "manufactured" are distributed into the air, falling and settling on surrounding surfaces now subject to multiple federal, state, and local laws.[Photo 2.3] Not to be overlooked is the multitude of other government regulations they are subject to, which include the Department of Defense, Army, Navy, Air Force, FBI,

Department of Homeland Security, local sheriff and police departments, and so on. This includes the operating procedures required set in place by civilian ranges and other firearms-related businesses required by state and federal law.[3]

Once produced or manufactured, the dust captured in the army tests is highly flammable and toxic. Federal law classifies this as hazardous material (hazmat) or hazardous waste (hazwaste). Per federal law, this dust and all items contaminated with it:

1. Are classified by EPA hazardous waste codes as D003 "Highly Reactive" (to heat) and D008 "Toxic Lead" per the Resource and Recovery Act (RCRA) of 1976.[15]
2. Shall be manufactured, handled, and collected by fully trained employees wearing approved personal protective equipment (PPE) at facilities in full compliance with the Occupational Safety and Health Act of 1970.[3]
3. Shall be manufactured, collected, containerized, labeled, stored, transported, and disposed of from "cradle to grave" per the Resource and Recovery Act (RCRA) of 1976.[15]
4. Shall be transported per applicable Department of Transportation and US Coast Guard regulations.
5. Shall be reported and accounted for from production to final disposition per the Emergency Planning and Community Right-to-Know Act (EPCRA) of 1986.[12]

Sounds like our government has it handled, right? *Wrong.* You see, Congress passed the Toxic Substances Control Act (TSCA) in 1976.[14]

The Toxic Substances Control Act (TSCA) of 1976 Section 3, (2), (B), (v) bans the EPA from enforcement of any regulations over *shot shells, cartridges, and components of shot shells and cartridges.*

That's right, the government is actually prevented from enforcing government regulations on bullets and their components by law. Unbelievable, right? I wonder what member of Congress introduced that little piece of legislation and what their motives were. We will examine this and similar laws and regulations contrary to public safety in more detail later.

Why is this dust so important, and what makes it so dangerous? For one, the unexploded gunpowder in it is highly flammable. It is directly responsible for burning down indoor ranges and starting wildfires at outdoor ranges when ignored and allowed to accumulate. If you see dust accumulated on the floor of an indoor range, I recommend you leave immediately. Why, you may ask?

1. You run the risk of igniting that unexploded gunpowder with a spark created by the copper, zinc, or other bullet-gilding materials impacting the minerals contained in the concrete floor. It is gunpowder! It burns extremely hot and fast, igniting anything flammable around it. That includes the flammable TSP that has permeated and accumulated in the walls, ceiling, and every nook and cranny of that range, sometimes for years!

2. Visible levels of toxic compounds on the floor indicate the range is not in compliance with the OSHA regulations required to protect range employees from poisoning. If they are not protecting their employees, they are not protecting you!

Furthermore, as I will identify here, this dust is directly responsible for wasting billions of taxpayer dollars per year, the increase in veteran suicides, out-of-control violence, and birth defects. And other than cigarettes, it is responsible for the sickness, disease, and deaths of more people per year than any government agency will currently acknowledge.

So how does this happen?

Remember the OSHA General Duty Clause at the beginning of the chapter? Since 1970,[3] the army, Department of Defense, and US government, as an employer, were and are directly responsible for complying with 29 U.S.C. § 654, 5(a)1 and 2 for protecting their employees from the hazardous and toxic compounds it recognized that ordnance produces. To date, they have failed to:

> "Furnish to each of his employees employment and a place of employment which are free from **recognized hazards** that are causing or are likely to cause death or serious physical harm to his employees."

Want proof? The government has known since testing began in 1999 that 146 hazardous and toxic compounds in the form of gases, fumes, particles, and dust smaller than a human red blood cell were poisoning us from ordnance.[2] Did you know that for lead alone federal regulations require:

> OSHA 1910.1025(n)(1)(iii): *The employer shall maintain these monitoring records for at least 40 years or for the duration of employment plus 20 years, whichever is longer.*

How about toxic hexavalent chromium? It is one of the compounds listed in the army's test results:

1910.1020(d)(1)(i) states: *"Employee medical records." The medical record for each employee shall be preserved and maintained for at least the duration of employment plus thirty (30) years . . .*

There are OSHA regulations for the majority of the hazardous and toxic compounds we government and military employees have been exposed to that the government and Department of Defense have *recognized* but failed to take action to protect us from.

I was first employed by the United States Navy in 1985, thirty-five years ago. I was fired for whistleblowing in 2014. That means my records and those of every range I worked on are required by federal law to be maintained by the Navy until 2054 and beyond. Do you think the Navy can provide records from my first exposure in basic training back in 1985? I have requested records via both the FOIA and Privacy Act, which the Navy has failed to provide.

Why? Because the Navy failed to conduct the monitoring required by federal, Department of Defense, and Navy laws and regulations.

What about firing ranges used by civilians? Federal law requires all firing ranges and businesses with employees that are exposed to lead to perform monitoring and "maintain these monitoring records for at least 40 years or for the duration of employment plus 20 years, whichever is longer."

Again, each of the 146 hazardous and toxic compounds have similar regulations whose compliance is mandatory, requiring records to be kept for up to forty years or more. If the Navy can't or won't produce these records, how about the local police departments? Do you think that civilian firing range down the street can provide those records for their firing range employees?

How about the person who reloads or recycles bullets and shells? Local gun shops selling used firearms? Local government surplus dealers selling contaminated military uniforms, clothing, equipment, and vehicles? All are *recognized* by the government as trafficking in lead and firearms-poisoning contaminated items—hazmat and hazwaste.

How about military housing? The government recognizes these are contaminated by lead and firearms poisoning as well. I'll get into that more later. All organizations producing or trafficking in contaminated materials are subject to complying with numerous federal, state, local, and agency laws and regulations. Think they do?

Were you aware that these compliance records are available to you through the Freedom of Information, Privacy, and the Emergency Planning and Community Right-to-Know Acts?[12]

Do you think that any of the organizations that manufacture or are contaminated with these hazardous and toxic compounds are in complete compliance with all federal, state, and local regulations? Do you think they can provide the compliance records that they must maintain for forty or more years?

I have received FOIA responses documenting that the United States Navy is not complying with these regulations. These FOIA responses chronicle that they concealed this information and then falsified statements and documents, committing perjury during a federal hearing to cover it up.

Do you think that any of these organizations can provide compliance records for all 146 hazardous and toxic compounds recognized by the Army, Department of Defense, EPA, and our government beginning in 2000[2] and published in 2004?[6] Government reports and documents that recognize these hazardous and toxic compounds as "causing or are likely to cause death or serious physical harm to his employees"?[8] They can't. Not all of them have to. The Department of Defense doesn't.

Executive Order 12196,[16] signed by President Ronald Reagan on February 26, 1980, requires all of government to comply with OSHA regulations with one notable exception. It states in section 1-101:

> *This order applies to all agencies of the Executive Branch except military personnel and uniquely military equipment, systems, and operations.*

Mind blown yet? That's right, "military personnel and uniquely military equipment, systems, and operations" do not have to comply with OSHA regulations. What do you think of good ol' Ronnie Reagan now?

This one-liner relieves the Department of Defense and government from any responsibility for knowingly poisoning veterans and their families with the hazardous and toxic compounds they have recognized since 1975. But it does not exempt them from compliance and maintaining exposure records for civilian employees working within the same facilities—not in the small arms range I was fired from. It gets much worse. I will get deeper into this later, but first, let's take a look at where this hazardous and toxic dust comes from.

"Lead Exposure and Design Consideration for Indoor Firing Ranges," NIOSH, December 1975[17]

The National Institute for Occupational Safety and Health (NIOSH) was established by the Occupational Safety and Health Act (OSH Act) of 1970. It established NIOSH as the research agency focused on the study of worker safety and health. Not to be confused with OSHA, NIOSH was established as part of the US Centers for Disease Control and Prevention (CDC) within the US Department of Health, Education, and Welfare (HEW). Today, NIOSH and the CDC are part of the Department of Health and Human Services (HHS).

In 1975, NIOSH published HEW Publication No. 76–130, *Lead Exposure and Design Consideration for Indoor Firing Ranges.* Over forty-five years ago, the US government identified and recognized the source of firearms poisoning and the many health hazards it is responsible for today.

This report recognizes the *Source of Contamination* and poisoning. It correctly lists one source of firearms poisoning as the bullet primer. The bullet primer is the small circular component centered in the round, shiny end of the bullet or shotgun shell (see Photo 2.2). The primer contains lead in the form of lead styphnate and lead peroxide.

Lead styphnate and lead peroxide, when tightly contained in a small metal container or primer, are extremely sensitive to impact or crushing forces. When crushed by a gun's firing pin, friction and heat are generated, creating a tiny spark or flame. This flame is directed into the gunpowder contained within the bullet or shotgun shell casing.

The casing is the shiny metal part of a complete round of ammunition. A complete round consists of a casing that holds the primer on one end, the gunpowder inside, and the bullet at the pointy end. The gunpowder, once ignited by the primer, burns at a preengineered speed, or velocity.

The burning gunpowder creates gases that expand to accelerate and propel the bullet or payload out of the gun's barrel at speeds above or approaching the speed of sound. Contrary to popular belief, there is no "explosion." The entire process is a controlled burn engineered within the gunpowder for its specific purpose. That loud bang you hear is caused by the bullet or projectile breaking the sound barrier as it leaves the barrel, combined with the immediate release of the compressed gases following behind it.

As an example, there are two kinds of "explosives." Low explosives are engineered as propelling charges. Used in firearms, large military guns, rockets, missiles, and so on, they are used to accelerate projectiles and push payloads. High explosives are engineered to cut and shatter—this is called brisance.

For instance, a low explosive would be used to push and remove a tree stump from a field without shattering it. A high explosive would be used to cut the steel beams of a building or bridge during demolition. High explosives would be used to shatter a giant boulder blocking a highway into manageable pieces for removal without damaging the road underneath. Gunpowder could also push the boulder away, but it would damage the road.

Burn rates, or velocities, are engineered into explosives and gunpowder for their specific uses by the chemical compounds listed in Table 2.1.[6] High-explosive detonation cord, or *det cord*, burns at just over four and a half miles per second. Gunpowder burns at just under a half mile per second. While they both may appear as violent explosions, they actually burn at the rate they are designed to.

NIOSH reported as early as 1975[17] that the gunpowder used in firearms produces temperatures as high as two thousand degrees Fahrenheit and pressures as high as twenty thousand per square inch (PSI). Actually, today we know a .357 Magnum handgun can produce pressures as high as thirty-eight thousand pounds per square inch (PSI) and M16/AR15s sixty-two thousand PSI.

What this government report recognized was the source of lead and firearms poisoning they would document twenty-five years later[2,6] consisted of 145 other hazardous and toxic compounds.

The source of lead and firearms poisoning was first recognized by the government in this 1975 report[17] as:

1. Lead styphnate and lead peroxide from the primer
2. Lead generated at the firing point from the heat of the firing process and friction experienced as the bullet travels down the gun barrel at high speed
3. Lead generated at the firing point from bullet fragmentation due to gun-barrel-to-cylinder misalignment and gaps from wear and manufacturing tolerances
4. Side blast at the firing point. NIOSH defines "side blast" as dust and fumes blown out of the barrel at right angles, in the turbulence created by the immediate release of pressure as high as twenty thousand PSI between gun barrel-to-cylinder misalignment, and when the bullet leaves the barrel. The report states, "The side blast creates turbulence in the breathing zone of the shooter, thus increasing his exposure to lead dust and fumes." Again, unbeknownst at the time, the report was describing the *toxic particulate* matter identified as TSP in the 2000 through 2006 army tests, discussed earlier.[2,6]
5. Lead generation from bullet *fragmentation at the impact point.* This report also identifies:

   The problem of personal exposure from this source [bullet fragmentation at the impact point] *is believed to be minimal since the distance between the shooter and the bullet trap is normally seventy-five feet or more away.*

   As previously pointed out, from 2000 to 2006, DoD, army, and EPA reports and test results would document the poisoning from toxic and hazardous compounds produced within the first fifteen feet of the firing point only—not the point of impact.
6. Lead poisoning occurring at the firing point through the inhalation and/or ingestion of lead fumes and dust (dust documented in size as smaller than a human red blood cell, as early as 2000[2])

The government further recognized in the report:

Toxicology and Hygienic Standards

1. *Lead poisoning may occur through the inhalation and/or ingestion of lead fumes or dust. This results in the deposition of lead in the bones and tissues of the body and alterations in normal physiological functions.*

2. *Lead poisoning may present itself such symptoms as a metallic taste in the mouth, loss of appetite, indigestion, nausea, vomiting, constipation, abdominal cramps, nervousness, and insomnia* (all symptoms I first began experiencing shortly after enlisting in the Navy in 1985).

Physiological

The physiological stresses associated with the position of range officer should be considered . . . By its very nature the job demands close confinement, constant watchfulness for violations, rote repetition, and exposure to high noise levels and to lead dust and fumes.

Floors

The floor is the place where most of the lead dust and fumes and any other particulate contaminate finally comes to rest.

Work Practices

A rotation system should be instituted for the range officer position. It is suggested that a one month of duty be followed by three months of alternate activity. This change is suggested not only to alleviate any possible lead absorption . . . but also **to prevent undue psychological stresses associated with the position**.

Eating, drinking, and smoking on the range should be prohibited.

Other considerations identified in this report include:

In all the firing ranges surveyed, the ventilation was inadequate to keep airborne lead levels below the standard of 0.20 mg/m³.

Indoor ranges can and do present health hazards in the form of lead poisoning and high noise levels. In addition, there may be problems with exposures to carbon monoxide and oxides of nitrogen.

Most ranges surveyed employ one or more full-time range officers who are always present when any firing takes place. In many instances, the range officers also serve as instructors requiring them to remain in the firing area and outside of the range office for extended periods of time. Therefore, a range officer's overall exposure to lead and noise is greater than any other individual using the range.

We have clearly established that the government has recognized:

1. Its responsibility to *furnish to each of his employees with employment and a place of employment which are free from recognized hazards that are causing or are likely to cause death or serious physical harm to his employees* per OSHA 29 U.S.C. § 654, 5(a)1 in 1970.[8]
2. Its responsibility to comply with and its role in ensuring each employer shall comply with the OSHA,[3] CAA,[9] CWA,[11] RCRA,[15] EPCRA,[12] and other mandatory laws and regulations.
3. The source, psychological, and physiological hazards of lead poisoning, noise, and stress of firearms exposure since 1975.[17]
4. The 146 hazardous and toxic compounds contained in lead and firearms poisoning since 2000.[2,6]

In the next few chapters, we will take a closer look at how these toxic compounds spread from the firing point to poison everyone and everything they come into contact with.

CHAPTER 3
Spreading the Poison

Now that you know what *firearms poisoning* is and where it comes from, let's take a look at how the government *recognizes* that it spreads from the source into the homes, communities, and lives of those who have never even handled a gun. After you read this chapter, I recommend reviewing the documents presented on the website URLs provided in the "References" at the end of the book.

These documents and others that I unearthed hit me pretty hard. As a thirty-year warrior, firing range officer, weapons instructor, supervisor, husband, and father, I now realize the extent to which I have poisoned myself, my coworkers, our homes, vehicles, families, friends, surrounding communities, and the environment.

Despite these reports published decades ago, documenting how our military and government recognized these hazards, I was never informed of the reports and their content, nor was I required to take the precautions identified in them.

US Marine Corps Department of the Navy Engineering Study: "Reducing Lead Contamination and Exposure on Military Firing Ranges through the Practical Application of Ballistic Containment Systems," Fourth Edition, 1999[18]

This report was produced after much testing and evaluation to review and publish findings in an attempt to mitigate the exposure of Department of Defense personnel to toxic lead in indoor ranges. For the purpose of this book, it confirms the dangers of lead poisoning and how it affects those exposed during the shooting process. It establishes that toxic lead spreads into the surrounding communities, homes, and families of those who did not participate in firing a weapon or have ever held a gun.

It supports that in 1999, the Department of the Navy, Department of Defense, and the federal government further *recognized the hazards* of lead and firearms poisoning to its employees, their loved ones, their unborn children, the surrounding communities, and the environment.

In addition, this report and others we will review here establish and recognize the route and extent of poisoning caused by the TSP documented in the last chapter, dust and particulate matter produced by all manners of weapons and ordnance used by the military, law enforcement, and anyone exposed to firearms, as well as the contaminated materials and facilities that result.

Most importantly, it establishes full culpability of the government for our poisoning and their failure to stop it.

This report contains permission for us to use it here:

Distribution Statement: Approved for public release. Distribution is unlimited.

Therefore, the following is reproduced, in full, from the first seven pages.

PURPOSE

In today's environment of increasing pressure within the Department of Defense (DoD) to meet ever more stringent environmental requirements in an equivalent manner to the private sector, it has become necessary to assess the issue of reducing or eliminating lead contamination at military firing ranges. It is in this spirit of searching for solutions to decreasing the overall effects of this environmentally dangerous element that this study has been conducted. The information that follows is intended as a guide for understanding the causes and effects of general lead contamination and for choosing or analyzing different types of Ballistic Containment Systems (BCS) intended to reduce or eliminate lead contamination.

HISTORICAL BACKGROUND

For decades, the presence of lead in the environment has been widespread and uncontrolled, beginning with lead smelting factories and continuing to the present day with the manufacture of glazed pottery, batteries, leaded gasoline, and firearms ammunition. Only recently has it been acknowledged that the presence of lead poses a threat to public health serious enough that it warrants government control.

In 1971, the Environmental Protection Agency (EPA) began enforcing the Lead-Based Paint Poisoning Prevention Act, which restricts the amount of lead used in paints. Seven years later, in October of 1978, the EPA went on to set the National Ambient Air Quality Standards for airborne lead. This would serve as the primary mechanism to reduce the content of lead in gasoline. However, even with these standards and other controls, the residue of lead in food, water, and soil can elevate a person's Blood Lead Level (BLL) of lead to unacceptable levels.

LEAD

The U.S. Environmental Protection Agency (EPA) classifies lead as a highly toxic heavy metal. It exhibits no biological benefit in the body. When a person inhales or ingests lead, it is absorbed into the bloodstream. Once lead is in the body, it becomes very difficult to remove. Continual exposure to lead results in the accumulation of lead in the body, and measurable amounts of lead exposure can accumulate over a lifetime.

The EPA has determined that lead poses a serious health hazard to everyone who comes in contact with it. Unfortunately, individuals who work with and around firearms have entirely ignored the harmful effects of lead up to this time. Therefore, firearms range personnel, and those individuals using firing ranges, must take precautions to control all unnecessary exposure to this highly toxic element. For most people involved in shooting, just knowing the hazards of lead is a primary responsibility; taking the necessary precautions to minimize unnecessary exposure is a duty.

EFFECTS OF LEAD ON THE BODY

A simple look into the overall near and long-term effects lead contamination has on the human body is in order to understand the seriousness of this problem.

Approximately 6 percent of all lead ingested or inhaled is immediately deposited in the blood or soft body tissues, such as the kidneys, brain, or other vital organs. The remaining 94 percent is more deeply deposited in bone matter. Unfortunately, the body mistakes lead for calcium. In doing so, it presumes that, once deposited, the lead needs to be stored forever.

The body does, however, break down lead so that it can be removed. The time required for this process is measured by the term "half-life," which means the amount of time the body needs to excrete one-half of the total accumulation of stored lead.

Lead in the bloodstream and in soft body tissue has a half-life of approximately 30–40 days and is excreted from the body through urine, bile, sweat, hair, and nails. However, lead deposited in bone has a half-life of approximately twenty (20) years. That is, one-half of the lead dosage absorbed by the body through only one exposure and deposited in bone matter would still be present in the body after a time-lapse of twenty (20) years.

EXPOSURE TO LEAD THROUGH FIREARMS

The exposure to lead on firing ranges (military or civilian) occurs as soon as a shooter pulls the trigger on a firearm. This action causes the primer of the cartridge in the weapon's chamber to explode, which—in turn—ignites the main powder charge. At this point, a respirable cloud of lead particulates is expelled from the cartridge primer into the air, with minute particles of lead dust spraying the shooter's hands, face, and clothing.

With exposed lead types of projectiles, minute lead particles also shear off from them as the projectile travels through the barrel of the weapon. In jacketed ammunition with exposed lead bases, minute particles are shed from the small exposed base area. When the projectile leaves the barrel, a second cloud of contaminants, in the form of the muzzle blast, bursts into the air. These contaminants contain particles of lead and other chemicals from the projectile and the residue of un-burnt powder and burnt powder gasses. Then, as the bullet travels through the air and strikes the impact area, another contaminated cloud rises if the projectile strikes a solid object causing it to break up, releasing small particles of lead dust into the air.

When shooters inhale these various clouds of contaminants, lead particles travel directly into their lungs and are quickly absorbed from there into the bloodstream. The blood then transfers this inhaled lead into soft body tissue and bone. Heat from smoking, sweating, or physical activity accelerates this process.

Lead can also settle on the skin and hair, and in turn, be absorbed through the pores of the skin. If lead particles reach the mouth, they can be ingested directly into the digestive system.

Exposure increases when it is time for the individual to clean up, because handling empty casings can result in lead being transferred to the skin, or to clothing and other garments from where it will eventually find its way into the body. The actual cleaning process for the weapon also removes much of the remaining lead in the barrel and lead particulates from other parts of the weapon and transfers it to the cleaner's hands. Oils and solvents used to clean and lubricate weapons cause the natural oils in the skin to evaporate, leaving dry skin and open pores through which the lead can more easily pass.

SYMPTOMS OF LEAD POISONING

The numerous symptoms of lead poisoning mimic various diseases, often making diagnosis confusing and difficult. Most commonly, individuals experience abdominal pain, fatigue, nausea, subtle mood changes, headaches, constipation, irritability, and depression. More seriously, muscle pain, muscle weakness, weight loss, impotence, convulsions, anemia, and renal (kidney) failure may also occur with increased lead levels in the body.

TESTING FOR LEAD

Testing for lead can be performed in several ways. The BLL test detects recent exposure to lead but does not provide information regarding long-term or past exposure. The BLL measures the quantity of lead in micrograms per deciliter of blood, written as ug/100 dL, that is, micrograms of lead per 100 deciliters of blood.

The Occupational Safety and Health Administration (OSHA) standards state that the median blood levels for adults should be about 15 ug/100 dL; children and pregnant women should have blood levels below 10 ug/100 dL. For reproductive health, the blood level should stay below 30 ug/100 dL. OSHA recommends removal from the workplace of any employee whose BLL measures 40 ug/100 dL or higher.

In order to determine deeper exposure, the zinc protoporphyrin (ZPP) test can be performed in conjunction with the BLL. Lead interferes with the absorption of iron into the blood, which is needed to transport oxygen, thereby allowing zinc to replace the iron. The ZPP measures the amount of zinc in the blood, which remains elevated longer than the BLL. The normal range for the ZPP is 0–100 ug/100 dL. An elevated ZPP indicates concentration in the bone marrow.

The only effective test used for bone lead levels is the disodium edetate (EDTA) chelating agent test. EDTA, a solution administered intravenously, bonds with the lead in bone and clears it from body compartments so that it is excreted through the urine. EDTA both tests and treats an individual, but medical personnel use it only in extreme cases of lead poisoning because of potentially harmful side effects.

SPECIAL LEAD CONTAMINATION RISKS

In males, high levels of lead can decrease the sex drive and cause sterility. Lead can also alter the structure of sperm cells, thereby causing birth defects.

Pregnant women are especially vulnerable to rapid absorption of lead, along with calcium, from the blood into the bone. This rapid lead migration occurs due to hormonal changes caused by pregnancy. Of greater danger, in pregnant women, lead passes unimpeded through the *placenta to the fetus, potentially causing miscarriages of the fetus and/or birth defects.*

Tragically, children are more vulnerable to lead toxicity than adults. Children exposed to lead may manifest slow learning, mental drifts, slight retardation in development, hypertension, and behavioral problems, while excessive blood lead levels can seriously and irreversibly damage a child's brain and nervous system during crucial development years. Because the symptoms mirror those of many childhood diseases, many doctors do not test for lead exposure.

PRECAUTIONS ON THE FIRING RANGE

Precautions can be taken both on and off the range to protect shooters, instructors, and their families from the effects of lead poisoning. Administrative controls and good hygiene are two necessary tools. In addition, all shooters and instructors should practice the following "do's and don'ts" of range safety.

- *Don't smoke on the range: Smoking any type of tobacco products on the range should be prohibited to prevent acceleration of inhaled lead into the bloodstream and ingestion of lead transferred from hands to the cigarette, cigar, etc.*
- *Don't eat on the range: Lead dust on hands and face can be ingested through contact with food. Airborne lead expelled from the weapon can also contaminate food.*
- *Don't collect fired brass in hats: Many shooters use their hats to collect spent brass; this contaminates the hat with lead particles. When the hat is placed back on the head, the lead is deposited into the hair and absorbed into the skin. Providing boxes for the brass prevents this practice.*
- *Do be aware that face, arms, and hands are covered with lead particles: Shooters and instructors should wash thoroughly with cold water and plenty of soap. Cold water is preferred because warm water enhances the absorption of lead by opening the pores of the skin. If no water is available, shooters should consider carrying*

a box of wet handwipes or a bottle of cool water and a washcloth for this purpose.

- *Do be aware that hair and clothes are still contaminated: Shooters and firearms instructors should wear an outer garment, such as a jumpsuit or coveralls, or change clothes before going home. Contaminated clothes should not be cleaned by blowing, shaking, or other means that dispense lead into the air. To prevent cross-contamination, range clothes should be washed separately from the family's regular laundry. Families with infants should be particularly careful, since infants are most vulnerable to lead contamination. Changing to clean clothing before leaving the range prevents recontamination of the hands and any contamination of the family vehicle.*
- *Do change shoes before entering residence: Shoes can also transport lead into the home. Shoes should be left at the door to prevent tracking lead onto floors and carpets. As an alternative, disposable shoe coverlets can be used while firing and cleaning, then discarded when leaving the range. Ordinary vacuuming does not remove lead from the home, but redistributes it by blowing it into the air to be inhaled and/or resettled onto the carpet.*
- *Do avoid physical contact with family members until after a shower, shampoo, and change of clothes: Lead can be transferred by casual contact. Family and friends should not be hugged or kissed until after a shower and a change of clothes. Any physical contact should be avoided while the shooter is still in range clothing.*

REDUCING INDOOR FIRING RANGE CONTAMINATION

Most indoor ranges have a greater lead dust contamination problem than outdoor ranges due to the closed environment. There are two general areas where lead contamination occurs:

- *At the firing line from primer ignition and muzzle blast.*
- *At the terminus end—the bullet trap—from projectiles striking the trap and breaking up.*

In spite of these problems, range personnel can institute several controls to lower the amount of lead dust in firing ranges from these two major areas. First, lead controls from the firing line end of the range:

- *The careful choice of ammunition is one such control for lead. Non-jacketed ammunition produces the most lead dust and fumes. Jacketed ammunition produces the least contaminates. Shotgun shells produce more airborne lead dust than any handgun round. Currently, many ammunition manufacturers, and DoD, are working to develop lead-free ammunition. Until sufficient lead-free ammunition is available, precautions should be taken.*
- *Indoor ranges should not be carpeted, since lead dust settles and contaminates the rugs. Sealed concrete or a similar media is most desirable for floor designs.*
- *Floors should be cleaned by vacuuming or washing contaminants into an industrial treatment/capture facility. The best vacuum to use for lead would be a high-efficiency particulate (HEPA) vacuum with a 3-stage particulate air filter.*
- *Because water cannot be treated for lead contamination, personnel should use water sparingly to remove lead when cleaning ranges. If water is used for lead removal, minimizing the amount of water used will result in less pollution.*
- *Range maintenance employees should wear disposable coveralls and air purifying masks while cleaning and/or repairing indoor ranges that show signs of lead contamination . . .*

The first time I read this report, I was in disbelief. I had never seen nor heard of any of these things. It is a Navy report that was completed and published in 1999. Beginning in 1985, I served as a Navy and Department of Defense weapons and firing range expert and employee through 2014. My son enlisted in the Navy and instructed fellow military personnel at firing ranges too—the same ranges that I had used.

My fellow employees and friends continue to work in those fields. Not one of them had ever seen or heard of this report either. As of this book's writing in 2021, the Navy and Department of Defense still have not addressed these findings, informed its personnel of them, or instituted the very precautions the report identified in 1999!

Instead, they allow this poisoning to continue. They allow us to continue poisoning our fellow employees, our homes, vehicles, families, and the surrounding communities and environment. They allow us to continue poisoning our unborn children, resulting in stillborn babies, miscarriages, and birth defects. In 1999, when this report was published, I was already experiencing the symptoms documented in the report.

The second time I read it, I became sick to my stomach, thinking of my wife's three premature births, as well as the miscarriages my friends and coworkers had endured—not to mention the birth defects of my oldest son and the children of our closest friends and coworkers. And then there are all the female soldiers, sailors, airmen, and Marines who have been poisoned. My God! The more I thought about it, the harder it hit home.

The Navy and Department of Defense took none of the precautions they outlined in this report to stop the poisoning of every female in the military, including that of their fetuses and children—poisoning they would experience and pass on in future pregnancies for a minimum of forty years after leaving the service. Newborn children that will experience the side effects of this poisoning and the permanent behavioral and physiological changes that will continue to occur until they turned forty or older. Poisoning that continues today.

I then researched lead in blood and in bone. This report is correct: forty years or more after last exposure, lead continues to poison our bodies, causing sickness, disease, and death even into our retirement years. A recent blood test indicates I still have lead coursing through my veins, poisoning me. My wife and son have lead in their veins as well. We lived in military housing through 2009.

This same housing was also contaminated by generations of military personnel who lived there before us—personnel who unknowingly brought lead and the other 145 hazardous and toxic compounds home, which contaminated the carpeting, washing machines, and clothes dryers . . . every surface they and their contaminated gear and clothing came into contact with.

Lead in my home, carpet, and vehicles? Lead in my clothing and wardrobe? Lead in my family's laundry? The more I researched and thought about it, the more despondent I became.

Betrayed by the very country and government I had pledged to serve and had blindly followed orders for. For eighteen consecutive years, I deployed, leaving my wife to raise our children alone. I served in five wars and did seven tours in war zones from the Middle East to South America. I also completed twenty-plus other deployments under ninety days, which the Navy doesn't even recognize as tours—hundreds of special operations and contingencies not even documented.

I've had nearly a dozen surgeries, with more to come, as well as painful nerve conduction testing to diagnose lead poisoning. I take twenty pills a day to mitigate the lead and firearms poisoning symptoms I continue to suffer from today. I would have given my life in service to my country. What I did not realize, what I did not know, was that the Navy had willfully taken my life anyway. My resolve strengthened, and I vowed to reveal what I'd discovered and ensure that the poisoning was stopped so future generations could be free of this betrayal. As you will see, it got much worse.

Before I get started, I would like to draw attention to three names I have run across that feature prominently in lead and heavy metal research for the CDC and NIOSH: Eric J. Esswein, Mark F. Boeniger, and Kevin Ashley. The research and publications presented next establish that our government recognized the dangers of this poisoning more than fifteen years ago.

"Preventing the Toxic Hand-Off," September 2005[4]

This 2005 report, which was brought to my attention by a NIOSH employee I'd contacted, validates and reconfirms the earlier

1999 Department of the Navy report.[18] Ironically a naval reserve officer himself, he was concerned with Navy personnel's exposure to lead
at firing ranges. As he is still employed, he will remain anonymous.
Before I start, let me make one important point: this naval officer and
NIOSH employee was unaware of the other 145 hazardous and toxic
compounds produced by ordnance that the army and Department
of Defense had recognized in 2000. Although this 2005 report had
been published ten years earlier, at the time, neither of us had any
knowledge of the army's test results. We'd only discussed lead exposure and contamination.

He pointed out the highlights of this interesting and very important report, substantiating them as fact. "Preventing the Toxic Hand-
Off" identifies research conducted confirming three main points:

1. lead particles, and all those from firearms poisoning, adhere to
   clothing and skin to be redistributed by contact to anything it
   touches;
2. lead particles embed themselves deep into any porous surface;
   and
3. soap and water are ineffective at removing these particles.

The document, like the 1999 report, reaffirmed that even after washing hands with soap and water, lead remains on the hands,
"equivalent to the permissible exposure dose for a full 8-hour work-
day."

Think about that. The 1999 report[18] stated, "Lead can also settle
on the skin and hair, and in turn, be absorbed through the pores of
the skin." Remember, US Army tests in 2000 documented lead and
firearms poisoning particles smaller than 2.5 microns, smaller than
bacteria.

This 2005 report documents that even though the hands and
surfaces workers touched were washed and looked clean, they were
redistributing lead onto doorknobs, metal railings, tables, soda machine buttons, and various other places that had not been exposed to

lead contamination by any other source. This is the same redistribution recognized and documented in the Department of the Navy's 1999 report.[18]

This 2005 report also discusses a cleanser that NIOSH developed that would remove 98.9 percent of lead and toxic metals from the skin. Those cleansers are available for purchase and use by the public today.

So if the government developed this cleanser, why aren't they requiring their employees to use it? The government, via these reports, "recognize[d] hazards that may cause death or serious physical harm,"[8] developed a product that can prevent or stop lead poisoning,[4] and then doesn't provide or require its use by its own employees. Why?

"Handwipe Method for Removing Lead from Skin," 2005[19]

This article confirms that after developing a cleanser that would remove lead and heavy metals from the skin, NIOSH employees developed a hand-washing procedure that would remove 98.9 percent of these compounds from the skin. The same NIOSH employee that had provided the above two reports[4,19] established that this hand-wiping method was later adopted as a recognized technical standard for the removal of heavy metals from the skin and is available from ASTM International. ASTM STP1533[91] identifies this procedure as a decontamination procedure, not a hand-washing step.

The authors of this report, working for the CDC and NIOSH, go into great depth discussing how heavy metal particles adhere and are even absorbed into the skin, and yet the government did not require its employees to comply with this "handwipe method."[19,91] Why?

Skin Absorption of Inorganic Lead (PbO) and the Effect of Skin Cleansers, 2006[20]

This is yet another article published identifying how these minute particles are absorbed straight through the skin. Please note that

Mark F. Boeniger contributed to this research as well. This article, published in 2006 by the *Journal of Occupational and Environmental Medicine*,[20] identifies a number of easily understood conclusions that are highly important in comprehending how we are poisoned by exposure to lead and firearms poisoning. What's easily understood is that the poisoning is a result of breathing contaminated air, consuming contaminated food and beverages, and so on, which are preventable within the workplace.

The article establishes for me, as a thirty-year weapons and firing range expert and employee, a far more dangerous source of our poisoning. The article states that even the use of NIOSH-formulated decontamination cleansers and procedures does not prevent the absorption of lead through the skin and into the bloodstream. What it does confirm is that *lead that comes into contact with the skin will be absorbed to poison those exposed.*

You can't stop it.

So after the NIOSH-developed cleansers were used to decontaminate skin, lead absorption into the skin still continued after its use. We can easily draw the conclusion that, upon contact with the skin, particles from lead and the other 145 hazardous and toxic compounds produced by ordnance will be absorbed in the same manner. The CDC must agree.

Late in the summer of 2021, while editing this book and conducting research for future publications, I came across the CDC's Office of Science website. It contained information I had to include here. Last reviewed in 2017, it includes the following:

Combatting the Dangers of Heavy Metal Contamination: the CDC Can Lead the Way![88]

The first paragraph from this website is produced here in full:

"Exposure to lead has long posed serious health risks, but dangers from occupational and environmental skin exposures to lead and other toxic metals proved difficult to assess until now. Skin contamination (and ingestion) typically occurs from exposure at work including smelters, construction, battery making, and firearm use on the battlefield. It can also result from the environment during recreation, and from lead paint in old homes and buildings. Detection and decontamination in the field remains a daunting challenge to quantify. Ingestion of lead from skin exposure can adversely impact every organ in the body; the kidneys, blood, nervous, and reproductive systems are most affected. There is no known lower threshold limit for lead exposure and harmful health effects."

Did you pick up that last sentence? "There is no known lower threshold limit for lead exposure and harmful health effects." How about "skin contamination (and ingestion) typically occurs from exposure at work including smelters, construction, battery making, and firearm use on the battlefield"?

The CDC also identifies "detection and decontamination in the field remains a daunting challenge to quantify." Maybe on the battle fields of the Middle East and Asia but not in training on military gun ranges here in the States. I have dozens of official reports identifying the Navy knew the levels of poison on the ranges I trained on for twenty-nine years. Many that were concealed. The DoD and military recognize this poison and what it is doing to us yet fails to "follow the science." As the next book *Conspiracy and Cover-up* will reveal, the military and government have robust laws and regulations in place to protect veterans and their families but fail to comply with them.

But, why is skin absorption so important to me? Working in an environment exposed to lead requires repeated handwashing, which dries out the skin. Each time I washed my face, hands, and arms at work, I applied a moisturizing lotion afterward. I now understand that using that lotion actually accelerated and ensured the rapid absorption of these toxic compounds into my skin and bloodstream. Why should this be so important to you?

Lead and the hazardous and toxic compounds produced by firearms will be absorbed through the skin from contact with any contaminated

source through both initial and repeated secondhand contact.
You can't stop it!

Secondhand contact with items and places contaminated by those who have no knowledge they have been contaminated. Secondhand contact by those who do not know they have toxic materials on their skin, nor do they have the resources necessary to remove it. Secondhand contact that will remain on the skin, clothing, items, and places contaminated until absorbed into the body, physically removed, or spread elsewhere to poison others. Secondhand contact spreading throughout our communities and environment, poisoning those who have never even been in contact with a gun. Last, secondhand contact from the spread of 146 toxic and hazardous compounds throughout our communities and environment recognized by our government in 1975,[17] 1999,[18] and 2005[4,19] that continue to be ignored by our government today.

CHAPTER 4
Chronicling the Spread

In this chapter, I present photos chronicling the production and spread of the hazardous and toxic compounds produced by the weapons in use today. As a good friend pointed out, nothing compares to seeing photos of how the poison spreads through both first- and secondhand contact. First, let's take a look at the primary source of firearms poisoning in our country today—the military's M16 and civilian AR15 assault rifle.

Photo 4.1 illustrates my civilian version of the M16 assault rifle. This particular rifle is patterned after the M4 and Model 727 M16 carbine. The M4A1 and 727 are smaller, shorter versions of the M16. Introduced in 1994, the M4 is still in use today by Navy special operations personnel like me. Go online and look up images of "Navy SEAL M4 rifle wikimedia."[89] You will see a Navy SEAL allowing a child to fire an M4.

I purchased my M4 years ago and use it primarily for maintaining proficiency as a small-arms instructor.

As discussed earlier, the AR15/M16 assault rifle is the primary villain involved in this poisoning. Why? Because of a dated and inherent design flaw that blows these hazardous and toxic compounds straight into the face and breathing zone of the shooter with every bullet fired.

The AR15/M16 was first designed and submitted for US military service in the fall of 1956 as the AR10. Eventually, it was redesigned to become the AR15 and began service in early 1963. Not long after, following a final redesign, the new M16 was adopted by our armed services as its main battle rifle.

Designed as a "direct gas impingement operated rifle," the rifle uses gas pressure bled out of the barrel to directly operate (cycle) the weapon for automatic reloading. Gas pressure, just under sixty-eight thousand PSI and consisting of the toxic compounds I have identified, is directed via the gas tube to the bolt carrier, where it cycles the weapon.

Photo 4.2 shows the large hole on the side of the weapon (in yellow) where these gases exit the gun and are blown directly into the face of the shooter.

Photo 4.3 shows a partially disassembled AR15 revealing the shiny gas tube that ports gas above the barrel from the front of the gun back to the rear of the weapon. The included bolt-carrier group and a disassembled gas tube above the rifle illustrate where gas pressure is released to blow (or impinge) against the gas key on top of the bolt-carrier group. Gas pressure pushes the bolt-carrier group to the rear, thus reloading the weapon. The toxic gases and particles are then released directly into the face of the shooter to be inhaled, swallowed, and absorbed directly into the eyes and pores of the skin. The only other poison-delivery vehicles that are more direct include cigarettes, e-cigarettes, or just plain injection via syringe.

The M16 was developed to replace the M14. The M14 also uses gas pressure to cycle the weapon but does so through an operating rod. Photo 4.4 shows the gas piston hanging under the end of the barrel. This piston pushes the operating rod to the rear, releasing the gas pressure under the front of the weapon away from the shooter. The operating rod cycles the bolt to reload the weapon.

Better, safer, and more modern weapons have been developed and tested by the military. Despite these weapons being safer, they have not replaced the M16 and its variants and remain in limited use by the military. Photo 4.5 shows one such gas piston–operated weapon. I purchased this gun to replace my M4. Similar to the older M14, this weapon siphons off gas at the front of the barrel to cycle a short-stroke piston. Gas is not blown into the face of the shooter with every bullet fired but released away from the shooter instead.

With this knowledge, why is the AR15/M16 and its variants still being purchased and used by the military? Simple: the gas impingement design is cheaper to produce. Why is the AR15 the most widely available and used weapon in the US civilian marketplace today? There are a number of reasons.

First, retired military men and women are familiar with and proficient in their use and maintenance. We tend to purchase these guns for hunting, home defense, and competitive shooting events. The gun then becomes a staple in the home favored by other family members who become proficient as well. This has been going on since the beginning of time. Rocks, sticks, spears, bow and arrow, rifle—it doesn't matter. What works in war works for putting meat on the table and self-defense.

The hunting rifle in Photo 4.6 belonged to my grandfather. First produced in 1952, it is a direct derivative of the Browning Automatic Rifle (BAR) used in World War II and Korea. It is chambered in .30-06. As with the M14's .308 (7.62), both the BAR's .30-06 and the M16/AR15's .223 (5.56) caliber cartridges were adopted by civilians, as they were cheap and widely available after the wars they were developed for and used in.

Second, pick up any first-person shooter video game, and you will find various M16/AR15 variants used in gaming. Popular in video games, these weapons can be purchased legally. Mk12 Navy SEAL Sniper Rifles, M4, Mk18, M16A1, 2, and 3 are all available for sale here in the United States. Adam Lanza, the Sandy Hook Elementary School shooter, is probably the most infamous video gamer who used one of these assault rifles. Of course, you can't purchase the machine guns in these games. But that didn't stop Stephen Paddock from rapid firing more than eleven hundred rounds into a crowd of twenty-two thousand in Las Vegas, did it? As you will learn later in the book, these two killers and others are also victims of the firearms poisoning that I am revealing here.

Third, cottage industries produce large quantities of these weapons, as well as parts and accessories so that you, too, can adorn your assault rifle and play SWAT, Army Ranger, Navy SEAL, or Marine Corps Recon at your local shooting range, while playing video games, or while just showing off in your living room, she shed, or man cave at home.

Fourth, shooting ranges and clubs organize and host massive paramilitary-style competitions, where hundreds of rounds are fired using three guns—the AR15, a handgun, and shotgun. They have competitive classes for women and children as well. Look up "competition using 3 guns" online.[90] Note the images of men, women, and children all firing AR15 assault rifles. Do you think those people realize how badly they are poisoning themselves or the children they are encouraging to compete? How about their homes, families, unborn children, or surrounding communities? You will understand the consequences in the next chapters.

In the previous chapter, I revealed numerous reports documenting how the government recognized toxic particles distributed to contaminate everything they blanket at the firing point. *Everything— hands, face, skin, hair, hat, clothing, footwear, equipment, the ground, vehicle, home, carpet, and laundry.* Let's take a look at how it spreads from the range and into our daily lives.

With every pull of the trigger, every bullet fired, the AR15/M16 shooter is being poisoned. My AR15/M4? Knowing what I know today, it sits in the gun safe, and it's unlikely that I'll ever fire it again.

First- and Secondhand Exposure

Photos 4.7 through 4.18 portray how toxic compounds are issued from a gun and carried into the home and surrounding community. Remember the 1999 Navy report from the previous chapter?[18] How about the 2005 report, "Preventing the Toxic Hand-Off"?[4] Remember, the army tests that identified particles at the firing point range in size from visible particles down to dust so fine it cannot be seen. Particles so small and light the Navy stated in 1999, "Ordinary vacuuming does not remove lead from the home, but redistributes it by blowing it into the air to be inhaled and/or resettled onto the carpet."[18]

Earlier, we saw the shooter in Photo 4.2 lying in the prone position, firing his gun. Whether standing, sitting, kneeling, or lying on the ground, up to sixty-two toxic compounds[Table 2.1] are being ground into his skin, clothing, and footwear. That goes for shooters firing weapons at the range while resting on tables or benches. Everything at the firing point is covered with these poisons by the fumes and fine dusts manufactured by the firing process.

The photos illustrate how these compounds are further transferred to the shooter's hands and hat while picking up the empty cartridges. Remember the 1999 Navy report we revealed earlier that stated, "Don't collect fired brass in hats: Many shooters use their hats to collect spent brass; this contaminates the hat with lead particles. When the hat is placed back on the head, the lead is deposited into the hair and absorbed into the skin."[18]

How about the hazwaste and hazmat produced at the range? Aside from the contaminated dirt at the firing line, what about the used bullet casings? The government has already classified them as lead-contaminated waste.

Hazwaste and hazmat identified since 1975[17] contaminated with up to 146 hazardous and toxic compounds recognized in 2000,[2] compounds recognized to poison and even kill our troops and their families in numerous Department of Defense and government reports identified throughout this book and the references compiled to produce it.

Hazwaste and hazmat governed by the following:
1. Occupational Safety and Health Act of 1970[3]
2. Resource and Recovery Act (RCRA) of 1976[15]
3. Emergency Planning and Community Right-to-Know Act (EPCRA) of 1986[12]
4. Numerous other federal, state, and local laws and regulations

Let's not forget, though, that due to Congress and the exemption in the Toxic Substances Control Act (TSCA) of 1976,[14] the Environmental Protection Agency is forbidden from enforcing those laws over "shot shells, cartridges, and components of shot shells and cartridges." And then Ronald Reagan exempted the military from compliance in 1980.[16]

The contamination on the shooter's hands does not just come from the shooting range. Photo 4.9 demonstrates how the contamination spreads to the area in which weapons are maintained. Note how the toxic particles penetrate deeper into the shooter's hands and clothing from the oils and degreasers he is using.

Recall the Navy stating in 1999:

"Exposure increases when it is time for the individual to clean-up, because handling empty casings can result in lead being transferred to the skin, or to clothing and other garments from where it will eventually find its way into the body. The actual cleaning process for the weapon also removes much of the remaining lead in the barrel and lead particulates from other parts of the weapon and transfers it to the cleaner's hands. Oils and solvents used to clean and lubricate weapons cause the natural oils in the skin to evaporate, leaving dry skin and open pores through which the lead can more easily pass."[18]

How many photos have you seen of troops eating or sleeping with their weapons in past wars? We have already chronicled that soap and water do not remove lead and other toxic compounds from the skin.[4] Photo 4.10 shows a typical soldier eating a meal ready to eat (MRE) in the field after having fired and cleaned his weapon. Remember the Navy stating:

"Do be aware that face, arms, and hands are covered with lead particles: Shooters and instructors should wash thoroughly with cold water and plenty of soap. Cold water is preferred because warm water enhances the absorption of lead by opening the pores of the skin. If no water is available, shooters should consider carrying a box of wet handwipes or a bottle of cool water and a washcloth for this purpose . . . and . . . Don't eat on the range: Lead dust on hands and face can be ingested through contact with food. Airborne lead expelled from the weapon can also contaminate food."[18]

How about heading home after working at the range or maintaining weapons?

- *Changing to clean clothing before leaving the range prevents recontamination of the hands and any contamination of the family vehicle . . .*
- *Do avoid physical contact with family members until after a shower, shampoo, and change of clothes: Lead can be transferred by casual contact. Family and friends should not be hugged or kissed until after a shower and a change of clothes. Any physical contact should be avoided while the shooter is still in range clothing . . .*
- *Do change shoes before entering residence: Shoes can also transport lead into the home. Shoes should be left at the door to prevent tracking lead onto floors and carpets . . .*
- *Contaminated clothes should not be cleaned by blowing, shaking, or other means that dispense lead into the air. To prevent cross-contamination, range clothes should be washed separately from the family's regular laundry. Families with infants should be particularly careful, since infants are most vulnerable to lead contamination.*

Everything the above soldier's boots, uniform, and skin touches gets contaminated, poisoning everyone, everything, and every place he comes into contact with.[Photos 4.11-18]

How about hugging and kissing your family and poisoning them? What about sex? Those same toxic compounds now in your blood and semen are transferred to create a baby, the lead crossing the placental barrier to build up in the bones of the baby. All of you are being poisoned as the lead leaches out for forty years or more after a person's last exposure, forever altering the health, mind, and body of those poisoned.

Take a look at those pictures again. I lived like this for my entire career not knowing any better. The Navy didn't notify me of its findings in 1999.[18]

My uniforms hung in our closet. They were washed with the same laundry as my wife's and children's. We had one family vehicle that I drove to and from work. Recreating these photos for you made me sick to my stomach. I couldn't use real photos, as the Navy and Department of Defense would have had an excuse to bury this book.

What about the grocery store, restaurant, rental cars, and hotels used by those in contaminated uniforms coming from the range?

See those veterans flying home from overseas in camouflaged uniforms? Think they are contaminating those airline seats? Every veteran you see in camouflaged uniforms or flight suits out in town could be spreading these poisons without even knowing it. That was me and all those I worked with.

Not just first- and secondhand exposure from firearms, how about the innocent civilians you see in the media of late? Recognize the heavy white smoke you see in the media used by law enforcement to combat the riots occurring across the country?

Whether a flash-bang stun or smoke or tear gas grenade, it doesn't matter. The Department of Defense, EPA, and government recognized almost twenty years ago that the ordnance used by law enforcement to combat the protests and riots of today consist of

a. fifteen hazardous and toxic chemical compounds in GG09, nonlethal stun hand grenade[6(Ch 15.5.13)] (chemical compounds that are *lethal*),

b. fifty-nine hazardous and toxic chemical compounds in G930, White Smoke Grenade[6(Ch 15.5.5)], and

c. forty-one hazardous and toxic chemical compounds in G963, M7A3 CS Riot Control Agent Hand Grenade (Tear Gas).[6(Ch 15.5.10)]

Let's understand three important points:

1. Lead contamination doesn't break down to something benign from exposure to the sun, water, or over time. It will be lethal forever, poisoning everything it comes into contact with until physically removed.
2. Every contaminated person will deposit lead wherever they go. With every new contact, it accumulates in increasing amounts until physically removed. One veteran contaminating one airline seat won't necessarily poison you. How about ten, twenty, or one hundred veterans? What about that aircraft being used to transport entire planeloads of soldiers to and from war? How about that restaurant or grocery store down the street from a military base that caters to hundreds of customers a week in camouflaged uniforms or flight suits?
3. In the body, poisoning is cumulative. One dose doesn't just go away overnight. It takes forty years to leave the body. Every contact with this poison increases the amount of lead in your body and bones with each dose, and that forty-year countdown resets until your body is completely free of lead.

How many people do you know who have been or are being exposed? How many who are being poisoned daily? Is it in your home? The store or restaurant you and your family frequent? How about that used vehicle you just bought? What about that cool, hip army surplus jacket or boots your daughter or niece is wearing?

Does your family wear the old uniforms a military member in your family kept after leaving the service?

Will you allow that service member in camouflaged uniform or flight suit into your place of business, vehicle, or home?

We have some tough choices ahead.

CHAPTER 5
Recognizing the Symptoms

Let's begin this chapter by listing many of the lead poisoning symptoms recognized by our military and government. Here are a few:

- 1975 NIOSH[17]—metallic taste in mouth, loss of appetite, indigestion, nausea, vomiting, constipation, abdominal cramps, nervousness, and insomnia.
- 1999 Department of the Navy[18]—abdominal pain, fatigue, nausea, subtle mood changes, headaches, constipation, irritability, depression, muscle pain, muscle weakness, weight loss, impotence, convulsions, anemia, renal (kidney) failure, decreased sex drive, sterility, birth defects, miscarriages of the fetus, and/or birth defects; and in children, slow learning, mental drifts, slight retardation in development, hypertension, and behavioral problems.
- 2014 EPA[97]—brain, liver, and kidney damage; slowed development; learning or behavior problems; lowered intellect (or IQ); hearing loss; restlessness; headaches; stomachaches; nausea; tiredness; and irritability.
- 2018 CDC/NIOSH[21]—abdominal pain, constipation, fatigue, headache, irritability, loss of appetite, memory loss, pain or tingling in the hands and/or feet, anemia, weakness, kidney and brain damage, death, high blood pressure, heart disease, kidney disease, reduced fertility, miscarriage, stillbirths, infertility (in both men and women), and affected behavior and intelligence;

in children, all of the above plus neurological effects and mental retardation.

- 2019 VA[22]—metal-taste in mouth, frequent stomachaches, nausea, abdominal cramps, muscle pain or weakness, frequent stomachaches (lead colic), joint and muscle pain, weakness, and loss of memory; changes in personality, motor skills, and learning ability.
- 2019 OSHA[23]—metal taste in mouth, frequent stomachaches, nausea, abdominal cramps, and muscle pain or weakness; changes in personality, memory, learning, motor skills.

Additionally, the Occupational Safety and Health Administration stated: *Epidemiological and experimental studies indicate that chronic exposure resulting in blood lead levels (BLLs) as low as 10 µg/dL in adults are associated with impaired kidney function, high blood pressure, nervous system and neurobehavioral effects, cognitive dysfunction later in life, and subtle cognitive effects attributed to prenatal exposure. Pregnant women need to be especially concerned with reducing BLL since this can have serious impact on the developing fetus.*

Chronic exposures leading to BLLs above 20 µg/dL can cause subclinical effects on cognitive functions as well as adverse effects on sperm/semen quality and delayed conception. BLLs between 20 to 40 µg/dL are associated with effects such as cognitive aging as well as deficits in visuomotor dexterity, lower reaction time, and attention deficit. At BBLs above 40 µg/dL, workers begin to experience symptoms such as headache, fatigue, sleep disturbance, joint pain, myalgia, anorexia, and constipation.

While much less common today, workers can be exposed to high lead levels resulting in BLL over 60 µg/dL. Health effects at these very high BLLs can range from acute effects such as convulsions, coma, and in some cases, death, to more chronic conditions such as anemia, peripheral neuropathy, interstitial kidney fibrosis, and severe abdominal cramping.[23]

Despite multiple federal government departments and agencies having conducted research recognizing this poisoning and the symptoms it creates, no effort has been undertaken to address, mitigate, or stop it. The worst offender by far is the Department of Defense. Let me introduce you to the most recent and comprehensive government report documenting the extent of our poisoning.

Department of Defense Contract W81K04-11-D-0017, "Potential Health Risks to DoD Firing Range Personnel from Recurrent Lead Exposure," National Academy of Sciences and Medicine, 2012[24]

Funded under contract by the Department of Defense, this report was produced by the National Academy of Sciences and Medicine. On Monday, December 3, 2012, at 2:00 p.m. EST, a prepublication advance copy was released for public review. Its existence should have resulted in massive changes within our military and government to mitigate our exposure and stop the poisoning, right? Wrong—nothing happened. The Department of Defense did nothing.

The National Academy of Sciences is a private, nonprofit, nongovernmental organization composed of the country's leading researchers. The National Academy consists of the National Academy of the Sciences, Engineering, and Medicine. Signed into law by President Abraham Lincoln on March 3, 1863, as an Act of Congress,[25] it established the National Academy, stating:

> *The Academy shall, whenever called upon by any department of the Government, investigate, examine, experiment, and report upon any subject of science or art, the actual expense of such investigations, examinations, experiments, and reports to be paid from appropriations which may be made for the purpose, but the Academy shall receive no compensation whatever for any services to the Government of the United States.*

The National Academy of Sciences is charged with providing independent, objective advice to our leaders on matters related to science and technology. When called upon, the National Academy of Sciences and its foreign associates gather the best and brightest that our nation and the world have to offer to examine any subject on which our government identifies a need for information.

First published in December 2012, this report identified a number of disturbing conclusions and further confirmed gross willful negligence committed by the US government and Department of Defense.

Gross willful negligence for failing to "furnish to each of his employees employment and a place of employment which are free from recognized hazards that are causing or are likely to cause death or serious physical harm to his employees" per 29 U.S.C. § 654, 5(a)1.

Gross willful negligence in taking no action to protect the public, our communities, and environment from "recognized hazards that are causing or are likely to cause death or serious physical harm."

Upon discovering this report in late 2017, I had the answers I'd desperately searched for to explain the sickness and disease my family and I have suffered as a result of my employment as a warrior and Navy and DoD weapons expert, technician, and firing range employee. Immediately apparent and disturbing are the conclusions presented in Chapter 6 of the report, but first let me share this little tidbit: Congress was briefed on this report's findings in 2012[26] and the Department of Defense in 2013[24] that the standards in use to protect its employees from lead poisoning are insufficient to protect us. Not just veterans and government employees—all of us. (Standards being the laws and regulations in use by the government.)

That's right. Congress and the DoD were informed by the world's leading experts, who provided evidence primarily consisting of government reports,[27,28] substantiating that OSHA and DoD regulations in use were obsolete and failed to protect us from poisoning. These regulations are in use by every government and civilian organization in the United States today. Let me rephrase:

Congress and the DoD were informed and provided evidence[24,26] substantiated by the EPA,[28] the Department of Health and Human Services (NIH, NIEHS, CDC, NIOSH),[27] and the Food and Drug Administration[27] identifying that Department of Defense and OSHA regulations were obsolete and failed to protect us from lead poisoning. Regulations that all other government agencies and civilian organizations rely upon to safeguard their employees and the public from lead poisoning. All of us.

So what did they do about it? *Nothing.* There was an election going on back then, remember? It did not fit the narrative for the Democrats in charge or the Republicans challenging them to do anything. So they did nothing, thus allowing our poisoning to continue today.

This National Academy of Sciences report[24] referenced over 261 peer-reviewed and validated scientific research reports produced by the world's foremost authorities to identify that the standards in use today, established by the Department of Labor's OSHA in 1978, were outdated and did not sufficiently protect employees. It identified that despite advances in medicine, detection, and lead mitigation, government and military standards have not been updated for over forty years. Why forty years? It is 2021, and those standards are still in use today.

Further, Congress and the Department of Defense were notified that the Department of Health and Human Services National Toxicology Program and the Environmental Protection Agency had completed research and issued reports *recognizing these hazards* and identifying this in 2012 as well,[27,28] research referenced by the National Academy of Sciences in its report.[24] What does that tell us?

In 2012, the government further *recognized hazards that may cause death or serious physical harm to its employees* and were responsible for immediately addressing it to *provide a place of employment free from recognized hazards* per federal law.[3,8] Instead, they did nothing.

The National Toxicology Program (NTP) consists of the National Center for Toxicological Research (NCTR) of the Food and Drug Administration (FDA), the National Institute of Environmental Health

Sciences (NIEHS) of the National Institutes of Health (NIH), and the National Institute for Occupational Safety and Health (NIOSH) of the Centers for Disease Control and Prevention (CDC). These 2012 National Academy of Sciences, NTP, and EPA reports document adverse health effects at blood lead levels under 5 and 10 µg/dL of blood. OSHA, Department of Defense, and Veterans Affairs (VA) regulations state that 40 µg/dL of lead in blood is safe. You may recall mine was found to be 66 µg/dL in 2014.

Despite Congress and the Department of Defense's decision to ignore the results of these 2012 findings, reports by multiple other agencies and departments of the US government chronicle the culpability of our government and its leaders for allowing the continued poisoning of its employees, their families, our citizens, and the country. Our government has already recognized the OSHA standard of 40 µg/dL of blood ineffective at protecting employees from lead poisoning but has taken no action to stop it. OSHA and the VA also still use this standard today.

This report goes into great detail establishing the science necessary to update the standards in use today. A brief review of the references used to compile this report reveal multiple official government reports and documents used from the Departments of Defense, Health and Human Services, the Environmental Protection Agency, Labor, and their subordinate agencies, again, clearly establishing the government's culpability for recognizing hazards that are causing or are likely to cause death or serious physical harm to his employees.[8]

This and the EPA and NTP reports are fantastic resources that document the cause of symptoms suffered by those who experience poisoning from lead. They break tradition, establishing that low levels of lead, thought to have been benign in the past, are responsible for the sickness, disease, and death suffered by veterans, law enforcement, firing range and associated employees, and their families the world over. This includes all those exposed to firearms and the secondhand exposure and contamination caused by them.

Before we continue, let me briefly touch on and answer a question you are likely asking. If the Department of Defense had known since 2000 that its troops and employees were exposed to a total of 146 hazardous and toxic compounds[2] and that DoD firing range personnel like me were exposed to chronic stress,[17] why did the DoD contract the National Academy of Sciences to research only the dangers of our exposure to lead poisoning?

A better question would be, if the Department of Defense, Departments of the Army, Navy, and Air Force employ thousands of medical doctors, toxicologists, industrial hygienists, and other safety and occupational health professionals in hundreds of medical, research, laboratory, and safety and occupational health medical facilities around the world, and if they have access to the medical records of the largest single demographic of exposed personnel on the planet, why did they contract out for a report from the outside and only for lead? Why not do it themselves?

Simple: they do not have to officially agree with and accept this report, thus avoiding liability and therefore maintaining legal plausible deniability and protection from accountability. The Department of Defense knew what it was doing. Conspiracy? Yes. Evidence and answers to these questions will be presented in Volume 2 of this edition.

This 2012 report[24] documents the OSHA blood lead level standard of 40 μg/dL (or mcg/dL) of blood fails to protect us from the sickness and disease caused by lead poisoning. What does a BLL of 40 μg/dL mean? Forty micrograms of lead per deciliter of blood is the maximum amount of acceptable lead in the blood established by OSHA in 1978. This "standard" is written into law as regulations in OSHA 1910.1025(j)(2)(i) and is still used today by various agencies to include the VA. As long as this OSHA standard exists, government and industry can continue to legally poison us free from accountability.

What is a deciliter of blood? A deciliter of blood is one-tenth of a liter. If an average adult has 5 liters of blood, this means OSHA, the VA, and other government organizations allow an average adult's blood to contain as much as 2,000 micrograms of lead. I had 3,300 micrograms of lead in my blood in 2014. So how much lead was in my body during that one test in 2014? Remember the 1999 US Marine Corps Department of the Navy Engineering Study,[18] which stated:

> "Approximately 6 percent of all lead ingested or inhaled is immediately deposited in the blood or soft body tissues, such as the kidneys, brain, or other vital organs. The remaining 94 percent is more deeply deposited in bone matter."

That means OSHA allows 31,340 micrograms of lead to be deposited in bone at the time that a blood test is taken. I had 51,510 deposited in my bones in 2014 when my blood test revealed 66 micrograms per deciliter in my blood. That is enough lead to completely cover a dime, maybe even a penny. How did it get there?

A Freedom of Information Act request response provided a 2015 industrial hygiene report of my place of employment. It documented test results taken to investigate my poisoning that registered lead dust distributed on every surface throughout the building I worked in. Lead in the air. Lead on my desk. Lead on my computer keyboard, mouse, and telephone. It documented lead dust on the fresh air supply vent above my desk. It documented lead dust on areas where the Navy SEALs and I trained and daily stood, kneeled, sat, and lay down to fire weapons. Over three hundred times the maximum Navy allowed limit.

Daily, every minute of every day I worked there, lead was absorbed through the pores of my skin. I breathed it, drank it in the coffee I brewed at work next to my desk, and ate it in my lunch. FOIA responses revealed reports back to the opening day of the range I worked in reporting the same. Worse, they reported that I was completing tasks that exposed me to large amounts of lead and that required immediate testing. Testing the Navy failed to conduct while they continued requiring me to perform those tasks. Tasks I performed for years until finding out how seriously poisoned I was in 2014.

Federal law and naval regulations require that Naval Special Warfare Command notify me that I was being poisoned. They concealed this and many other reports from me. I only know about it from FOIA and Privacy Act request responses attained years after I was fired for whistleblowing.

Worse, it's cumulative. That number represents only the lead deposited in my bones from that single blood test that day. I have experienced poisoning daily, with lead deposited in my bones throughout my entire Navy career. How much was deposited? I will never know. During the twenty-nine years I served, before that 2014 blood test, the Navy had only tested me twice despite regulations requiring it every six months. Remember also that the 51,510 (or 66 μg/dL) deposited in my bones that day will take forty years or more to completely clear out of my body,[33] which means that it is still poisoning me today.

So what does this report chronicle? Building on the NTP,[27] EPA,[28] and the over 261 research reports reviewed by the National Academies in 2012,[24] these reports establish:

- adverse renal effects (kidney failure) beginning at 8–9 μg/dL;
- adverse cardiovascular effects that include increased blood PSI, hypertension, and hypertensive vascular disease at under 10 μg/dL;
- increased cardiovascular mortality (heart failure and death) at 8 μg/dL or higher;
- adverse nervous system effects in cognitive and psychomotor performance at about 18 μg/dL and higher;
- hearing loss at under 10 μg/dL;
- changes in balance at about 14 μg/dL;
- changes in visual function at 17 μg/dL;
- slowed auditory-evoked potentials at 26 μg/dL;
- changes in autonomic nervous system function at 20 μg/dL;
- changes in peripheral sensory nerve function at 30 μg/dL;

- adverse hematologic effects (blood production and life span) at about 20–30 μg/dL;
- adverse developmental effects in infants and children at maternal levels at under 10 μg/dL; and
- reduced fetal growth and low birth weight at under 5 μg/dL.

My last VA lead blood test in June 2019 listed the range of 0–40 μg/dL as acceptable. This standard of acceptable amounts of lead in blood was established in 1978 by the Department of Labor's OSHA. The Department of Defense and Congress were notified that it was insufficient to protect us from poisoning in 2012 by this DoD contracted report.[24] The EPA and NTP reports did the same.[27,28] Remember, the CDC even stated in 2017, "There is no known lower threshold limit for lead exposure and harmful health effects."[88] So why does the VA, military, and OSHA continue to state that 40 μg/dL of lead in blood is acceptable when the medical and research subject matter experts of the US government have already established that standard to be grossly outdated and ineffective? Why are they ignoring the science?

That 2019 blood test further documented that lead is still leaching out of my bones after a career of constant exposure. The military and VA refuse to test for this.

When I asked for a lead-in-bone test, both VA neurology and toxicology departments refused my request, stating that:

"It wouldn't correctly reflect my lead exposure as it would reflect my lifetime exposure to other sources not affiliated with my military service as well. Sources like exposure to paint chips in the paint of my house."

"Funny," I responded. "I resided in military housing my entire career; I don't care about then; I just want an explanation and treatment for my symptoms now."

It is constantly being reported in the news how military housing is poisoned with lead,[32] the same military housing my family lived in, which was built at the turn of the century and contained lead water pipes and lead paint chips. The same military housing that the Navy documented in 1999[18] was contaminated with the lead from dust shooters and range workers brought home from work. Despite this fact, the VA still refuses to test for levels of lead in bone. Why? Conspiracy? Yes, but, how about gross willful negligence, misdiagnosis, and malpractice?

This 2012 DoD report[24] also inadvertently identifies shortfalls in testing procedures. Let me explain: Let's say a lead blood test registers 50 μg/dL of lead in a worker's blood. OSHA then requires that the person be placed in a job with no possible exposure to lead until the lead level recedes to under 40. The half-life of lead in the blood is roughly twenty-eight days.[33]

With a half-life of four weeks, one month later with no exposure to lead, that 50 μg/dL would be roughly halved to a blood lead level of 25 μg/dL. Given no exposure to lead, a month later it should drop by half again to roughly 12 and so on, until 0 μg/dL is registered around three months later.

The point is that unless testing is performed immediately after every exposure, the likelihood of detecting a blood lead level that exceeds the current regulation of 40 μg/dL from a blood test is highly unlikely. That test result of 50 μg/dL of blood only documented the level of lead at the time it was taken. Under current regulations, if that test were conducted a week or more later, it would have registered an acceptable reading of under 40 μg/dL of blood. No action would have been taken nor would the employee be made aware that they had been poisoned at a level that exceeds current regulations.

No investigation done, no report filed, and yet the employee still gets sick and maybe dies without ever knowing why. Worse, had that employee tested at 40 μg/dL, they could very well have been exposed to a lethal dose of 80 μg/dL four weeks earlier and never even been aware of it. The system of standards, checks, and balances is flawed and does not work.

All this is further complicated by the diagnosis of lead poisoning symptoms. As documented in the Navy's 1999 report:[18]

"The numerous symptoms of lead poisoning mimic various diseases, often making diagnosis confusing and difficult."

And:

"Because the symptoms mirror those of many childhood diseases, many doctors do not test for lead exposure."

As I have experienced, the VA Medical Center's Departments of Neurology and Mental Health in La Jolla, California, do not recognize lead poisoning in diagnosis and treatment at all despite being presented with evidence of a career's worth of chronic long-term exposure and poisoning.

If lead exposure is not identified or is ignored in diagnosis, misdiagnosis then occurs, leading to the tragic consequences of mistreatment, malpractice, and the continued onset of poisoning symptoms. Keep in mind this occurs for all toxic and hazardous compounds identified in the army tests[2] and EPA's AP 42.[6] Let's take a closer look at the DoD National Academy of Sciences report[24] and the symptoms veterans suffer from documented in it.

All the effects of lead poisoning documented by this 2012 DoD report,[24] the National Toxicology Program's report,[27] and the EPA's report[28] highlight the damaging effects of multiple systems throughout the body taking place at under the 40 μg/dL standard used by OSHA, the VA, the DoD, and the government today. They include damage to the:
- kidneys,
- hematology (normal production of blood),
- bone marrow,
- thymus,

- lymph nodes and various other lymphoid organs and tissues,
- cardiovascular (heart, arteries, and circulatory system),
- cancer effects,
- male and female reproductive organs,
- developmental (physical and neurological birth defects),
- central nervous system,
- peripheral nervous system,
- autonomic nervous system,
- sensory organ function,
- brain, and
- psychological development and progression.

Renal Effects

Kidney disease and kidney failure are symptoms recognized to be caused by lead poisoning. The kidneys filter waste from the body and also produce hormones and enzymes involved in blood regeneration in bone marrow and other functions such as the regulation of blood pressure. In addition to filtering lead and other waste products from the body, the kidneys and blood-regeneration systems in the body are codependent on each other's healthy function.

In short, the adverse effects on the hematopoietic system by lead poisoning result in heme proteins injuring the kidneys. Lead poisoning of the kidneys results in their failure to filter waste from the body and produce the hormones and enzymes required by the blood and cardiovascular system to function normally. This contributes to hypertension and abnormal blood regeneration times (see Hematopoietic Effects).

If not recognized and diagnosed early, kidney disease and kidney failure will result. A by-product of this failure results in high blood PSI, hypertension, heart disease, and heart failure. Sound familiar?

Hematopoietic Effects

What does hematopoietic mean? Like you, I am not a doctor, so I had to look it up.

It means the system in adult mammals involved in the production and maturation of red blood cells, white blood cells, and platelets. It consists of the bone marrow, thymus, lymph nodes, and other lymphoid organs and tissues. The 2012 report[24] presents evidence supporting the symptoms identified above that includes anemia and other symptoms, which are a result of inhibited heme production.

Heme is the substance necessary to produce the hemoglobin that transports oxygen throughout the body. Compromising the integrity and production of the components necessary to transport oxygen places more stress on the cardiovascular system. The cardiovascular system is then called upon to transport more blood containing less oxygen than a normal, healthy system of blood production would produce.

These reports[24,27,28] conclude that there is sufficient evidence to infer that lead poisoning affects the body's ability to normally produce hemoglobin and therefore transport oxygen throughout the body. They also note the shortened survival times of red blood cells within the body.

They present evidence[24,27,28] that red blood cells in normal humans, who have not been exposed to lead poisoning, live approximately 120 days. Red blood cells in lead-poisoned humans live about 101 days. What does this mean?

For the human body to continue transporting the needed amount of oxygen demanded by the body, it must produce roughly 17 percent more red blood cells in a lead-poisoned individual. To make up for the loss, and until the needed blood is produced, the cardiovascular system is tasked with providing increased blood flow through increased heart rate and blood flow management.

Translated, that means high blood pressure, hypertension, and an increase in cardiovascular mortality (increased death rates at earlier ages due to heart failure, stroke, etc.), just like those identified in Chapter 1.

Keep in mind that interrupting the normal flow of blood throughout the body also interferes with the flow of waste materials produced by normal cell activity. This waste is toxic. These toxins are filtered and discarded by the kidneys and liver.

Think of each living cell in our body as a tiny human. It needs food, water, and oxygen to survive and do its job. It then produces carbon dioxide, urine, and feces. The blood transports these to and from each cell. When the body is not removing waste material, it accumulates in the blood and organs, systemically poisoning the body and resulting in further symptoms not associated with lead poisoning.

Cardiovascular Effects

As identified above, the cardiovascular system has to work harder, putting stress on the heart and system of veins and arteries to maintain the supply of oxygen to the body. Despite Special Operations Soldiers, Sailors, and Marines like me, who worked hard our entire careers and live to maintain ourselves in top physical condition, we are dying at a much higher rate than our peers.

This 2012 DoD report[24] concludes that evidence is sufficient to infer lead poisoning causes increased blood pressure, hypertension, and an increase in cardiovascular mortality. The medical term *cardiovascular mortality*, in short, means death from heart failure. This same type of heart failure that has killed my fellow teammates is killing me through hypertensive heart disease today.

Recently, I had a heart attack scare. After an overnight stay in the hospital and enduring a multitude of tests, doctors determined that my heart has stiffened and therefore does not relax between beats. What does that mean?

The heart must fully relax to allow its chambers to completely fill up with blood. If it does not relax, the chambers don't fill and the heart pumps less blood, creating a shortage of oxygen throughout the body. This also means the heart cannot maintain good blood pressure. The result?

Hypertension and diastolic heart failure. Heart failure with preserved ejection fraction (HFpEF). This is the increase in cardiovascular mortality due to poisoning that killed my brother and sister veterans as discussed in Chapter 1. Why doesn't the heart relax? There are a few causes that I will cover in the next chapters.

How am I doing? The doc says what has saved me so far is that I have a large "athletic" heart. Years of taking care of my body and working out have produced a large, strong heart that pumps enough blood to keep my body going. I now know that I have to manage my heart rate throughout the day. Hopefully, this knowledge will allow me, and those who read this book, to outlive those who didn't have it. The problem is that as the lead leaches out of my bones over the next 34 years, my cardiovascular system will continue to deteriorate. Maintaining a blood lead level over twice that of an average adult doesn't help.

Cancer Effects

Despite the well-documented effects on the renal system, this report does not conclude that it has sufficient evidence to link renal cancer in humans to lead poisoning. Sufficient evidence links it in other mammals but does not yet exist for humans. Why not, you may wonder? After all, our government has recognized this poisoning for over fifty years. Why haven't they conducted the testing? What I will tell you is that in the case of the poisoning revealed here, it doesn't matter.

Multiple government reports document that the hazardous and toxic compounds produced by ordnance and the guns we fire contain recognized Group One Carcinogens. Group One Carcinogens are known cancer-causing compounds in humans recognized by the International Agency for Research on Cancer (IARC), Department of Health and Human Services, EPA, and NTP agencies (NIOSH, CDC, FDA, NIH, etc.). Further evidence will be revealed later in the book.

You'll likely recognize some of these Group One Carcinogens as well:

Acrolein   Furans
Benzene   Hexavalent Chromium

Beryllium   Toluene

Dioxins

Trimethylbenzene

Take a look at Table 5.1 below. You will recognize a number of toxic compounds you didn't know were produced by firearms and ordnance. Table 2.1 lists 62 of the 146 that are produced by pistols, rifles, and shotguns commonly used by the military, law enforcement, and the roughly fifty million shooting participants in America each year.[5] The other 84 are produced by the pyrotechnics used in tracer rounds, grenades, flash bangs, smoke grenades, illumination rounds, explosives, and propellants used in the big guns, rockets, and guided missiles.

Those in the military who serve on ships, in army tanks, and Marine Corps armored vehicles or who fire or maintain any of the numerous weapons systems, armories, range facilities, etc., that these compounds are produced at and contaminate are exposed to the hazardous and toxic compounds identified in Table 5.1. This happens for many of these personnel and their families daily, for entire careers, and forty years after leaving the service.[24,27,28]

Table 5.1 Hazardous and Toxic Compounds Produced by Ordnance

Note: This table contains only the 146 hazardous and toxic compounds listed in the EPA's AP 42 Chapter 15.[6] Compounds produced by all manner of military ordnance to include small arms, large guns, tanks, rockets and missiles, grenades, and pyrotechnics. It does not include all of the compounds listed.

Acenaphthene

Acenaphthylene

Acetaldehyde

Acetonitrile

Acetophenone

Acrolein

Acrylonitrile

Allyl Chloride

Aluminum

Ammonia

Anthracene

Antimony

Arsenic

Barium

Benzene

Benzenev

Benzo[*a*]pyrene

Benzo[*a*]anthracene

Benzo[*b*]fluoranthene

Benzo[*k*]fluoranthene

Benzo[*g,h,i*]perylene

Benzo[*g,h,i*]perylene

Benzo[*e*]pyrene

Beryllium

Bromomethane

1,3-Butadiene

t-Butyl Alcohol

Butanal

Butyl benzyl phthalate

Butyraldehyde

2-Butoxy Ethanol

Cadmium

Carbon disulfide

Carbon Tetrachloride

Carbonyl Sulfide

Chlorine

Chlorobenzene

Chloroethane

Chloroform

Chloromethane

Chromium

Chrysene

Cobalt

Copper

Crotonaldehyde

Cumene

Cyclohexane

Particulate Cyanide

Dibenz[*a,h*]anthracene

Dibutyl phthalate

Di-*n*-butyl phthalate

Dichlorodifluoromethane

1,2-Dichlorobenzene

1,3-Dichlorobenzene

1,4-Dichlorobenzene

Dichlorodifluoromethane

1,2-Dichloroethane

Dimethyl Phthalate

Diphenylamine

2,6-Dinitrotolulene

Total Dioxin/Furan Compounds

Ethyl Acrylate

Ethylbenzene

Ethylene

bis(2-Ethylhexyl)phthalate

Fluoranthene

Fluorene

Formaldehyde

Freon
Freon 113
Hexachlorobutadiene
Hexachloroethane
Hexane
n-Hexane
Hexavalent Chromium
1,2,3,4,6,7,8-Heptachlorod-
ibenzofuran
1,2,3,4,6,7,8-HpCDD
1,2,3,4,6,7,8-HpCDF
1234789-HPCDF
1234789-HPCDF
1234789-HPCDF
123478-HXCDD
123678-HXCDD
123789-HXCDD
1,2,3,4,7,8-HxCDF
1,2,3,6,7,8-HxCDF
2,3,4,6,7,8-HxCDF
Hydrochloric Acid
Hydrogen Cyanide
Indeno[1,2,3-cd]pyrene
Isopropyl Alcohol
Isothiocyanato Methane
Manganese
Methacrylonitrile
Methylene Chloride
Methyl Isobutyl Ketone
Methyl Methacrylate
2-Methyllactonitrile
2-Methylnaphthalene
Methyl t-Butyl Ether
Methylene Chloride

Mercury
Naphthalene
Nickel
Nitric acid
Nitroglycerin
2-Nitrophenol
4-Nitrophenol
OCDD
1,2,3,4,6,7,8,9-Octachlorod
ibenzo-p-dioxin
1,2,3,4,6,7,8,9-Octachlorod
ibenzofuran
1,2,3,7,8-Pentachlorodibenzo-
p-dioxin
12378-PECDF
23478-PECD
Pentachlorobenzene
Phenanthrene
Phenol
Phosphorus
Propanedinitrile
 (Phenylmethylene)
Propionaldehyde
Propylene
Pyridine
Pyrene
Selenium
Silver
Styrene
Sulfuric Acid
Tetrachloroethylene
1,1,2,2-Tetrachloroethane
2,3,7,8-Tetrachlorodibenzo-
p-dioxin

2,3,7,8-Tetrachlorodibenzofuran
2,3,7,8-TCDF
Thallium
Toluene
1,1,1-Trichloroethane
Trichlorofluoromethane
2,4,6-Trichlorophenol
1,2,4-Trimethylbenzene
2,2,4- Trimethylpentane
Vanadium
Vinyl Chloride
Vinylidene Chloride
m-Xylene
o-Xylene
p-Xylene
Zinc

US Army Environmental Center (USAEC) Contract No. GS-10F-0131K, Order No. W911S0-04-F-001 test results published in the US Environmental Protection Agency Office of Air Quality Planning and Standards "Air Emissions Factors and Quantification" report, Chapter 15, "AP 42 Section 15" sections below:

i.	12ga shotgun	15.1.2, 15.1.3
ii.	9mm pistol	15.1.21
iii.	.38 cal pistol	15.1.23, 15.1.24
iv.	.45 cal pistol	15.1.25
v.	5.56mm rifle and machine gun	15.1.4, 15.1.5, 15.1.6, 15.1.7, 15.1.8, 15.1.9
vi.	7.62mm rifle and machine gun	15.1.12, 15.1.13, 15.1.14, 15.1.15, 15.1.16
vii.	.50 cal machine gun	15.1.26, 15.1.27, 15.1.28, 15.1.29
viii.	20mm machine gun	15.1.30
ix.	25mm chain gun	15.1.31, 15.1.32
x.	40mm grenade launcher	15.2.2, 15.2.3, 15.2.4, 15.2.5, 15.2.6, 15.2.7, 15.2.13, 15.2.15
xi.	60mm mortar	15.2.8, 15.2.9, 15.2.10, 15.2.11, 15.2.12, 15.2.14
xii.	75mm naval gun	Not Available
xiii.	81mm mortar	15.3.1, 15.3.2, 15.3.11, 15.3.12, 15.3.22, 15.3.29
xiv.	84mm mortar	15.3.13
xv.	105mm artillery gun	15.3.4, 15.3.5, 15.3.17
xvi.	120mm Abrams tank gun	15.3.3, 15.3.7, 15.3.8, 15.3.9, 15.3.10, 15.3.15, 15.3.25, 15.3.26
xvii.	5-inch naval guns	not available
xviii.	155mm artillery gun	15.4.1, 15.4.3, 15.4.4, 15.3.5
xix.	grenades	15.5.2, 15.5.3, 15.5.4, 15.5.5, 15.5.11, 15.5.12, 15.5.13, 15.5.14
xx.	guided missiles	not available
xxi.	rockets	15.6.5, 15.6.6

Table 5.1

Reproductive and Developmental Effects

We opened this chapter by listing symptoms recognized by a number of government agencies, reports and resources documenting the effects of lead poisoning, including those on the reproductive system, fetuses, and our children. They include reduced fertility, miscarriage, stillbirths, infertility (in both men and women), slow learning, mental drifts, slight retardation in development, hypertension, behavioral problems affecting behavior and intelligence, neurological effects, and mental retardation.

This 2012 DoD-contracted report[24] concluded that evidence is sufficient to infer that lead poisoning affects sperm and semen, including decreased sperm count, reduced sperm movement, and increased sperm structure defects. The report also concludes evidence is sufficient to infer that BLLs of under 10 μg/dL affect and impair the normal development of infants and children, and there is evidence of an association between maternal BLLs under 5 μg/dL and reduced fetal growth and low birth weight.

As we have learned,[18,24,27,28] and in terms easier to understand, when a female is poisoned with lead, the body deposits lead into bones, believing it to be calcium. There it will reside for forty years or more as it slowly leaches out from the body. During pregnancy, a woman's body will remove that lead and calcium from her bones to build the bones of the fetus in the womb.

As that lead crosses the placental barrier in her blood, it is circulated throughout the developing fetus, where it poisons the unborn child, hindering its growth and damaging its brain and nervous system. Not only does it reside in the mother for forty years or more, but it also now resides in the infant's bones for forty years or more, until the infant's body disposes it. All the while, that lead continues to poison the developing child into adulthood.

If the fetus is damaged enough to become unviable, the mother's body will kill and reject it, aborting the pregnancy in miscarriage or stillbirth. Regardless, lead circulating through the fetus is recognized to cause neurological, behavioral, and/or physical birth defects.[18,24,27-29] Irreversible effects that will plague the child for its entire life. My son was diagnosed with severe autism at age two.

Knowing this, why does our government and the Department of Defense actively recruit and allow women to serve in the armed forces performing jobs requiring their constant exposure to this poisoning? Why would they allow them to work with a BLL of up to 40 µg/dL? Does the government and DoD conceal this poisoning from these women? The answer is yes.

In addition, let's not forget our government is aware that *lead can also alter the structure of sperm cells, thereby causing birth defects.*[18]

Why hasn't our government taken steps to protect the unborn children and family plans of both their female and male employees, as well as veterans and their families?

In the next chapter, I will examine the effects of this poisoning on behavior and the body's nervous system. These have the most impact on our daily lives, as well as on those who have never even fired a gun.

CHAPTER 6

The Effects on the Nervous System and Behavior

As I continued examining the findings of the Department of Defense,[24] National Toxicology Project,[27] and EPA,[28] I began to see a pattern in my own symptoms.

Those reports document in great detail the signs, symptoms, sickness, and disease caused by poisoning that my fellow veterans and I suffer from. Reading these reports and their references revealed the source of the excessive white and gray matter anomalies, which magnetic resonance imaging (MRI) tests have shown in my brain. They identified the source of the numbness, itching, burning, and sensation of ants crawling around, including pain in our forearms, hands, lower legs, and feet—diabetic nerve pain without the diabetes.

They established that the hearing loss we have experienced is caused by lead poisoning. Most importantly, they established the cause of the hypervigilance that I was misdiagnosed with upon retiring from active duty in 2009, severe posttraumatic stress disorder (PTSD) that I was misdiagnosed with seven years later, and my high blood pressure, hypertension, and heart problems that are worsening.

One of the easier-to-understand reports that I have found is from the National Library of Medicine (NLM). The 2014 report "Pb Neurotoxicity: Neuropsychological Effects of Lead Toxicity"[34] lays it out in language I can understand. Combined with the findings of the EPA, NTP, and DoD reports, here is what I discovered:

The Peripheral Nervous System

A quick online search identifies the brain and spinal cord as the central nervous system, and the peripheral nervous system includes the ganglia and nerves throughout the rest of the body. Think of the peripheral nervous system as the back roads and highways that connect the far reaches of the body to the superhighway of the spinal cord and the big city that is the brain.

Ganglia are a mass of nerves and nerve tissue. They are little control centers outside the brain (small towns). They make decisions and initiate actions without input from the brain.

Nerve Damage and Reduced Nerve Conduction Velocity and Amplitudes

The studies I have participated in confirm damage to my peripheral nervous system. In a nutshell, my nervous system now transmits electric signals slower than it did before. How do they test for this?

They use probes with wires connected to instruments that measure the speed that electricity travels down a nerve. On one end of a nerve root, they inserted a probe—a big needle—into my upper arms and legs in the vicinity of the medial nerves. The medial nerve is the main nerve root serving the arms and legs. Think of it as the highway that branches off from the spinal cord into the back roads of our limbs.

Next, they placed a probe connected to the same machine down around my wrists and lower legs. The machine then generated electricity that blasted through the nerve root. The instruments then measured the speed at which the electric signal traveled through the nerve. The results were compared to tests conducted on healthy nervous systems.

Let me just say, submitting myself to repeated electric shock was one of the most excruciating things I have ever experienced. The result: confirmation of damage to my peripheral nervous system and the median motor nerves as identified in the National Academy, NTP, and EPA reports.[24,27,28] My VA toxicologist identified lead poisoning as a cause of my carpal tunnel and other symptoms. How does this happen?

One cause is lead poisoning that damages or inhibits the production of myelin.[24,27,28,36] Myelin is the fatty tissue that forms the insulative protective coating around nerve fibers within the brain and body. Take a look at any electrical device or appliance connected to an electrical source by a cord. The rubber coating on the cord insulates you from being shocked by the electricity flowing through the wire within the cord. More correctly, it prevents electricity from escaping. In the nervous system, myelin does the same thing.

Both the rubber-coated appliance cords and the myelin surrounding the nerve fibers protect the electrical signals, ensuring that they transmit at full strength, unimpeded, directly from the source to their destination. To measure the integrity of the insulation in electric wire, an electrician uses a megger.

A megger generates an electric signal to measure the insulation resistance in a wire. An ohm meter then reports the results. The machine used by neurologists basically does the same thing, only on a much smaller scale.

Old, cracked, or damaged wire can leak or increase the resistance to electricity traveling through it, slowing and weakening the signal. The same thing happens in the nervous system. When myelin deteriorates, electricity leaks out, which slows and weakens the signal traveling through the nerve fiber. This is referred to as *demyelization.*

Demyelization (the removal of myelin or absence of sufficient myelin) causes delays in signal transmission from the brain to the motor nerves.[24] It also slows the signal from the sensory organs to the brain and creates the poisoning symptom identified as "Slowed-Evoked Potential." What symptoms are we talking about here?

Hearing loss, blurred or double vision, poor posture and balance, foot and wrist drop, a decrease in coordination, essential tremor, muscle weakness, joint pain, myalgia, numbness and pain (usually in the hands and feet), ataxia (gait abnormality, speech changes, slurred speech, abnormal eye movements), hyperesthesia (excessive sensitivity of the skin), and decreased autonomic nervous system function, to name a few.[24,27,28]

Autonomic Nervous System (ANS): The ANS consists of a complex set of neurons contained in the ganglion that mediate and perform functions within the body without conscious intervention or voluntary control.[35] In other words, the ANS controls processes within the body without you having to think about them. The ANS controls and regulates blood pressure, breathing, digestion, urination; modulates sexual arousal; and so on. It also controls the body's reaction to stress and the fight-or-flight reaction. Damage to the autonomic nervous system is responsible or partially responsible for the following poisoning symptoms: high blood pressure, hypertension, hypertensive heart disease, disturbances in menstrual cycles, abdominal pain, constipation, diarrhea, shortness of breath, cardiac arrhythmia, abnormal EKG, a decrease in sex drive, decreased sperm count, infertility, fatigue, headache, drowsiness, anemia, labored breathing, and more.[24,27,28]

Ganglia, plural for ganglion, are clusters of nerve cell bodies within the nervous system. I will examine autonomic ganglion here. There are two types within the ANS: sympathetic and parasympathetic. Ganglia within the sympathetic and parasympathetic nervous systems control and initiate complex functions within the body automatically.

The sympathetic nervous system's primary process is to stimulate the body's fight-flight-or-freeze response. You will understand the significance of this in the next few chapters.

The parasympathetic nervous system is responsible for stimulation of processes involved in activities that occur when the body is at rest. Eating, salivation, swallowing, digestion, urination, defecation, lacrimation (secretion of tears), and sexual arousal are processes controlled by the parasympathetic nervous system.

Damage to the myelin protecting these ganglia of nerve fibers results in the symptoms listed above and more.

Central Nervous System: The central nervous system consists mainly of the brain and spinal column. The DoD report[24] concluded that lead poisoning symptoms of the central nervous system occurring as a result of oxidative stress are inhibition of enzymes needed for energy production, increased permeability of the blood-brain barrier, decreased levels of neurotransmitters, and altered neurotransmitter release.[28]

Government research and reports in 2012[24,27,28] document changes in behavior, cognitive and psychomotor performance and mood, neurodegenerative diseases, and neurophysiologic changes in the auditory, visual, and balance systems. Government reports and other sources do the same.[34,38,39]

Oxidative stress is the physiological stress placed on the body and brain caused by cumulative damage of free radicals that antioxidants have failed to stop, which are associated with aging. Oxidative stress contributes to the poisoning symptoms of premature cognitive aging, demyelization, and others. Associated symptoms include forgetfulness, attention deficits, brain fog, impaired short-term memory, memory loss, and so on.

In 2014, Lisa H. Mason, Jordan P. Harp, and Dong Y. Han stated in "Pb Neurotoxicity: Neuropsychological Effects of Lead Toxicity"[34]:

> *Lead-related changes in effect are less researched than other functional domains. A study of 526 older adults in the Normative Aging Study found that anxiety, depression, and phobia were positively correlated with bone lead level. Lead workers with high blood lead levels have been reported to experience greater interpersonal conflict than their less-exposed counterparts, and a review of 14 studies of low-level lead exposure concluded that lead-related interpersonal problems may be mediated by irritability and fatigue.*
>
> *There is also growing evidence of early lead exposure linking to increased frequency of antisocial behavior including violent behav-*

*ior. A number of studies are revealing that antisocial tendencies like violent and aggressive behaviors correlate with environmental stressors like **lead** or **polychlorinated biphenyls** (PCBs), beyond that of socioeconomic factors.*

"Inhibition of enzymes needed for energy production" is easier to understand. If the required numbers of enzymes within the central nervous system are not present, processes within the brain slow down, causing fatigue and hindering thought and action. The body is queued to rest until enzyme levels can replenish. Chronic fatigue, myalgia, and fibromyalgia result.

"Decreased levels of neurotransmitters and altered neurotransmitter release" is a bit more complex to understand. Neurotransmitters are chemicals created in the body that enable communication within the nervous system and between the nervous system and the rest of the body. They allow individual nerve cells to relay information between them along the nerve fibers throughout the body. Nerve cells protected by the myelin discussed above.

Without those chemicals, information is lost, not transmitted, or corrupted. The brain and remainder of the central nervous system do not function normally. Within the brain, this causes symptoms that include behavior changes, learning difficulties, forgetfulness, attention deficits, anxiety, aggressive behavior, brain fog, impaired short-term memory, memory loss, insomnia, impaired judgment, racing mind, decreased sex drive, and so on.

"Increased permeability of the blood-brain barrier" is what it says. The blood-brain barrier allows only the required chemicals, hormones, enzymes, and other materials to enter or leave the brain. When that barrier becomes more permeable, allowing excessive quantities to pass, oxidative stress and other physiological changes occur, opening up a myriad of possible conditions. As an example, excess glucose could trigger diabetes.

Ultimately, as a result of poisoning, changes occur in brain structure and neurochemistry, including white matter changes, reduction in gray matter, and alterations in brain metabolites,[24] the same conditions that MRIs have revealed within my brain. What is white matter and white matter disease?

A quick online search[37] explains that white matter appears as a white or pale-colored tissue due to the fatty materials contained in myelin, the same myelin discussed above that protects the electrical signals traveling through the nerve fibers of the body, brain, and spinal cord. White matter disease occurs due to the demyelization of nerve fibers in the largest and deepest part of the brain and is normally attributable to aging.

White matter disease affects problem solving, focus, and mood, resulting in behavior changes, learning difficulties, forgetfulness, attention deficits, anxiety, aggressive behavior, brain fog, impaired short-term memory, memory loss, insomnia, impaired judgment, racing mind, and more, the same premature cognitive aging symptoms identified above. Also affected are normal everyday functions like balance and the ability to walk in a straight line.

So I went for the simple explanation most of us can understand by looking it up on the internet. While white matter disease generally is recognized in older people as a normal by-product of aging, as demonstrated here, it also manifests as a result of the hormone and chemical imbalances caused by chronic poisoning. Recognize some of the symptoms we reviewed before? Symptoms documented throughout the numerous Navy,[18] CDC,[21,29,33] NIOSH,[17,30] EPA,[28] NTP,[27] VA,[22] and DoD[24] reports reviewed so far. Do you see the pattern?

Ready? Poisoning increases the permeability of the blood-brain barrier, allowing excessive free radicals and other compounds exposure to the brain, causing premature aging and damage to the myelin sheathing surrounding nerve fibers and their neurons. This decreases the levels of neurotransmitters and alters neurotransmitter release, interrupting communication within the brain, nervous system, and between the nervous system and the rest of the body. White matter changes are the visible damage to the myelin sheathing of nerve bundles that join parts of the brain. Whew! I actually understood what I just said.

Damage to the neural pathways that join different regions within the brain result in the neurobehavioral changes, destructive behaviors, and poor decision-making associated with this poisoning. The news (over the past few years) has reported on the effects of damage to the brain by traumatic brain injury and concussions experienced by football players.

"Depressive Symptoms and White Matter Dysfunction in Retired NFL Players with Concussion History"[38] is another good source of information linking white matter changes within the brain to the symptoms associated with it—the same symptoms linked to the poisoning I've discussed here.

Unfortunately, little research is available or has been conducted to identify the relationships of all the body's systems and processes affected by poisoning from the other 145 hazardous and toxic compounds listed in the army's test results,[2,6] which are absorbed, inhaled, and ingested by exposure to ordnance. Therefore, we are forced to rely on the symptoms we can identify from lead.

Table 6.1 provides a basic compilation of symptoms caused by all the hazardous and toxic compounds recognized by the government in AR15/M16 A059 ball ammunition.[6 Ch 15.1.4] Why did I pick this particular bullet to illustrate the sickness and disease it causes? The AR15/M16 and its A059 ball ammunition is simply used by more military, law enforcement, and civilian shooters in the United States today than any other firearm. As revealed earlier, it is responsible for directly poisoning every shooter with every bullet fired.

Table 6.1 Symptoms of AR15/M16 Poisoning

The below symptoms are presented from the hazardous and toxic compounds listed in the army's 2000 test results[2] published in 2004 by the EPA[6] for AR15/M16 assault rifle A059 ball ammunition. Chapter 15.1.4 "A059 (M16A1 rifle) EF Calculations" spreadsheet summary page documents tests were conducted at the US Army Aberdeen Proving Grounds 3/23/2000. Two tests of twenty rounds each were conducted.

Note 1: The primary reference documents used to identify the toxicity of the toxic and hazardous compounds of A059 here were sourced directly

from the EPA at EPA.gov. In odd cases of missing toxicity documents, only Department of Health and Human Services Centers for Disease Control, National Library of Medicine, National Institute of Health, and National Institute of Occupational Safety and Health documents are referenced.
Note 2: Only the symptoms for humans are presented.
Note 3: This list is not all-inclusive.

Neurobehavioral and Effects on the Nervous System

Adrenal burnout	Alzheimer's
Anxiety	Apprehension
Ataxia	Attention deficit
Blurred or double vision	Brain fog
Cognitive aging	Cognitive dysfunction
Confusion	Convulsions
Decrease in visuomotor speed and accuracy	Decrease in sex drive
Depression	Developmental delay
Distraction	Dizziness
Drowsiness	Fatigue
Forgetfulness	Headache
Hearing loss	Hyperactivity
Hyperesthesia	Hypertension
Insomnia	Impaired judgment
Impaired short-term memory	Impotence
Irritability	Joint pain
Learning difficulties	Loss of coordination
Lower IQ	Memory loss
Metallic taste in mouth	Mood disorders
Muscle pain, cramps, spasms	Myalgia
Narcosis	Nervous irritability
Panic attacks	Paranoia

Performance decrements
in numerical ability
Peripheral neuropathy
PTSD
Restlessness
Slowed reaction time
Tremor
White matter changes
in the brain

Problems with balance

Physical weakness
Racing mind
Schizophrenia
Slurred speech
Uncoordinated movements

Cardiovascular, Circulatory, and Immune System Effects

Anemia
Bone marrow damage
Chronic bronchitis
Cyanosis
Dyspnea
High blood pressure
Impaired pulmonary function
Increased heart palpitation
Labored breathing
Pleural adhesions
Severe chest pain

Abnormal EKG
Cardiac arrhythmia
Chronic emphysema
Delayed bone formation
Heart muscle damage
Hypertension
Inactive tuberculosis
Increased risk of leukemia
Leukocytosis
Pulmonary edema
Shortness of breath

Gastrointestinal, Glandular, and Other Effects

Abdominal pain, spasms
Cataracts
Colitis
Hemorrhagic gastritis
Liver damage and disease
Nausea
Stomach and intestinal
inflammation

Cancer
Constipation
Diarrhea
Hypothyroidism
Loss of appetite
Profound hypokalemia
Renal cancer

Renal disease	Retina damage
Metallic taste in the mouth	Vomiting
Weight loss	

Reproductive System Effects in Women

Disturbances in the menstrual cycle	Birth defects
Infertility	Miscarriage
Still birth	Premature birth
Increased risk of spontaneous abortion	

Reproductive System Effects in Men

Decreased sperm count	Infertility
Degenerative changes in testis	
Birth defects from affected sperm cells	

Table 6.1

The myriad of studies and tests and their resultant reports presented here document the effects of lead and other toxic compounds produced by weapons and their effects on our nervous system, brain, behavior, and the neurodevelopment of our fetuses, children, and youth. Good reads include:

- *Pb Neurotoxicity: Neuropsychological Effects of Lead Toxicity*[34]
- *Neurotoxic Effects and Biomarkers of Lead Exposure: A Review*[36]
- *Toxicity of Lead: A Review with Recent Updates*[39]
- *Lead, Arsenic and Manganese Metal Mixture Exposures: Focus on Biomarkers of Effect*[40]
- *Information for Workers, Health Problems Caused by Lead*[41]

As stated above, what I have not been able to find is any study that documents the effects of concurrent exposure of our veterans to all of the hazardous and toxic compounds listed by the army tests and EPA[2,6] twenty years ago. This forces me to reference data for lead poisoning only.

Lead Poisoning in Children and Our Youth

Note the statement by the CDC and NIOSH within *Information for Workers, Health Problems Caused by Lead*, 2018[41]:

"Generally, lead affects children more than it does adults. Children tend to show signs of severe lead toxicity at lower levels than adults. Lead poisoning has occurred in children whose parent(s) accidentally brought home lead dust on their clothing. Neurological effects and mental retardation have also occurred in children whose parent(s) may have job-related lead exposure."

The effects of lead poisoning are well documented, as it affects the brain and nervous system and the way it hinders our neurodevelopment. The EPA reports significant increases in symptoms directly related to lead and poisoning by firearms.

In 2019,[42] the EPA's *America's Children and the Environment (ACE)* "Health -Neurodevelopmental Disorders" report stated:

Neurodevelopmental disorders are disabilities associated primarily with the functioning of the neurological system and brain. Examples of neurodevelopmental disorders in children include attention-deficit/hyperactivity disorder (ADHD), autism, learning disabilities, intellectual disability (also known as mental retardation), conduct disorders, cerebral palsy, and impairments in vision and hearing. Children with neurodevelopmental disorders can experience difficulties with language and speech, motor skills, behavior, memory, learning, or other neurological functions.

Several widespread environmental contaminants are associated with adverse effects on a child's developing brain and nervous system in multiple studies. The National Toxicology Program (NTP) has concluded that childhood lead exposure is associated with atten-tion-related behavioral problems (such as inattention, hyperactivity, or attention-deficit/hyperactivity disorder) and increased incidence of problem behaviors (including delinquent, criminal, or antisocial behavior). EPA has determined that methylmercury is known to have neurotoxic and developmental effects in humans. A wide variety of other environmental chemicals have been identified as potential con-cerns for childhood neurological development based on animal stud-ies and observational studies in humans.

The article goes on to report significant increases in these behav-iors and behavioral deficits in our children and youth. Missing is any relationship to the exposure to guns, firearms, or the contamination and poisoning caused by them—or is it? In Table 5.1, you'll note that in addition to lead, the methyl and mercury compounds mentioned in this report[42] are present in firearms poisoning as well.

This becomes personal for me, as all three of my children were born prematurely and were of low birth weight. My oldest was diag-nosed at two as severely autistic. Close family friends (who are veter-ans) have children who are autistic as well: two boys in one family and an autistic daughter in another. Another family has twin boys born with *cerebral palsy* and *impairments in vision and hearing.*[42] The twins also suffer from a number of maladies that are statistically impossi-ble. Their father has Gulf War Syndrome and was exposed to fire-arms poisoning and military burn pits as well. None of these families report any "family history" associated with their kids' birth defects. That includes my wife and me. Where did we meet these families?

We all lived on the same street, within a half block of each oth-er, in military housing. Coincidence? The military didn't group us together in housing because of our disabled children. I have since learned that a very large number of my fellow veterans have children born with developmental disorders and other birth defects, many who experienced multiple miscarriages and premature births, includ-ing good friends and my wife.

In 2014, the National Institutes of Health released *Lead in Kids' Blood Linked with Behavioral and Emotional Problems.*[43] It references research documenting lead poisoning effects on children at much lower levels than previously accepted. Doctor Kimberly Gray, former Health Scientist Administrator, National Institute of Environmental Health Sciences (NIEHS), is quoted as saying:

"This research focused on lower blood lead levels than most other studies and adds more evidence that there is no safe lead level."

The article goes on to say:

In this study, children with higher blood lead levels had internalizing problems, such as anxiety and depression, as well as some externalizing problems.

And:

U.S. studies have reported that lead exposure causes what psychologists call externalizing behavior problems, such as aggressiveness and bullying, which may lead to truancy and even jail time as children get older.

Are you seeing a behavioral pattern from our exposure yet? As you will see here and in later chapters, it gets worse.

My VA toxicologists informed me in 2019 that damage to the brain and nervous system from lead poisoning is permanent. I looked it up online and confirmed their statements. That said, my psychologist told me it is possible to build new pathways and strengthen older, unused pathways in the brain to combat memory loss and other issues. I confirmed his statement as well.

The problem facing our poisoned children and youth is that this poisoning degrades their cognitive abilities by damaging areas of the brain responsible for "emotional regulation, impulse control, attention, verbal reasoning, and mental flexibility," saddling our youth with lower intelligence and hampering their decision-making ability. This doesn't affect just our youth but our seasoned veterans as well.

What is the end result? Confusion, anxiety, depression, anger, irritability, and so on, culminating into externalizing behaviors (taking it out on those around them). Do you recognize these symptoms from earlier?

Do you remember in Chapter 3 the 1999 Navy engineering report[18] stating:

> "The numerous symptoms of lead poisoning mimic various diseases, often making diagnosis confusing and difficult."

And:

> "Tragically, children are more vulnerable to lead toxicity than adults. Children exposed to lead may manifest slow learning, mental drifts, slight retardation in development, hypertension, and behavioral problems, while excessive blood lead levels can seriously and irreversibly damage a child's brain and nervous system during crucial development years. Because the symptoms mirror those of many childhood diseases, many doctors do not test for lead exposure."

Case in point, the National Institutes of Health National Library of Medicine presents a 2016 NIOSH report[44] documenting a sixteen-year-old girl who was misdiagnosed with appendicitis. After her appendix was removed, her symptoms persisted. Later, it was determined that she suffered from lead poisoning. In diagnosing her symptoms, it was ignored that her father had been treated two years earlier for lead poisoning—lead he had brought home to poison his family, just as the Navy and government had identified we do over ten years earlier.[18,4] In addition, in 2020, I was contacted by a veteran's wife familiar with the research I was doing for this book. Her husband was experiencing the same symptoms as this sixteen-year-old girl.

Knowing that her husband had served in the Navy doing the exact same things I did, she suspected lead poisoning. Ironically, his VA doctor's first response was to remove his appendix. Cooler heads prevailed when a copy of this 2016 report and evidence of a career's exposure to lead were presented to his doctors. VA toxicology and a civilian second opinion confirmed his symptoms caused by a toxin or toxic substance. To date, the VA still refuses to recognize his lead exposure as the cause. Instead, he is forced to live with the pain and discomfort of an undiagnosed condition.

If lead and poisoning symptoms from the other 145 hazardous and toxic compounds produced by firearms and ordnance are unknown or ignored, misdiagnosis and mistreatment will occur as well.

Traumatic Brain Injury, Multiple Sclerosis, PTSD, and Chronic Stress

In 2013, I began experiencing symptoms that included slurred speech, saying things that I did not wish to say, short-term memory loss, brain fog, and other symptoms. I would forget and pass the freeway exit I normally took to get home—an exit I had taken every day for seventeen years. I could not remember my ATM PIN number or computer passwords. I could not grasp words to use in speech or texts that I had used almost daily throughout my life. My friends and family noted something was wrong. While at an appointment at the VA, I spied a brochure listing these symptoms associated with traumatic brain injury (TBI).

I sought out my doctor, and in early 2014, began testing for TBI at the local VA hospital.

Traumatic Brain Injury

The VA's Office of Research & Development: Traumatic Brain Injury (TBI),[45] states:

> *TBI can include a range of comorbidities, from headaches, irritability, and sleep disorders to memory problems, slower thinking,*

and depression. These symptoms often lead to long-term mental and physical health problems that impair Veterans' employment and family relationships, **and their reintegration into their communities** (remember this one).

The severity of the TBI is determined at the time of the injury and is based on evidence of a positive computed tomography (CT) scan (evidence of brain bleeding, bruising, or swelling), the length of the loss or alteration of consciousness, the length of memory loss, and how responsive the individual was after the injury.

Most TBI injuries are considered mild, but even mild cases can involve serious long-term effects on areas such as thinking ability, memory, mood, and focus. Other symptoms may include headaches, endocrine, vision, and hearing problems.

In 2014, as part of the testing for TBI, the VA also performed an MRI on my brain. The result? Excessive white matter and gray matter anomalies were noted. Both are lead poisoning symptoms and are consistent with traumatic brain injuries, multiple sclerosis (MS), poisoning, and other medical conditions.

I then completed testing for cognitive issues and loss of memory at the VA Medical Center in La Jolla, California. The result? It was explained that I exhibited symptoms experienced by your average fifty-year-old. I was fifty-two. The problem with that diagnosis is I was not your average fifty-year-old.

I explained and provided official Navy documentation to my doctor chronicling my intelligence, mental capacity, and cognitive abilities from 1985 to the present. Scoring a ninety-three on the armed forces quotient test far exceeds the average of those tested. That means I scored better than 93 percent of test takers.

The score of the average test taker is in the midthirties. It should be fifty, but it's not. Further, your average person fails to meet the criteria to even enter the Armed Forces to take that test in the first place.[46] How tough is the test?

My son's friend from high school asked him to take the test for him. His friend could not pass the exam and was denied entry into the Navy. He continually scored a thirty-three, despite recently graduating from a San Diego state university with a college degree. The Navy requires a minimum of thirty-five. He failed the test three times. Instead of working as a nurse, paramedic, or EMT making use of that degree, he now works as a greeter at a local fitness club.

At fifty-two, I could not keep up with my peers. I grasped for common words that I have used all my life. I searched for military regulations that I have quoted verbatim my entire career. I had a problem remembering a good friend's last name, a man I had known for many years.

The brain fog, confusion, and memory loss could not be explained. As I stated earlier, VA Mental Health does not even recognize lead and poisoning from the hazardous and toxic compounds identified by the government and military since 1975. The VA determined I did not suffer from TBI and began looking elsewhere for the cause.

A good friend, retired Navy Master Chief Jeff Caldwell, is disabled and suffers from MS. He knew of my itching, burning hands and feet. Combined with the other symptoms I'd identified, these were all symptoms he, too, suffered from. Jeff recommended testing for MS.

Multiple Sclerosis

The National Institute of Neurological Disorders and Stroke states that MS is[47]:

> *An unpredictable disease of the central nervous system, multiple sclerosis (MS) can range from relatively benign to somewhat disabling to devastating, as communication between the brain and other parts of the body is disrupted. Many investigators believe MS to be an autoimmune disease—one in which the body, through its immune system, launches a defensive attack against its own tissues.* **In the case of MS, it is the nerve-insulating myelin that comes**

under assault. Such assaults may be linked to an unknown environmental trigger, perhaps a virus.

Most people experience their first symptoms of MS between the ages of 20 and 40; the initial symptom of MS is often blurred or double vision, red-green color distortion, or even blindness in one eye. Most MS patients experience muscle weakness in their extremities and difficulty with coordination and balance. These symptoms may be severe enough to impair walking or even standing. In the worst cases, MS can produce partial or complete paralysis. Most people with MS also exhibit paresthesias, transitory abnormal sensory feelings such as numbness, prickling, or "pins and needles" sensations. Some may also experience pain. Speech impediments, tremors, and dizziness are other frequent complaints. Occasionally, people with MS have hearing loss. Approximately half of all people with MS experience cognitive impairments such as difficulties with concentration, attention, memory, and poor judgment, but such symptoms are usually mild and are frequently overlooked. Depression is another common feature of MS . . .

A physician may diagnose MS in some patients soon after the onset of the illness. In others, however, doctors may not be able to readily identify the cause of the symptoms, leading to years of uncertainty and multiple diagnoses punctuated by baffling symptoms that mysteriously wax and wane.

So how many symptoms identifiable as lead poisoning symptoms did you spot? "Blurred or double vision, muscle weakness, difficulty with coordination and balance, numbness, prickling, or 'pins and needles' sensations, pain, speech impediments, tremors, hearing loss, cognitive impairments such as difficulties with concentration, attention, memory, poor judgment, depression . . ."

How about the explanation "communication between the brain and other parts of the body is disrupted"? And: "Many investigators believe MS to be an autoimmune disease—one in which the body, through its immune system, launches a defensive attack against its own tissues. In the case of MS, it is the nerve-insulating myelin that comes under assault. Such assaults may be linked to an unknown environmental trigger, perhaps a virus."

What about the environmental trigger of chronic poisoning over a period of years? Decades, even? Recall the earlier discussion of the effects on the central and peripheral nervous systems? Poisoning causes multiple disruptions in the autoimmune system caused by disruptions of the autonomic nervous system, which also results in oxidative stress, premature cognitive aging, demyelization, inhibition of enzymes needed for energy production, decreased levels of neurotransmitters and altered neurotransmitter release, and increased permeability of the blood-brain barrier. Remember demyelization? The National Institute of Neurological Disorders and Stroke states:

"In the case of MS, it is the nerve-insulating myelin that comes under assault. Such assaults may be linked to an **unknown environmental trigger**, perhaps a virus."

I personally don't think you have to be a rocket scientist or hold a PhD to make the connection. My good friend with MS served twenty-two years in the Navy right alongside me. It is not genetic. As we learned earlier, myelin is composed of fatty tissues. You'll note the significance of that very soon.

In 2014 and 2015, I was diagnosed with carpal tunnel in both arms and peripheral neuropathy. Itching, nerve tingling, pins and needles stabbing me in the feet, crawling-with-ants-feeling in my lower legs, uncontrollable itching in my forearms, and so on. My medical records note these symptoms as early as the mid-1990s, which were misdiagnosed as athlete's foot without evidence of fungi. My Navy doctors prescribed foot powder that—surprise, surprise—never worked. Recognize the symptoms? They are the same as MS, but . . .

The VA tested me for MS, concluding that I did not present with symptoms indicating MS. VA neurology testing did, however, confirm peripheral neuropathy, carpal tunnel syndrome, and ulnar neuropathy. MRIs in 2014 and 2019 identified both white and gray matter anomalies within my brain, symptoms, VA toxicology would later conclude, of lead poisoning.

In 2015, the VA would not diagnose me with MS. Later, in 2019 out of confusion, VA neurology did, however, state that they could not discount symptoms of MS. As I stated earlier, the VA Medical Center La Jolla Neurology still refuses to recognize poisoning from lead or the other 145 toxic compounds.

In 2016, I began experiencing an increase in irritability, anxiety, depression, and other symptoms to add to brain fog, forgetfulness, short-term memory loss, and so on I had experienced for years. In 2016, I was diagnosed with severe PTSD.

By early 2018, I had accumulated evidence, reports, and documents chronicling my poisoning from lead and the other 145 hazardous and toxic compounds over my entire Navy career. The symptoms are there in my medical records, and yet the VA still has failed to diagnose and treat it. In fact, they rigorously ignore it.

In late 2018, I began to see a clinical psychologist for these symptoms, one not associated with the VA. I presented him with my Navy and VA medical records as well as the evidence I have presented here. I now understand that my symptoms were caused by other comorbidities and poisoning, which the Navy chronically exposed me to since the beginning of my Navy career in 1985.

No longer a mystery, symptoms of depression, anxiety, and irritability have faded away with my understanding of the cause of my symptoms, symptoms that over twenty veterans per day seek relief from through suicide.

It isn't PTSD. It never was. It is poisoning from the ordnance we have been exposed to in service to our country. How did this happen?

What do lead and poisoning from ordnance, traumatic brain injury, multiple sclerosis, chronic stress, and PTSD have in common? Simple: they all manifest in the same symptoms. Back in 1999, the Navy recognized that "the numerous symptoms of lead poisoning mimic various diseases, often making diagnosis confusing and difficult."[18]

When Congress, the Department of Defense, and military and VA doctors go out of their way to ignore our exposure and poisoning, misdiagnosis and mistreatment can have devastating effects.

CHAPTER 7
Discovery

What came first, the chicken or the egg? Think about it. Without the egg the chicken could not hatch; without the chicken the egg could not be laid. So what came first: Suicide, PTSD, chronic stress, or lead and firearms poisoning? It's not meant as a joke, as you will see—it is a very serious, legitimate question.

When the VA diagnosed me with severe PTSD in 2016, I was upset and suffering from anxiety, depression, irritability, and more. I was told that my condition resulted from not being able to mentally cope with the traumatic events I must have seen or experienced during my military career, and I was incapable of reintegrating into a normal society. Remember that one from earlier? I was, therefore, nuts—that was the only explanation.

The VA didn't diagnose me with traumatic brain injury and said multiple sclerosis did not explain my symptoms. They stated they could find no physical reason that accounted for my memory loss, brain fog, loss of concentration, and so on. They completely ignored poisoning in diagnosis. The VA's playbook dictated it must, therefore, be PTSD. Like a good soldier, institutionalized to believe whatever my doctors told me throughout my three decades of military service, I took their word for it, didn't question it, and submitted to further testing.

Posttraumatic Stress Disorder (PTSD)

The US government's National Institute of Mental Health (NIMH)[48] identifies:

PTSD is a disorder that some people develop after experiencing a shocking, scary, or dangerous event.

It is natural to feel afraid during and after a traumatic situation. This fear triggers many split-second changes in the body to respond to danger and help a person avoid danger in the future. This "fight-or-flight" response is a typical reaction meant to protect a person from harm. Nearly everyone will experience a range of reactions after trauma, yet most people will recover from those symptoms naturally. Those who continue to experience problems may be diagnosed with PTSD. People who have PTSD may feel stressed or frightened even when they are no longer in danger.

Who develops PTSD?

Anyone can develop PTSD at any age. This includes war veterans as well as survivors of physical and sexual assault, abuse, car accidents, disasters, terror attacks, or other serious events. Not everyone with PTSD has been through a dangerous event. Some experiences, like the sudden or unexpected death of a loved one, can also cause PTSD.

According to the National Center for PTSD, about seven or eight of every 100 people will experience PTSD at some point in their lives. Women are more likely to develop PTSD than men. Some traumas may put an individual at a higher risk and biological factors like genes may make some people more likely to develop PTSD than others.

What are the symptoms of PTSD?

Symptoms usually begin within 3 months of the traumatic incident, but sometimes they begin later. For symptoms to be considered PTSD, they must last more than a month and be severe enough to interfere with functioning in relationships or work. The course of the illness varies from person to person. Some people recover within 6 months, while others have symptoms that last much longer. In some people, the condition becomes chronic (ongoing).

A doctor who has experience helping people with mental illnesses, such as a psychiatrist or psychologist, can diagnose PTSD.

To be diagnosed with PTSD, an adult must have all of the following for at least 1 month:
At least one re-experiencing symptom
• *At least one avoidance symptom*
• *At least two arousal and reactivity symptoms*
• *At least two cognition and mood symptoms*

Re-experiencing symptoms:
• *Flashbacks—reliving the trauma over and over, including physical symptoms like a racing heart or sweating*
• *Bad dreams*
• *Frightening thoughts*

Re-experiencing symptoms may cause problems in a person's everyday routine. They can start from the person's own thoughts and feelings. Words, objects, or situations that are reminders of the event can also trigger re-experiencing symptoms.

Avoidance symptoms:
• *Staying away from places, events, or objects that are reminders of the experience*
• *Avoiding thoughts or feelings related to the traumatic event*
• *Things or situations that remind a person of the traumatic event can trigger avoidance symptoms. These symptoms may cause a person to change his or her personal routine. For example, after a bad car accident, a person who usually drives may avoid driving or riding in a car.*

Arousal and reactivity symptoms:
• *Being easily startled*
• *Feeling tense or "on edge"*
• *Having difficulty sleeping, and/or having angry outbursts*

Arousal symptoms are usually constant, instead of being triggered by something that brings back memories of the traumatic event. They can make the person feel stressed and angry. These symptoms may make it hard to do daily tasks, such as sleeping, eating, or concentrating.

Cognition and mood symptoms:
* *Trouble remembering key features of the traumatic event*
* *Negative thoughts about oneself or the world*
* *Distorted feelings like guilt or blame*
* *Loss of interest in enjoyable activities*

Cognition and mood symptoms can begin or worsen after the traumatic event. These symptoms can make the person feel alienated or detached from friends or family members.

After a dangerous event, it's natural to have some of the symptoms mentioned on previous pages. Sometimes people have very serious symptoms that go away after a few weeks. This is called acute stress disorder, or ASD. When the symptoms last more than a month, seriously affect a person's ability to function and are not due to substance use, medical illness, or anything except the event itself, the person might be experiencing PTSD. Some people with PTSD don't show any symptoms for weeks or months. PTSD is often accompanied by depression, substance abuse, or one or more anxiety disorders.

How many poisoning symptoms can you pick out from the above? More importantly, why is it that veterans, law enforcement officers, and so on are diagnosed with PTSD primarily only *after retiring*, long after a traumatic event has been experienced? I was first diagnosed with it immediately after retiring in 2009. It had been many years since I'd experienced any traumatic event.

Like me, the majority of veterans I've spoken with were also diagnosed with PTSD many years—even decades—after a traumatic event. NIMH, the government, has determined that symptoms can be delayed for months but not years or decades. That is *not* posttraumatic stress syndrome.

I was diagnosed with what's called PTSD hypervigilance. Why? When at restaurants or sitting in public, I choose a spot where I can see those around me, often close to doors, windows, and exits. When staying in a hotel, I never stay in a room on the first floor or higher than the third floor, and I familiarize myself with the fire exits and so on before going to sleep.

When walking down the street, I scan for threats in my surroundings, strange behaviors, facial expressions, etc. When the stoplight turns green, I look both ways before walking or driving away. That is Navy training and conditioning practiced for over thirty years—not PTSD.

"Operational Risk Management[49]" is a mandatory Navy program requiring all of us to mentally examine and conduct risk mitigation for everything we do. Every service, as well as many industries, have similar programs in varying degrees. Navy OPNAVINST 3500.39[49] states:

"The naval vision is to develop an environment in which every individual (officer, enlisted and civilian) is trained and motivated to personally manage risk in everything they do on and off duty, both in peacetime and during conflict, thus enabling successful completion of all operations or activities with the minimum amount of risk."

The Navy's program states that every individual is trained and required to perform and execute this five-step process *in everything they do on and off duty, both in peacetime and during conflict* to:
- *identify hazards,*
- *assess the hazards,*
- *make risk decisions,*
- *implement controls, and*
- *supervise and watch for change.*

In basic training, recruits are first taught these five steps and to critically examine everything they do to mitigate the risks associated with doing it. Careers spanning as many as thirty years doing this, day in and day out, condition and institutionalize us to mitigate risk in our daily lives *in everything we do.*

Years, decades, of participating in risky actions and situations for the Navy, working and living with my family in Central and South America, the Middle East, and Asia as well as being responsible for the health and safety of others conditioned me to be constantly aware of my surroundings. Is that a bad thing? The VA says so.

The VA says that I suffer from extreme anxiety with an inability to adjust and *reintegrate into a normal society.* With no frame of reference or will to understand, these young, store-bought "professionals," armed with fresh degrees, ignore the decades of conditioning of our way of life and misdiagnose us with anxiety and PTSD hypervigilance.

It is a way of life for all military, law enforcement, firefighters, emergency service personnel, responsible parents, day-care providers, and more. It's a way of life for anyone who works in a hazardous, dangerous, or threatening environment, or has those who depend upon them for their safety. Intelligent thought and actions once prized by the Navy immediately upon retirement are now falsely mislabeled as a mental health illness, a mental disorder, PTSD.

In 2016, after my symptoms worsened, the VA diagnosed me with severe PTSD and blamed it on incidents that occurred in 1994 and 2005, neither of which I had paid any attention to until the VA forced me to reexamine my career for an event they perceived as traumatic enough to use in order to meet the criteria for a predetermined, explainable diagnosis.

I had served almost thirty years and experienced death and tragedy on numerous occasions during my entire career. Things much worse than the two events the VA chose to use for my diagnosis: seven tours, some twenty-plus other deployments, hundreds of high risk and special operations, and six years living and working in countries where many wanted us dead. Doesn't compute, does it? At least, not by the above NIMH standards for PTSD.[48]

A PTSD diagnosis dictated that I was suffering from an illness, a mental health disorder that prevented me from successfully returning to a normal life because of two traumatic events, which had occurred ten to twenty years earlier. I was then judged somehow mentally deficient by young VA interns filling in the blanks on VA-provided questionnaires, young VA doctors, fresh out of medical school, and old, over the hill, institutionalized federal employees who refuse to stay current with new discoveries in medicine. Both who had never served a day in the military, let alone experienced combat.

VA doctors and medical professionals who went out of their way to ignore the evidence I presented of my lead poisoning and the other 145 toxic compounds I'd been exposed to during my career. VA doctors who completely ignored complications, which were a result of more than a decade of severe tinnitus and thirty years of living with constant stress and physical pain. Despite the multitude of symptoms documented in my medical records, the VA decreed that my symptoms were caused by a mental illness—a deficiency, a disorder.

Unable to accept that I was somehow nuts, mentally deficient, and incapable of rejoining a normal society, I continued researching my symptoms. And then it happened.

In 2019, I noticed one of my good friends had lost quite a bit of weight. Thinking something was catastrophically wrong, I asked him if he was all right.

A retired Navy SEAL lieutenant commander I'll call Richard was the last executive officer I served with before retiring. Rich often drops by for tea early in the morning. We discuss art, history, nature, agriculture, current events—all the things we missed out on while deployed and serving the nation. One morning he told me about a book he'd recently read and how it had changed his life.

Always a proponent of eating healthy and maintaining our bodies, Rich explained what he'd learned from this book and how he had integrated that knowledge into his daily routine. He lost weight, had more energy, required fewer drugs and supplements—it was an all-around win-win. The book was called *The Rain Barrel Effect* by Dr. Stephen Cabral.[50]

In his book, Dr. Cabral examines the damaging effects to our bodies from the environment we live in, including additives in our food and water. There are hazardous and toxic compounds that leach into our bodies through the dental fillings in our teeth, cosmetics, fabric softeners, scented candles, and so on.

The book is a comprehensive study of things in our everyday lives that are detrimental to our health, such as toxins and poisoning from sources the average person is completely unaware of—things that are slowly killing us. It details the multiple physiological effects to our bodies and the numerous systems within.

While reading Cabral's book, I made a discovery that my PTSD diagnosis simply ignored. He provided the information I knew was out there but couldn't quite grasp. *Toxic Enemy #5—Stress* was the final piece of the puzzle I had been searching for.

Poisoning, chronic stress, the fight-or-flight response, and their effect on the whole body. As you will see, his book led to my discovering so much more.

Toxic Enemy #5 presents xenostressors and xenobiotics and how they trigger stress and the fight-or-flight reaction in the body. Dr. Cabral then breaks down the physiological effects and processes that occur within the body as a result of this poisoning.

As discussed in the previous chapter, the sympathetic nervous system of the autonomic nervous system responds to danger by preparing the body for fight or flight. His book identifies xenostressors as "outside stressors": things like stress at work, dealing with heavy traffic, a career spent in the military or law enforcement, and so on.

Xenobiotics are defined as substances, which are foreign to the body—toxic substances such as lead, herbicides in fruits and vegetables we consume, and so on. As I researched Dr. Cabral's book, I came across familiar references that further validated his work and led to several discoveries of vast importance to our veterans, their families, and our country.

When reading about xenobiotics, the chemical most often referred to was dioxins. Within the National Institute of Health's National Library of Medicine, I came across an article, "The Mechanism of Dioxin Toxicity: Relationship to Risk Assessment" by L. S. Birnbaum.[51]

It lists *2,3,7,8-tetrachlorodibenzo-p-dioxin* (TCDD) as the most toxic member of a class of related chemicals I'd seen before. This class of chemicals includes polyhalogenated dibenzo-p-dioxins, dibenzofurans, *biphenyls*, naphthalenes, azo- and azoxy-benzenes. Big scientific terms you have seen before.

Remember from the last chapter, Lisa H. Mason, Jordan P. Harp, and Dong Y. Han[34] stated the following:

"A number of studies are revealing that antisocial tendencies like violent and aggressive behaviors correlate with environmental stressors like lead or polychlorinated biphenyls, beyond that of socioeconomic factors."

Dioxins, Furans, and PCBs

Recall tables 2.1 and 5.1, where the hazardous and toxic compounds produced by M16/AR15 assault rifles, handguns, shotguns, rifles, and other ordnance were identified? Weapons and ordnance used daily by military, law enforcement, and civilians alike? Dibenzo-p-dioxins, dibenzofurans, biphenyls, naphthalenes, azo- and azoxy-benzenes, they are all there including *2,3,7,8-tetrachlorodibenzo-p-dioxin*. Straight out of the army's 2000 tests,[2] published by the EPA in 2004[6] and the number one most poisonous xenobiotic that Dr. Cabral and Dr. Linda Silber Birnbaum both discussed.[50,51]

Dr. Birnbaum is prominently featured in many of the research reports I've come across and is likely the nation's leading expert on the toxicity of this poison. In 1994, she is referenced as the number one contributor to the EPA's *Health Assessment Document for 2,3,7,8-Tetrachlorodibenzo-p-Dioxin (TCDD) and Related Compounds*.[53] The US government must also agree that she is the leading expert too.

In 1994, she was the director of the environmental toxicology division of the health effects research laboratory in the EPA. She then rose to become the director of the National Institute for Environmental Health Sciences and National Toxicology (NIEHS) program.

So what are these chemicals? Where do they come from and how do they affect us? In 2000, the army acknowledged that they come from weapons and ordnance.[2] More correctly, they are produced when burning the chemical compounds found in all manner of ordnance—you know, bullets, explosives, and pyrotechnics—which the EPA identified in 1999[52]:

> *Dioxins and furans are not made for any specific purpose; however, they are created when products like herbicides are made. They are also created in the pulp and paper industry, from a process that bleaches the wood pulp. In addition, they can be produced when products are burned.*
>
> *Dioxins and furans can enter your body through breathing contaminated air, drinking contaminated water, or eating contaminated food. About 90% of exposure to dioxins and furans is from eating contaminated food. Dioxins and furans can build up in the fatty tissues of animals.*
>
> *You can be exposed to dioxins and furans by eating contaminated food. Dioxins and furans typically stay and build up in the fatty tissues of animals. This means that eating beef, pork, poultry, fish as well as dairy products can be a source of exposure.*
>
> *There are several sources of exposure to dioxins and furans. If you work in or near a municipal solid waste incinerator, copper smelter, cement kiln, or coal-fired power plant you can be exposed to dioxins and furans. Individuals who burn their household waste or burn wood can be exposed as well.*

Today, the EPA states[54]:

Dioxins refer to a group of toxic chemical compounds that share certain chemical structures and biological characteristics. Several hundred of these chemicals exist and are members of three closely related families:

Chlorinated dibenzo-p-dioxins (CDDs),
Chlorinated dibenzofurans (CDFs) and
Certain polychlorinated biphenyls (PCBs).

CDDs and CDFs are not created intentionally, but are produced as a result of human activities like the backyard burning of trash. Natural processes like forest fires also produce CDDs and CDFs. PCBs are manufactured products, but they are no longer produced in the United States.

Where does dioxin come from?

Industrial activities: Dioxin is not produced or used commercially in the United States. It is a contaminant formed in the production of some chlorinated organic compounds, including a few herbicides such as silvex. Over the past decade, EPA and industry have been working together to dramatically reduce the production of dioxin in the environment.

However, it should be noted that though levels have decreased in the last 30 years, dioxins are extremely persistent compounds and break down very slowly. In fact, a large part of the current exposures to dioxins in the US is due to releases that occurred decades ago.

Even if all human-generated dioxins were eliminated, low levels of naturally produced dioxins would remain. EPA is working with other parts of the government to look for ways to further reduce dioxin levels entering the environment and to reduce human exposure to them.

Other ways dioxins are produced:

Burning: Dioxins are formed as a result of combustion processes such as waste incineration (commercial or municipal) or from burning fuels (like wood, coal, or oil).

Bleaching: Chlorine bleaching of pulp and paper, based on certain types of chemical manufacturing and processing, and other industrial processes this can create small quantities of dioxins in the environment.

Smoking: Cigarette smoke also contains small amounts of dioxins.

Drinking Water: Dioxin can get into drinking water from:

emissions from waste incineration and other combustion that get deposited into bodies of water; and

discharges into water from chemical factories.

How can dioxin affect my health?

*Dioxins are highly toxic and can cause cancer, reproductive and developmental problems, damage to the immune system, and **can interfere with hormones*** (remember this last one)

Did you see that dioxins accumulate in the fatty tissues of the body? How about the fatty tissues of the myelin protecting nerve fibers? Remember, the National Institute of Neurological Disorders and Stroke stated[47]:

"*In the case of MS, it is the nerve-insulating myelin that comes under assault. Such assaults may be linked to an **unknown environmental trigger**, perhaps a virus.*"

Like I said, it doesn't take a rocket scientist to conclude that it is likely that the lead, dioxins, and other toxic compounds we were exposed to in the military are responsible for our sickness and disease. Dr. Birnbaum must agree. Throughout her many research papers and reports, she confirms that low-dose exposure poisons those who are exposed, and susceptibility to disease can persist long after the initial exposure has ended.

My good friend with MS, Jeff Caldwell, worked on powerful radar systems and electronics for his entire career. He confirmed what I already knew: that he could smell the off-gassing from heated and burning electronic components and insulation in the spaces where he worked. He was exposed to it day in and day out—PCBs (polychlorinated biphenyl), dioxins, and furans, the same compounds those who work in indoor shooting ranges and with weapons and ordnance are exposed to daily.

Did you recognize the symptoms listed above from dioxins are the same as those caused by lead poisoning, MS—all the same symptoms with the exception of cancer. As I stated earlier, whether lead poisoning causes cancer or not is irrelevant; the other compounds that firearms poisoning exposes us to does. Dioxins, furans, and PCBs do.

Note the absence of exposure to firearms and ordnance in the above EPA reports despite the EPA first publishing AP 42 Chapter 15 in 2004, identifying dioxins, furans, PCBs, and so on.[6] Despite intently searching for a good list of symptoms associated with this poisoning, I did not come across one—or so I thought.

I continued my research, which revealed four of the largest and most controversial cases of poisoning by dioxins, furans, PCBs, etc., involving the poisoning of veterans and their families. Before getting to them, let's start with one of the largest known cases in history.

The **World Trade Center** poisoning continues to account for the deaths of firefighters, law enforcement, and other first responders. What poisoned them? A 2007 study[55] published by EPA scientists documented dioxin levels measured in the air close to the smoldering pile of debris as the "highest ambient measurements of dioxin ever recorded anywhere in the world."

Inside the Twin Towers, firefighters and other first responders were subjected to breathing lead and other toxic metals along with all manner of other hazardous and toxic compounds—heavy metals, dioxins, and PCBs released by burning electronics, plastic, rubber, insulation, and other materials. Many of the same hazardous and toxic compounds found in firearms poisoning.

Then there were the crews who removed the debris. They all brought those toxic compounds, which were in their blood and on their skin and clothing, home to their families. Everything around the site and throughout the city of New York was being poisoned, poisoning that is still claiming victims today, just like veterans who have been exposed to the same poisons. Poisons like Agent Orange.

Agent Orange: Executing the largest exposure to herbicides the world has ever seen, US military aircraft sprayed vast areas of Vietnam to destroy the jungles to prevent enemy troops from using the foliage to hide. It rained down on our veterans, Vietnamese citizens, their fields, and livestock. It not only decimated the jungles, but it also killed their crops and contaminated their food sources and water supply for decades. It killed our veterans too. Just like the firefighters dying from the poisoning they experienced in the World Trade Center fires, veterans are still dying from Agent Orange poisoning.

The Environmental Programs Directorate at the Navy and Marine Corps Public Health Center states[56]:

"Dioxin is an unwanted by-product of activities such as burning refuse, metal smelting, and producing some chemicals. Dioxin was present in small amounts in the herbicide Agent Orange."

Agent Orange is also acknowledged by the VA[57] to cause:

- *Chronic B-cell leukemia: A type of cancer that affects your white blood cells (cells in your body's immune system that help to fight off illnesses and infections)*
- *Hodgkin's disease: A type of cancer that causes your lymph nodes, liver, and spleen to get bigger and your red blood cells to decrease (called anemia)*
- *Multiple myeloma: A type of cancer that affects your plasma cells (white blood cells made in your bone marrow that help to fight infection)*
- *Non-Hodgkin's lymphoma: A group of cancers that affect the lymph glands and other lymphatic tissue (a part of your immune system that helps to fight infection and illness)*

- *Prostate cancer: Cancer of the prostate (the gland in men that helps to make semen)*
- *Respiratory cancers (including lung cancer): Cancers of the organs involved in breathing (including the lungs, larynx, trachea, and bronchus)*
- *Soft tissue sarcomas (other than osteosarcoma, chondrosarcoma, Kaposi's sarcoma, or mesothelioma): Different types of cancers in body tissues such as muscle, fat, blood and lymph vessels, and connective tissues*
- *Other illnesses we believe are caused by contact with Agent Orange*
- *AL amyloidosis: A rare illness that happens when an abnormal protein (called amyloid) builds up in your body's tissues, nerves, or organs (like your heart, kidneys, or liver) and causes damage over time*
- *Chloracne (or other types of acneiform disease like it): A skin condition that happens soon after contact with chemicals and looks like acne often seen in teenagers*
- *Diabetes mellitus type 2: An illness that happens when your body is unable to properly use insulin (a hormone that turns blood glucose, or sugar, into energy), leading to high blood sugar levels*
- *Ischemic heart disease: A type of heart disease that happens when your heart doesn't get enough blood (and the oxygen the blood carries). It often causes chest pain or discomfort.*
- *Parkinson's disease: An illness of the nervous system (the network of nerves and fibers that send messages between your brain and spinal cord and other areas of your body) that affects your muscles and movement—and gets worse over time*
- *Peripheral neuropathy, early onset: An illness of the nervous system that causes numbness, tingling, and weakness.*
- *Porphyria cutanea tarda: A rare illness that can make your liver stop working the way it should and can cause your skin to thin and blister when you're out in the sun*

Note that despite the VA recognizing damage to the central and peripheral nervous systems above, there is a complete absence of behavioral symptoms on the VA's website attributable to this poisoning. Curious, isn't it? Must be PTSD, right?

Gulf War Syndrome: Again, one of the largest exposures to dioxins, furans, and PCBs in modern history. Remember the photos of our veterans covered in oil and soot from the burning oil fields set ablaze by a crazed dictator? Like the Agent Orange that rained down from the sky, the debris from burning petroleum settled on everything. The deadly chemicals produced by burning petroleum contaminated the air, food, water, and skin of veterans. Everything they came into contact with and brought home with them in and on their bodies, uniforms, and gear.

Despite recognizing dioxins, PCBs, and other toxic compounds produced by the burning oil wells, the VA states[58] that:

- *A prominent condition affecting Gulf War Veterans is a cluster of medically unexplained chronic symptoms that can include fatigue, headaches, joint pain, indigestion, insomnia, dizziness, respiratory disorders, and memory problems.*
- *VA refers to these illnesses as "chronic multisymptom illness" and "undiagnosed illnesses." We prefer not to use the term "Gulf War Syndrome" when referring to medically unexplained symptoms reported by Gulf War Veterans. Why? Because symptoms vary widely.*
- *Military service connection.*
- *Gulf War Veterans who meet the criteria below do not need to prove a connection between their military service and illnesses in order to receive VA disability compensation.*
- *VA presumes certain chronic, unexplained symptoms existing for 6 months or more are related to Gulf War service without regard to cause. These "presumptive" illnesses must have appeared during active duty in the Southwest Asia theater of military operations or by December 31, 2021, and be at least 10 percent disabling. These illnesses include:*

- *Myalgic Encephalomyelitis/Chronic Fatigue Syndrome (ME/CFS), a condition of long-term and severe fatigue that is not relieved by rest and is not directly caused by other conditions.*
- *Fibromyalgia, a condition characterized by widespread muscle pain. Other symptoms may include insomnia, morning stiffness, headache, and memory problems.*
- *Functional gastrointestinal disorders, a group of conditions marked by chronic or recurrent symptoms related to any part of the gastrointestinal tract. Functional condition refers to an abnormal function of an organ, without a structural alteration in the tissues. Examples include irritable bowel syndrome (IBS), functional dyspepsia, and functional abdominal pain syndrome.*
- *Undiagnosed illnesses with symptoms that may include but are not limited to: abnormal weight loss, fatigue, cardiovascular disease, muscle and joint pain, headache, menstrual disorders, neurological and psychological problems, skin conditions, respiratory disorders, and sleep disturbances.*

Recognize these symptoms? They are lead and Agent Orange poisoning symptoms as well. But wait, there's more.

Military Burn-Pit poisoning has been in the news lately. You may have seen pictures of our veterans tending the fires that burned the war debris in Iraq and Afghanistan. How about pictures of veterans in Vietnam, Korea, and other wars burning "shit pits," drums and pits filled with feces, urine, vomit, blood, and menstrual cycle debris from latrines?

Soldiers and sailors would, and still do, pour diesel fuel over the top and ignite the waste with gasoline, slowly stirring to burn it down until it is gone. "Gone" meaning turned into vapor and soot that floated through the air to be breathed in and, again, redistributed onto everything in the vicinity. Pretty gross, isn't it?

In 2001, the Department of Defense and US Navy recognized the significance of dioxin and associated poisoning from burning debris, writing in "Navy Guidance for Conducting Human Health Risk Assessments—Dioxin"[59]:

"Dioxins are unwanted by-products of combustion and chemical manufacturing. As such, wind direction is often an important factor in determining deposition of dioxins. Therefore, where appropriate, a historic wind rose pattern should be used to focus sampling in areas that are predominantly downwind of a source."

The VA's War-Related Illness and Injury Study Center—Burn Pits (Trash and Feces Fires)[60] states:

Proper disposal of waste during deployment is essential to prevent health problems and protect service members. In certain situations, when sanitary and waste management facilities are not available, this waste may be burned in an open pit.

A main concern of service members is exposure to smoke from burning trash and feces. Burning solid waste may generate many pollutants including dioxin, particulate matter, polycyclic aromatic hydrocarbons, volatile organic compounds, carbon monoxide, hexachlorobenzene, and ash.

Health effects from burning waste smoke depend on several factors including the nature of the waste being burned, duration of exposure, and how close to the burning smoke an individual is. Service members who are actually burning the waste are at greater risk for possible health effects than those who may be in the vicinity of the smoke.

Most health effects related to solid waste burning are temporary, and resolve once the exposure is gone. These include:

• *Eye irritation and burning*
• *Cough and throat irritation*
• *Difficulties breathing*
• *Skin irritation and rashes*

At this time, research does not show evidence of long-term health problems from exposure to burn pits. A summary of research is on this website. VA continues to study the health of deployed Veterans.

Got it? The VA recognizes "dioxin, particulate matter, polycyclic aromatic hydrocarbons, volatile organic compounds, carbon monoxide, hexachlorobenzene," and "ash." That's it.

If you were exposed, you may have "eye irritation and burning, cough and throat irritation, difficulties breathing, or skin irritation and rashes."

Where are the myriad symptoms of sickness and disease recognized by the EPA and other federal agencies of the Department of Health and Human Services for dioxins, furans, PCBs, and the multitude of other toxic compounds identified in burning petroleum products and debris? The VA already recognizes many of them in Agent Orange and Gulf War Syndrome. Where is the disconnect over military burn pits? The VA recognized dioxins in them as well. The same things were burned in them as the World Trade Center and in the Gulf War.

I interviewed a retired Navy Seabee recently. Jason Marshal is sick and dying of heart disease and is younger than me. He's had two heart attacks and wears a heart monitor on his wrist. Jason told me about digging and operating shit pits and burn pits in Iraq. At lunch one day in 2020, he told me they burned whole vehicles, military hardware, computers, electronics, trash, uniforms, motor oil, tires—everything you can imagine was rolled into these pits, doused with fuel oil, and burned. The same stuff that burned in the World Trade Center.

He and Sal (from Chapter 1) both described the acrid, suffocating smoke from these pits wafting through their camps twenty-four hours per day. The Department of Defense and VA know what was burned there. They and the government have already recognized dioxins, furans, PCBs, and multiple other toxic compounds produced in those pits that they willfully exposed our troops and civilian contractor personnel to.

Did you know that dioxins have a half-life just like lead? The University of Texas's *Estimates of the Half-Life of 2,3,7,8-Tetrachlorodibenzo-p-dioxin in Vietnam Veterans of Operation Ranch Hand*[51] established that dioxins embed in your fatty tissues (like myelin) and will leach out, poisoning you for just under forty years after the last exposure. Operation Ranch Hand was the operation that sprayed Agent Orange over Vietnam fifty years ago. Where are the military and VA's in-depth studies of this?

The same burn pit fires were tended to by our veterans in Vietnam, during the Gulf War, in Iraq, in Afghanistan, and in every war in American history to date. See a pattern? Burn-pit exposure symptoms are not currently acknowledged by the VA. Why not?

The EPA has already recognized dioxins, furans, and a list of other hazardous and toxic compounds produced by herbicides and burning debris.[52-55] A database of symptoms already exists for Agent Orange, Gulf War Syndrome, and 9/11 in New York.

But wait a minute—all three of the above military demographics were also chronically exposed to lead and the other 145 toxic compounds identified by the army in 2000,[2] as well as dioxins, furans, PCBs, and so on. They fired, carried, and lived with their weapons in all three of the above wars as they walked through the Agent Orange–poisoned jungle or petroleum-polluted Gulf War desert. They carried their firearms while tending the burn pits and shit pits of all wars. My good friends Sal and Jason did too.

They carried weapons that contaminated and poisoned them and their families, as the Navy described in 1999.[18] Veterans were exposed to the same dioxins, furans, PCBs, and other toxic chemical compounds identified by the EPA, NIH, and NLM in multiple documents. Yet the VA, DoD, and government continue to ignore the sickness and disease they have caused and are denying our veterans treatment and benefits for them as well.

In all four exposed demographics above—Agent Orange, Gulf War Syndrome, military burn pit, and firearms poisoning—veterans were exposed to the same hazardous and toxic chemicals and compounds produced by the military and the service that was demanded of them.

Toxic chemicals identified by the army in 2000[2] that include 2,3,7,8-tetrachlorodibenzo-p-dioxin (TCDD); polyhalogenated dibenzo-p-dioxins; dibenzofurans; biphenyls; naphthalenes; azo- and azoxy-benzenes; and polychlorinated biphenyls (PCBs). The same toxic chemicals produced and found in herbicides (Agent Orange), burning petrochemicals, burning debris, firing weapons, and expending ordnance.

But that's not all; as I examined Dr. Cabral's xenostressors, or "outside stressors," in combination with the above xenobiotics, I learned even more.

Chronic Long-Term Stress

The xenostressor of concern here plagues our veterans from day one in basic training throughout their entire military careers. It plagues law enforcement officers, firefighters, first responders, nurses, construction workers, truck drivers, day-care providers . . . the list goes on.

What is chronic stress?

In 1975,[17] NIOSH first recognized the effects of chronic stress and the psychological effects it has on gun firing range personnel. In "Lead Exposure and Design Consideration for Indoor Firing Ranges," NIOSH confirmed:

"The psychological stresses associated with the position of range officers should be considered when designing a new range. By its very nature the job demands close confinement, constant watchfulness for safety violations, rote repetition, exposure to high noise levels and to lead dust and fumes."

NIOSH then makes recommendations to mitigate stress within range design to reduce psychological stress stating:

"A rotation system should be instituted for the range officer position. It is suggested that one month of duty be followed by three months of alternate activity. This change is suggested not only to alleviate any possible lead absorption . . . but to prevent undue psychological stresses associated with the position."

Forty-five years ago, NIOSH had unwittingly identified what would become known today as a major cause of the sickness, disease, and death being covered here.

Today, the National Institute of Mental Health (NIMH) acknowledges[62] that:

"Long-term stress can harm your health."

And:

Coping with the impact of chronic stress can be challenging. Because the source of long-term stress is more constant than acute stress, the body never receives a clear signal to return to normal functioning. With chronic stress, those same lifesaving reactions in the body can disturb the immune, digestive, cardiovascular, sleep, and reproductive systems. Some people may experience mainly digestive symptoms, while others may have headaches, sleeplessness, sadness, anger, or irritability.

Over time, continued strain on your body from stress may contribute to serious health problems, such as heart disease, high blood pressure, diabetes, and other illnesses, including mental disorders such as depression or anxiety.

Recognize those symptoms? In keeping with my decision to present primarily government-related research and data, I have—again—come across a glaring *absence* of information from government sources. Despite decades of available data collected from treating veterans—the largest affected demographic—by the military and VA, the government ignores chronic stress in veterans and instead misdiagnoses it as PTSD. The two—chronic stress and PTSD—offer distinctions that are worthy of separate research, diagnosis, and treatment.

NIOSH, though, makes this distinction on its Job Stress website,[63] stating:

> "When job stress is high due to heavy demands and pressures or in response to a traumatic event, your body and mind can experience the "flight or fight" response. Your job performance and health may decline if your job stress is very high or lasts a long time. . ."

In attempting to research chronic stress, the VA and other government organizations lump it in with PTSD, stating that it is a mental illness, a disorder. The lack of government research into the chronic stress experienced by our military, law enforcement, and first responders is disappointing. You know the ones. These are the personnel experiencing the high suicide rates prevalent in the media today.

Written for civilian airline aircrews, this NIOSH report[63] sounds like it was written for veterans, stating:

> *Here crewmembers can learn more about how to recognize and manage job stress . . . Workplace conditions or events that cause job stress are called job stressors. Aircrew may face job stress from:*
> - *occasional or repeated heavy job demands*
> - *working long and irregular hours*
> - *sleep disruption*
> - *job insecurity*
> - *encounters with uncooperative or unpleasant passengers or co-workers/managers*
> - *unpredictable schedule disruptions*

* *extended time away from home and loved ones*
* *traumatic events, such as in-flight emergencies or disasters*

Acute Stress

Acute stress can occur when job demands, pressures, or uncertainties are higher over a relatively short period of time. This is generally followed by a return to low or more moderate levels. Examples might include working back-to-back flight segments with full passenger loads, flying during bad weather, or if a passenger medical event occurs in-flight. The symptoms of acute stress are generally mild to moderate and temporary. They can include:

* *physical and/or emotional tension*
* *digestive or sleep disturbances*
* *fear and anxiety*
* *irritability*
* *needing time to unwind after work before interacting with family and friends*
* *sleep disturbance*

Chronic Stress

Chronic or prolonged stress can develop from experiencing heavy demands and pressures over an extended period of time. There is also little or no control over those demands, limited resources to meet those demands, and/or limited relief or "down-time." Symptoms of chronic stress can range from mild to high and are generally persistent. Those with chronic stress may experience the symptoms associated with acute stress listed above, as well as:

* *difficulty making decisions*
* *loss of interest in normal activities*
* *sleep problems*
* *feeling powerless*
* *difficulty with relationships*
* *feeling sad and having other symptoms of depression*

Traumatic Incident Stress

Aircrew are responsible for the safety of passengers and must respond quickly to medical, mechanical, or other in-flight emergencies. Such emergencies can be considered traumatic incidents if they involve damage to physical structures or spaces, bodily injury, or death. Traumatic incident stress may occur at the time of the event or weeks or months later. It may include severe acute physical symptoms such as difficulty breathing, symptoms of shock, or chest pain that requires immediate medical attention. Visit the NIOSH Traumatic Incident Stress topic page to learn more signs and symptoms.

NIOSH's *Traumatic Incident Stress* topic page[64] identifies symptoms of stress as follows:

Chest pain
Difficulty breathing
Severe pain
Fatigue
Nausea/vomiting
Dizziness
Profuse sweating
Thirst
Headaches
Visual difficulties
Clenching of jaw
Nonspecific aches and pains
Confusion
Disorientation
Heightened / lowered alertness
Poor concentration
Poor problem solving
Memory problems
Nightmares
Anxiety

Guilt
Denial
Grief
Fear
Irritability
Loss of emotional control
Depression
Sense of failure
Feeling overwhelmed
Blaming others or self
Severe panic (rare)
Intense anger
Withdrawal
Emotional outbursts
Loss or increase of appetite
Excessive alcohol consumption
Inability to rest, pacing
Change in sexual functioning
Symptoms of shock (shallow breathing, rapid or weak pulse, nausea, shivering, pale and moist skin, mental confusion, and dilated pupils)
Difficulty identifying familiar objects or people

Recognize the symptoms of lead, dioxin, PCB, and firearms poisoning—as well as of TBI and MS—above?

Long-Term Effects of the Fight-or-Flight Response also affect veterans' long-term health. Veterans initially experience the physiological effects of the fight-or-flight response the very first day of basic training.

Arriving at the service's recruit training facilities late at night, after long plane and bus rides, recruits are sent to bed for the first time in a room with twenty-four or more total strangers. The majority of recruits have only slept in their own room, with mommy and daddy down the hall.

At five o'clock in the morning, after only a few hours of sleep, they are awakened by drill instructors banging on trash-can lids, yelling at the top of their lungs to get into formation. To this day, I still vividly recall that moment. The metallic taste in my mouth and the feeling of my entire body awakening, electrically charged with adrenaline to fight or take flight. This type of conditioning continues throughout basic training to desensitize veterans to the rigors of a life under stress in the military.

And it's not just in basic training. Navy SEALs, the most visible of the service's special operations personnel, are subjected to "Hell Week"—a week of sleep deprivation and physical exertion. And they are intentionally subjected to this same type of stress throughout their careers while training for that next deployment or last-minute contingency operation. Always on call, without sufficient time to rest and reset, and constantly exposed to poisoning from their weapons, uniforms, and gear, they have been involved in some of the most atrocious behavior to hit the news in a generation.

Veterans experience levels of stress that are unknown to the general public and to a much greater extent than the civilian personnel studied in the above-referenced reports. The stresses of combat and training with firearms, first identified by NIOSH in 1975,[17] are but a precursor to the stresses experienced by our military. Ironically, it is not the stress experienced in combat that is the problem. It is the stress experienced from the day they begin basic training and continue to experience throughout an entire career that is the problem.

The long-term effects of living in the stress-induced state of fight or flight without the body receiving the trigger to rest and reset is recognized by multiple sources, including the NIH's National Institute of Child Health and Human Development. NICHD states[65]:

> "Research now shows that such long-term activation of the stress system can have a hazardous, even lethal effect on the body, increasing risk of obesity, heart disease, depression, and a variety of other illnesses."

NICHD goes on to recognize that damage from chronic fight or flight without rest and reset results in:

Anxiety, loss of appetite, loss of sex drive, rapid heartbeat, high blood pressure, and high cholesterol and triglyceride levels . . . anorexia nervosa, malnutrition, obsessive-compulsive disorder, anxiety disorder, alcoholism, alcohol and narcotic withdrawal, poorly controlled diabetes, childhood sexual abuse, and hyperthyroidism . . . sleep disturbances, loss of libido, and loss of appetite as well as physical problems such as an increased risk for accumulating abdominal fat and hardening of the arteries and other forms of cardiovascular disease. These patients may also experience suppression of thyroid hormones, and of the immune system.

They further conclude:

Because they are at higher risk for these health problems, such patients are likely to have their life spans shortened by 15 to 20 years if they remain untreated.

Sound familiar? How about all my friends and coworkers from Chapter 1 dying in their fifties or earlier? How about what is happening to me?

Dr. Cabral's book identified and documented the physiological response on the human body to the stresses of both physical poisoning (xenobiotic) and outside stress (xenostressor). He successfully makes the case that both of these trigger the fight-or-flight response. Before reading his book and researching its conclusions, I never equated the effects of poisoning, chronic stress, and fight or flight to the symptoms that we as veterans, law enforcement, and other affected demographics suffer.

His book led to my discovery, which links five of the largest tragedies to befall our veterans and their families in the modern age and the gross willful negligence of our government failing to provide the necessary diagnosis and treatment to combat their effects—Agent Orange, Gulf War Syndrome, burn pits, firearms poisoning, and veteran suicide.

What do these all have in common? Chronic exposure to the hazardous and toxic compounds identified by the army and government from firearms and ordnance, Agent Orange, Gulf War Syndrome, military burn pits, and years of working in high-stress conditions, living in a constant state of fight or flight.

CHAPTER 8
Living the Lie

As I was preparing the book for submission to the publisher, additional information revealed itself worthy of adding to the book. Recently, I came across new articles and research questioning the cause of sleep apnea. It hit home as nearly every retired veteran I know has been diagnosed with it and is forced to sleep with a continuous positive air pressure (CPAP) machine. Let me rephrase that, every retired veteran I know who spent as much time in the service as I did away from home has been diagnosed with severe obstructive sleep apnea. As you will soon learn, the type of sleep apnea most veterans suffer is not recognized by the military and VA.

What is sleep apnea? The National Institute of Health's National Heart, Lung, and Blood Institute states[66]:

> Sleep apnea is a common condition in the United States. It can occur when the upper airway becomes blocked repeatedly during sleep, reducing or completely stopping airflow. This is known as obstructive sleep apnea. If the brain does not send the signals needed to breathe, the condition may be called central sleep apnea.
>
> Healthcare providers use sleep studies to diagnose sleep apnea. They record the number of episodes of slow or stopped breathing and the number of central sleep apnea events detected in an hour. They also determine whether oxygen levels in the blood are lower during these events.

Breathing devices such as continuous positive air pressure (CPAP) machines and lifestyle changes are common sleep apnea treatments. Undiagnosed or untreated sleep apnea can lead to serious complications such as heart attack, glaucoma, diabetes, cancer, and cognitive and behavioral disorders.

The government further states the causes as:

Sleep apnea can be caused by a person's physical structure or medical conditions. These include obesity, large tonsils, endocrine disorders, neuromuscular disorders, heart or kidney failure, certain genetic syndromes, and premature birth.

Got it? We all must be fat, have large tonsils, be genetically deficient, or be born prematurely. I will submit that we all snore.

What I have found curious all these years is that it does not matter if you are obese or skinny. Most of those I know with sleep apnea are skinny little guys with next to no body fat. Retired SWCCs, SEALs, and Sailors with seven or more deployments fighting the wars our politicians have volunteered us for. Health conscious workout machines, we all spent hours each day lifting weights, running, and swimming—maintaining our bodies in peak fighting form. Like PTSD, we were all diagnosed with sleep apnea just before or after we retired. Why?

The NIH goes on to say[66]:

Signs and Symptoms
Common signs of sleep apnea:
- *Reduced or absent breathing, known as apnea events*
- *Frequent loud snoring*
- *Gasping for air during sleep*
- *Common symptoms of sleep apnea:*
- *Excessive daytime sleepiness and fatigue*

- *Decreases in attention, vigilance, concentration, motor skills, and verbal and visuospatial memory*
- *Dry mouth or headaches when waking*
- *Sexual dysfunction or decreased libido*
- *Waking up often during the night to urinate*

And:

- *Complications*
- *Sleep apnea may increase your risk of the following disorders:*
- *Asthma*
- *Atrial fibrillation*
- *Cancers, such as pancreatic, renal, and skin cancers*
- *Chronic kidney disease*
- *Cognitive and behavioral disorders, such as decreases in attention, vigilance, concentration, motor skills, and verbal and visuospatial memory, as well as dementia in older adults. In children, sleep apnea has been associated with learning disabilities.*
- *Diseases of the heart and blood vessels, such as atherosclerosis, heart attacks, heart failure, difficult-to-control high blood pressure, and stroke*
- *Eye disorders, such as glaucoma, dry eye, or keratoconus*
- *Metabolic disorders, including glucose intolerance and type 2 diabetes*
- *Pregnancy complications, including gestational diabetes and gestational high blood pressure, as well as having a baby with low birth weight*

How many poisoning symptoms did you recognize? How about:

- *Excessive daytime sleepiness and fatigue.*
- *Headaches.*
- *Sexual dysfunction or decreased libido.*
- *Cancers, such as pancreatic and renal.*
- *Chronic kidney disease.*

Cognitive and behavioral disorders, such as decreases in attention, vigilance, concentration, motor skills, and verbal and visuospatial memory, as well as dementia in older adults. In children, sleep apnea has been associated with learning disabilities.

Diseases of the heart and blood vessels, such as atherosclerosis (hardening of the heart and arteries), *heart attacks, heart failure, and difficult-to-control high blood pressure.*

Metabolic disorders.

Pregnancy complications, including gestational diabetes and gestational high blood pressure, as well as having a baby with low birth weight.

Sleep Apnea and the VA

The VA has this to say about sleep apnea[67]:

Description: Sleep apnea (AP-ne-ah) is a common disorder in which you have one or more pauses in breathing, or shallow breaths while you sleep. Breathing pauses can last from a few seconds to minutes. Typically, normal breathing then starts again, sometimes with a loud snort or choking sound. The most common type of sleep apnea is obstructive sleep apnea. In this condition, the airway collapses or becomes blocked during sleep. When you try to breathe, any air that squeezes past the blockage can cause loud snoring. Not enough air flows into your lungs, and this can cause a drop in your blood oxygen level. Obstructive sleep apnea is more common in people who are overweight, but it can affect anyone. Sleep apnea usually is an ongoing condition.

When your breathing pauses or becomes shallow, you'll often move out of deep sleep and into light sleep. As a result, the quality of your sleep is poor, which makes you tired during the day. Sleep apnea is a leading cause of excessive daytime sleepiness. Frequent drops in your blood oxygen level and reduced sleep quality can trigger the release of stress hormones. These hormones raise your heart rate and increase your risk for high blood pressure, heart attack, stroke, and arrhythmias (irregular heartbeats). The hormones can also raise your risk for, or worsen, heart failure. Untreated sleep apnea can also lead to changes in how your body uses energy. These changes increase your risk for obesity and diabetes.

When you're awake, throat muscles help keep your airway stiff and open so air can flow into your lungs. When you sleep, these muscles relax, which narrows your throat. Normally, this narrowing doesn't prevent air from flowing into and out of your lungs. But if you have a smaller than normal airway, it can become partially or fully blocked, causing sleep apnea. If you are overweight, the extra soft fat tissue can thicken the wall of the windpipe and narrow the airway. If the oxygen drops to a dangerous level, it triggers your brain to disturb your sleep. This helps tighten the upper airway muscles and open your windpipe. Normal breathing then starts again, often with a loud snort or choking sound.

Signs and Symptoms: One of the most common signs of obstructive sleep apnea is loud and chronic (ongoing) snoring. Pauses may occur in the snoring. Choking or gasping may follow the pauses. The snoring usually is loudest when you sleep on your back; it might be less noisy when you turn on your side. You might not snore every night, but over time the snoring can happen more often and get louder. Not everyone who snores has sleep apnea. Here are some other common signs and symptoms of sleep apnea:

- *Fighting sleepiness during the day. You may find yourself rapidly falling asleep during the quiet moments of the day when you're not active.*
- *Memory or learning problems and not being able to concentrate.*
- *Morning headaches.*
- *Feeling irritable, depressed, or having mood swings or personality changes.*
- *Waking up frequently to urinate.*
- *Dry mouth or sore throat when you wake up.*

Recognize the symptoms? You have seen them before. Many of the same symptoms we reviewed earlier are the firearm poisoning symptoms listed in table 6.1.

Before I proceed, why do you suppose the VA ignores the symptoms and causes reported by various National Institute of Health agencies like the report referenced above? I think we both know the answer by now.

How about the cause? As we have documented, years of chronic poisoning by the 146 hazardous and toxic compounds, PTSD, and chronic long-term stress result in the majority of the symptoms recognized by the VA and the National Institutes of Health above.

I am not nor have I ever been obese. My tonsils were removed as a child, and I have been diagnosed with worsening *neuromuscular disorders, endocrine disorders, and* disorders leading to *heart failure.* So how does the VA and military treat veterans who exhibit sleep apnea symptoms?

Recently, I came across an article by Rob V. Rob founded the Operation Military Kids Foundation. OMK provides some of the most informative and in-depth content on military topics from writers that have actually served in nearly every branch of the US Military.

The December 2020 article[68] references the VA's own documents and data recording that one in four respiratory claims presented to the VA by veterans is linked to sleep apnea.

The VA's M21-1, Part III, Subpart iv, Chapter 4, Section F - Respiratory Conditions Topic 5. Sleep Apnea and Related Disabilities[69] lists the criteria for establishing the requirements for a sleep apnea diagnosis. Specifically, it states a veteran will not receive benefits unless a sleep study is performed. Further, if a sleep study was not performed prior to the veteran leaving the service, no service connection is established, and the VA will deny benefits to the veteran, resulting in a significant loss of income and benefits for the remainder of the veteran and their family's lives.

Further cases, such as with my own daughter, close family friends, and others who served, reveal a prejudice among military physicians and the VA in denying veterans the opportunity for diagnosis and benefits.

My daughter, having experienced severe trauma during her career and having trouble sleeping, requested a sleep study to rule out sleep apnea. Her Air Force doctor denied her request stating that *she was only interested in it to get money from the VA when she got out of the Air Force.* This is not the first time I have heard of these statements from military and VA doctors.

A close family friend is a retired Navy Chief. Exhibiting many of the symptoms of sleep apnea, he requested and received a sleep study at the VA shortly after retiring. Not obese at all, he spent his entire career deploying on Navy ships. Despite exhibiting the symptoms for the better part of his career, he was denied service connection and benefits by the VA after being diagnosed with severe obstructive sleep apnea. I have encountered many veterans who have experienced the same. Why? Before I answer, let's look a little closer at what causes sleep apnea.

The VA recognizes three types of sleep apnea.

- Obstructive Sleep Apnea is the most common. It occurs when throat muscles relax and block the upper airway.
- Central Sleep Apnea occurs when your brain doesn't send proper signals to the muscles that control breathing.
- Complex / Mixed Sleep Apnea occurs when someone has both obstructive sleep apnea and central sleep apnea.

Did you pick up on the second one? *Central Sleep Apnea occurs when your brain doesn't send proper signals to the muscles that control breathing.* Remember from earlier, we identified that breathing was a function of the autonomic nervous system? It's not the brain controlling breathing during sleep.

Sleep Apnea, Lead, and Dioxin Poisoning

Earlier, we reviewed data documenting our government recognizing how lead and dioxin poisoning affect the nervous system. Damage to the myelin sheathing on the nerves throughout the body slows the signals to and from sensory organs, ganglia, and the brain. Remember, ganglia are the small control centers outside the brain that make decisions and control the Autonomic Nervous System. To review:

The Autonomic Nervous System consists of a complex set of neurons contained in the ganglion that mediate and perform functions within the body without conscious intervention or voluntary control.[35] In other words, the ANS controls processes within the body without you having to think about them. The ANS controls and regulates blood pressure, breathing, digestion, urination, modulates sexual arousal, and so on. It also controls the body's reaction to stress and the fight-or-flight reaction. Damage to the autonomic nervous system is responsible or partially responsible for the following poisoning symptoms: high blood pressure, hypertension, hypertensive heart disease, disturbances in menstrual cycles, abdominal pain, constipation, diarrhea, shortness of breath, cardiac arrhythmia, abnormal EKG, a decrease in sex drive, decreased sperm count, infertility, fatigue, headache, drowsiness, anemia, labored breathing, and more.[24,27,28]

I am not a doctor, but it is pretty plain to me that damage to the autonomic nervous system from the chronic lead and dioxin poisoning we experienced will likely result in inhibiting the normal breathing our bodies rely upon during sleep. I searched but could find no reliable documentation making this connection. Why? Simple: the VA and military ignore our poisoning, misdiagnosing our symptoms.

The key is the snoring that causes obstructive sleep apnea. Snoring is caused by the inflated or relaxed tissues that restrict airways in the back of the throat. Airways restricted by the tongue, palate, or uvula. The uvula being the little worm-like thing that hangs down in the back of the mouth. All of these contain muscle tissue and, among other things, are used to breathe, swallow, and enunciate words in speech. I am not a rocket scientist but earlier we discovered that slurred speech is one of the symptoms of poisoning. Got it?

Evidence reliably infers that years of chronic exposure to poisoning results in damage to the autonomic nervous system resulting in the *slowed evoked potentials* of the brain and ganglion to respond to the sensory nerves controlling the actions of the muscle tissue within the tongue, palate, and uvula to allow normal breathing during sleep. Basically, the autonomic nervous system is tasked with coordinating the efforts of the lungs and airway while you sleep. If signals within this system are corrupted, slowed, or interrupted, the timing and coordination of this effort becomes confused resulting in *a loud snort or choking sound.*[67] Snoring!

The VA has the answer but ignores the poisoning that we have endured. Need proof? Remember above? The VA states[67]:

> *When you're awake, throat muscles help keep your airway stiff and open so air can flow into your lungs. When you sleep, these muscles relax, which narrows your throat . . . If the oxygen drops to a dangerous level, it triggers your brain to disturb your sleep. This helps tighten the upper airway muscles and open your windpipe. Normal breathing then starts again, often with a loud snort or choking sound.*

It's not rocket science. If the autonomic nervous system that controls sleep without you having to think about it is incapable of doing so, your brain has to wake up to get the job done. But is there another cause that the VA is aware of but, again, ignores?

Sleep Apnea, ORM, Chronic Long-Term Stress, and PTSD

Recently I read another article that got me to thinking about my own experience and Dr. Cheryl Spinweber.

In 2007, while on active duty, a knowledgeable Navy corpsman spotted my symptoms. I had been prescribed Valium and Ambien for sleep since 2003. I did not dream, snored loudly with choking sounds, was tired all of the time, and displayed various other symptoms. He and the Navy doc sent me for evaluation to the Sleep Clinic at Scripps Hillcrest Medical Center in San Diego, California.

At that time, Doctor Cheryl Spinweber was a clinical psychologist at the Sleep Disorders Clinic in Scripps Hillcrest Medical Center in San Diego, California. Today, I see, she is the director of their sleep programs in La Jolla, California.

Upon arriving for my sleep study, I was introduced to the "lab." It consisted of a comfortable bed placed in a room with cameras recording every angle of the event. The cameras would record the random eye movement I should experience in REM sleep. While I was lying on the bed and getting comfortable, sensors were attached to my head and body to record brain activity, oxygen levels, and other things. I took my normal meds and went to sleep. A few days later, after the study was completed, I met with Doctor Spinweber for a debrief.

The doc explained that I suffered from sleep apnea. She explained that it did not exactly meet the criteria accepted by the Navy and VA for severe sleep apnea. She explained that she'd had experience in dealing with the VA and knew of the strict requirements they place on veterans to receive benefits. Then she asked if I had been diagnosed with PTSD and about my military experiences.

I explained that I had not been diagnosed with PTSD and summed up my military career for her. I had been on sea duty and deployed every year from 1987 through 2005. Eighteen consecutive years, seven major deployments (tours), the Cold War, Drug War, three wars in the Middle East, and hundreds of deployments and high risk and special operations not even recorded. I had been a busy man.

The doc then asked if I could recount the events that had transpired during the test after I went to sleep. I recalled for her, in detail, the actions and conversations I had with the nurse until being released from the study the following morning. Afterward, she showed me the video taken during the study.

The video began with me falling asleep as soon as the nurse left the room. The doc indicated a complete lack of REM sleep over the next few hours. At one point, video recorded the nurse returning.

As soon as the nurse touched the door handle and began to open the door, I immediately sat bolt upright, wide awake, and held a conversation with nurse. The doc commented on the accuracy of the details I had recounted of that conversation. The nurse then attached a CPAP mask on my face. I immediately fell asleep once again.

A few hours later the nurse returned. Again, as soon as the nurse touched the door handle and began to open the door, I sat bolt upright, wide awake, and held another conversation with the nurse. Again, the doc commented on the accuracy of my recount of the conversation. The nurse adjusted the CPAP settings and left. The doc then showed me how I was beginning to enter REM sleep during that phase. At the end of the tests, upon the nurse touching the door handle, I would again immediately awaken. I was then released from the study and went home.

Doctor Spinweber explained that I had exhibited behaviors that she and other sleep specialists had observed veterans display. She explained that we exhibited behaviors similar to babies with Sudden Infant Death Syndrome (SIDS). She called it SIDS for adults.

In 2007, Doctor Spinweber would explain that veterans who had experienced years of living in dangerous surroundings, maintaining a constant state of vigilance, had become conditioned to stop breathing. We did this to listen and evaluate the safety of our surroundings. Any tiny noise, anything out of the ordinary would trigger this event. When required, we would then wake up, completely aware of our surroundings, ready to take immediate action. Afterward, we could then immediately fall back asleep. The problem was that we were not entering REM and getting the healthy, restful sleep our body and minds required. We slept in a constant state of fight or flight.

She then explained that when we stop breathing, oxygen levels in the blood deplete and, like a drowning man, drive processes within the brain triggering the fight-or-flight response to begin breathing. This prevents the brain from entering restful sleep and the REM sleep we all require. A CPAP machine would alleviate the oxygen depletion by maintaining the oxygen supply to the lungs during these episodes. The continuous positive airway pressure (CPAP) machine does so by maintaining air under slight pressure via a mask worn by the patient when sleeping.

She went on to explain that the Navy and VA did not recognize this type of "sleep apnea" and, since airway blockage was involved, wrote a diagnosis of severe obstructive sleep apnea for me.

Later, in 2021, I came across *The Connection Between Sleep Apnea and PTSD* by Logan Foley and Dr. Anis Rehman.[70] The article confirms what I had been told twelve years earlier. The article reports that roughly 17 to 22 percent of the population suffers from obstructive sleep apnea. Two studies referenced establish 69 percent of Vietnam veterans with PTSD and 69 percent of younger Iraq and Afghanistan veterans suffer obstructive sleep apnea. The article raises a number of interesting questions such as does sleep apnea contribute to PTSD or is it PTSD that contributes to sleep apnea. It is not rocket science to me. Remember, *when we stop breathing, oxygen levels in the blood deplete driving processes within the brain triggering the fight or flight response to begin breathing.*

Where does the VA stand on this subject? The VA reports[71]: *An additional consideration is obstructive sleep apnea (OSA), which has been found to be more common among individuals with PTSD than the general population. Estimates vary based upon measurement (e.g., self-report, Apnea Hypopnea Index (AHI) thresholds); and, a meta-analysis found OSA rates were significantly higher in individuals with PTSD (ranging from 43.6% to 75.7% based upon AHI threshold) than without the diagnosis. Of note, the classic predictors of OSA (Obstructive Sleep Apnea)—older age and body mass index (BMI) (being fat), in particular—may not be as relevant among Veteran samples, as indicated by a study of OEF/OIF/OND* (Gulf and Middle East Wars) *Veterans.*

Get it? The VA recognizes sleep apnea more common among individuals with PTSD than the general population and that age and body mass index (obesity) may not be as relevant among younger veterans. That's it. Within the entire article, that is the only mention of sleep apnea when reviewing sleep disorders among veterans with PTSD.

Then there is the VA National Center for PTSD *PTSD and Sleep* article in their PTSD Research Quarterly.[72] It states:

> It is important to be aware that insomnia and recurrent night-mares are often not the only sleep disorders that individuals with PTSD experience. There is growing evidence that this population also suffers from obstructive sleep apnea (OSA), a sleep-related breathing disorder, more often than the general population (Jaoude, Vermont, Porhomayon, & El-Solh, 2015) although not all studies have found an association with PTSD (Mysliwiec et al., 2015). OSA involves repetitive blockage of the airway that leads to fragmented sleep and reduced flow of oxygen to the brain. Given the impact of OSA on sleep, it is not surprising that studies are finding that treatment of comorbid apnea can improve not only sleep symptoms, but overall PTSD severity as well (Tamanna, Parker, Lyons, & Ullah, 2014). The primary treatment for OSA is continuous positive airway pressure (CPAP), in which a mask is worn at night that delivers pressurized air to keep the airway open. In some studies, patients with PTSD have lower adherence to CPAP (Collen, Lettieri, & Hoffman, 2012). A small body of evidence is beginning to show that parasomnias other than nightmares, such as sleep walking and rapid eye movement (REM) behavior disorder, are also more common in patients with PTSD, but it is not clear to what extent these represent comorbid disorders or are directly caused by trauma-related mechanisms (Mysliwiec et al., 2014). What is clear is that screening for sleep disorders beyond insomnia and recurrent nightmares needs to be routinely incorporated in the clinical assessment of PTSD.

I believe Dr. Spinweber, Ms. Foley, and Dr. Rehman are on the right track. Why? My VA records reveal that when first diagnosed, I experienced over thirty-one episodes per hour. Think about that for a moment. I stopped breathing every two minutes the entire time I attempted to sleep. For years, I had lived this way, never attaining restful sleep. My mind and body, suffocating like a drowned man, living in a constant state of fight or flight, for years, gasping for air just to survive every two minutes.

Immediately following my retirement in 2009, I was diagnosed with PTSD Hypervigilance (being constantly on guard and aware of my surroundings). As I write this in 2021, I called my VA Sleep Clinic to find that today, I suffer from an average of less than 1.1 episodes per hour. That is a significant reduction, wouldn't you agree?

Curious, I asked a few other veterans I know diagnosed with obstructive sleep apnea about their experiences. A retired Navy SWCC, SEAL and two Fleet Sailors with over seven deployments each, who all served as long as I did and retired about the same, reported similar findings. One reported that he was able to get away with not using his CPAP machine at all most of the time.

Why the gradual decline? Simple. First, having been out of the military and comfortably retired, we are all at ease with our surroundings in a manner that we were not years earlier when serving or recently retired. Remember, we all had been conditioned through years, decades of poisoning, chronic long-term stress, and conducting risk management (ORM), constantly having to reevaluate our safety and those we were responsible for. Second, the poisons are leaching out of our bodies, and the process has begun allowing our bodies to make repairs. Evidence infers that because the nerve damage in our autonomic nervous system is permanent, we will continue to suffer from sleep apnea for the rest of our lives to one degree or another.

Why is this a problem? Like the other things I have revealed and discovered, there are other obvious causes either unexplored or ignored that are not recognized by the military and VA. This results in veterans suffering from sleep apnea and being unable to achieve healthy, restful sleep—with many being denied the benefits for which they and their families are entitled. Veterans then left shouldering the financial burden with only one option to seek relief. Remember what the VA stated above?

> *What is clear is that screening for sleep disorders beyond insomnia and recurrent nightmares needs to be routinely incorporated in the clinical assessment of PTSD.*[72]

Veterans are forced to seek a diagnosis of PTSD.

CHAPTER 9

Epiphany: The Shame of Misdiagnosis and Resultant Veteran Suicide

Epiphany: epiph·a·ny | \ i-´pi-fə-nē
  Noun:
1: a usually sudden manifestation or perception of the essential nature or meaning of something
2: an intuitive grasp of reality through something (such as an event) usually simple and striking
3: an illuminating discovery, realization, or disclosure

Before I get started on this chapter, let me just state to all you veterans, law enforcement, and family members of those misdiagnosed with PTSD, suffering symptoms you cannot understand, denied treatment and benefits, afraid to come forward for fear of being labeled as suffering from mental illness—a disorder—with the stigma that comes along with it, contemplating or suffering from suicide by a loved one:

You are not nuts, going crazy, or mentally ill!
We have been poisoned!
We have been forced to work for weeks, months, years—
decades, even—
in high-stress conditions!

We suffer from poisoning and long-term chronic stress
symptoms!
We were removed from society and conditioned,
institutionalized from day one
to respond the way we have over years and decades;
We do not suffer from a "disorder"!
Every thought or action we have taken that has caused us, our
loved ones, and those around us harm was done so under the
influence of our conditioning, our poisoning, and the effects
of chronic long-term stress.
Years of operating daily in a fight-or-flight-induced
condition due to chronic stress (xenostressor) while under
the influence of these poisons (xenobiotics) have taken its toll
in the symptoms we are now forced to live with.
Years of our bodies and minds being denied sufficient
downtime to rest,
recoup, and reset have taken its toll!
You, we, they are not nuts!
We are not mentally deficient, crazy, going insane, unable
to cope with or rejoin "normal" society, or purposefully
destroying relationships around us.
We have been poisoned and injured; we simply suffer
from the symptoms and complications caused by it.
Symptoms, sickness, and disease caused by real, tangible things
that have physically harmed our bodies and our brains, resulting
in the behaviors we display.
We have been conditioned and institutionalized over decades
spent reacting the way we were trained, and our government
expected us to behave and react.
Do some of us suffer from PTSD? Yes!
For the vast majority of us, though, we suffer from behaviors
brought on by the physical, neurological, and hormonal damage
done to our brains. Behaviors brought on by years of
conditioning; training; and real, tangible injuries.

We do not suffer from a "disorder."
It is not our fault!
It is the fault of a government that has failed to comply with 29
U.S.C. § 654, 5(a)1:

> *Each employer shall furnish to each of his employees employment*
> *and a place of employment which are free from recognized hazards*
> *that are causing or are likely to cause death or serious physical harm*
> *to his employees.*

They know it, have recognized it, and have failed to stop it.

Instead, they ignore it, attempt to cover it up, and allow you
and society to believe that we are somehow mentally ill, suffering
from a "mental disorder."

How can I make these statements? I am not a doctor. I hold no degrees in psychiatry, psychology, neurology, pharmacology, or anything else, for that matter. It's the chicken-or-the-egg theory. The Socratic method, critical thinking.

Socrates, the stone mason who lived twenty-five hundred years ago. The man credited with developing the method of asking questions, gathering factual evidence, and then reaching a conclusion based on those facts. Plato, his "student," put it down on paper, established the Platonic Academy in 428 BC, and then taught it to Aristotle—three names familiar to most of us today. Scientists, doctors, mathematicians, and all major universities use these methods in research and education. At least, they used to.

Again, I am no doctor or author. I'm just a well-read guy armed with a computer who has been poisoned by his government, who refuses to die and is doing something about it. This information, unavailable just a few short years ago, is all over the internet. This is why I am primarily quoting government sources—to establish culpability and blame.

You are not to blame for your symptoms or the symptoms of your loved ones! The United States government is! Charged with protecting the safety and health of its employees and citizens, they have failed in their task. So what came first: suicide, PTSD, poisoning, or chronic stress?

Fact: According to the Department of Health and Human Services National Institute of Health's National Institute of Mental Health[62,74] and the Centers for Disease Control's National Institute for Occupational Health and Safety,[63,64] traumatic stress and PTSD are caused by a traumatic event that results in a person experiencing PTSD symptoms that:

> "Usually begin within 3 months of the traumatic incident, but sometimes they begin later. For symptoms to be considered PTSD, they must last more than a month and be severe enough to interfere with functioning in relationships or work. The course of the illness varies from person to person. Some people recover within 6 months, while others have symptoms that last much longer. In some people, the condition becomes chronic (ongoing)[62] . . ."

And:

> "Traumatic incident stress may occur at the time of the event or weeks or months later."[63]

A PTSD diagnosis two, five, ten, or twenty years later that results in suicide does not meet the government's criteria for PTSD. The physiological effects of the symptoms of chronic poisoning and chronic long-term stress in a person living for years in a poisoned and constantly induced state of fight or flight do. Remember the last chapter? NIOSH stated[63]:

Chronic Stress
Chronic or prolonged stress can develop from experiencing heavy demands and pressures over an extended period of time. There is also

little or no control over those demands, limited resources to meet those demands, and/or limited relief or "down-time." Symptoms of chronic stress can range from mild to high and are generally persistent. Those with chronic stress may experience the symptoms associated with acute stress listed above, as well as:

difficulty making decisions
loss of interest in normal activities
sleep problems
feeling powerless
difficulty with relationships
feeling sad and having other symptoms of depression

Acute stress symptoms listed above included:

- *physical and/or emotional tension*
- *digestive or sleep disturbances*
- *fear and anxiety*
- *irritability*
- *needing time to unwind after work before interacting with family and friends*
- *sleep disturbance*

To diagnose someone with PTSD for events that happened ten or twenty years ago—while ignoring the facts presented that document chronic poisoning, extreme conditioning, and chronic long-term stress over a five-, ten-, twenty-, or even my twenty-nine-year career—is grossly negligent and smacks of malpractice.

How about complications from years of tinnitus—the loud, noisy ringing in my ears that never goes away? I have suffered from it for close to two decades! What about chronic pain from injuries received during our service? I have been on opiates for pain, first prescribed by the Navy in 2003. I have had eleven surgeries, with more to come. I have the same symptoms as those above.

Decades of exposure to chronic pain and complications from years of tinnitus result in the same symptoms presented above from long-term chronic stress. Do you recognize the lead and dioxin poisoning symptoms listed above? They are the same symptoms!

When it comes to lead poisoning, there is all sorts of government research blaming lead paint or lead in gasoline for our woes but little to none on its effects on our veterans from guns and ordnance.

Take another look at the photos in Chapter 4, "Chronicling the Spread." Our veterans are covered in it—lead, dioxins, furans, PCBs, and other chemicals abound in the environment we are forced to train and live in.

Plenty of research has been done on children, which has concluded that lead poisoning is responsible for increased violence and destructive behavior—lead poisoning from lead in gasoline, paint chips, or water supplies from lead pipes. Where are the studies on veterans? Must be PTSD.

When it comes to firearms and ordnance poisoning,[2] where are the studies of its effects? None can be found for the combined effects of ordnance poisoning, burn pits, Gulf War Syndrome, and Agent Orange, despite veterans suffering from concurrent exposure to the toxic compounds of them all for more than fifty years. Chronic exposures experienced over entire careers to continue to be poisoned for forty years or more after their last exposure.

Where is the research on the effects of poisoning by dioxins, furans, and other toxic compounds produced in herbicides, the flaming oil wells of Kuwait and Iraq, and the burn pits of every war?

How about white matter dysfunction? The public is more interested in the effects on NFL football players than veterans. Remember from earlier? Traumatic brain injury indicates the same damage to the white matter of the brain as lead poisoning. NFL players suffer the same symptoms and commit suicide just like those reported in veterans.[38] Do you see hero football players misdiagnosed with PTSD to explain their symptoms? No! We can't label them mentally deficient, suffering from a mental disorder. That just wouldn't do, would it? They have sacrificed so much for our amusement and entertainment.

How about the effects of chronic long-term stress on veterans? Where are the government studies? I mean, hey, NIOSH identified the stress those who constantly fired guns were exposed to as early as 1975[17] and defined it for stewardesses and pilots in 2017.[63] You would figure with the vast resources and combined medical infrastructure of the Department of Health and Human Services, CDC, NIOSH, NIH, NTP, Department of Defense, Army, Navy, Air Force, and VA, someone would have conducted a study to come up with a definitive answer of the effects of all the above on our veterans, right? Wrong. PTSD is the accepted story line and catchall diagnosis.

So why are we suffering more as we age, and what is to blame for the massive increases in suicide of late? I know the answer. I am not even a doctor. It only took me a few weeks of research to figure it out using existing government research, and it cost you, the taxpayer, nothing but the price of this book.

Veteran Suicide

Not to leave out our law enforcement and first responder brothers and sisters and the increase in suicide they, too, have suffered, as I will reveal here: the same conclusions apply to them as well.

A good study to begin with is, once again, found in the National Library of Medicine[73]: *The Effects of Stress on Job Functioning of Military Men and Women*. Surprise, surprise, it was funded by a grant from the Department of the Army. The study concluded that women were more likely to experience and report stress while in the military than men. Hmm. The NIMH reported:

"Women are more likely to develop PTSD than men."[74]

Curious. How about the VA?

"Women are more than twice as likely to develop PTSD than men (10% for women and 4% for men). There are a few reasons women might get PTSD more than men: Women are more likely to experience sexual assault. Sexual assault is more likely to cause PTSD than many other events."[75]

This coincides with statistics published by the VA[76] documenting massive increases in veteran suicide since 2001. The VA reports female veteran suicide rates increased by 85.2 percent. Male veterans experienced an increase of 30.5 percent. Why? What changed in 2001? Before I answer, let me point out something I continue to discover throughout my research.

In July 2016, the VA reported an 85.2 percent increase in female veterans' suicide from 2001 to 2014.[66] In August 2017, the VA reported a 62.4 percent increase for the same years.[77] That is a 23 percent decrease. The first report was published in 2016 and the second in 2017. This is a pattern I've found in government reports and documents that indicates either gross incompetence on the part of senior government officials or a coordinated attempt within the government to downplay the significance of alarming or embarrassing facts to make them more palatable to the public in an effort to cover up the truth. In short, CONSPIRACY to COVER UP!

How about in the last chapter? The VA War Related Illness and Injury Study Center's *Burn Pits (Trash and Feces Fires)*[60] stated:

> "Proper disposal of waste during deployment is essential to prevent health problems and protect service members. In certain situations, when sanitary and waste management facilities are not available, this waste may be burned in an open pit."

Why is the VA soft pedaling and even justifying "proper disposal of waste during deployment is essential to prevent health problems and protect service members"? That statement has no place in a medical document used to identify the consequences of the poisoning caused by the military's actions. The vast majority of items burned in those pits weren't burned for sanitation purposes. You don't burn cars, military equipment, electronics, plastics, petroleum products, and so on to "prevent health problems and protect service members."

They burned it because it was simple, easy, and cost effective to do so. It required no effort on the part of senior leadership to plan, coordinate, and fund the disposal. They just ordered their subordinate enlisted men and women to burn it. Senior military leadership damn sure did not suffer the stench or poisonous effects from the burning debris that their subordinates did. Besides, no one would or could be held accountable despite having already *recognized* that they were poisoning everyone in the vicinity.[59] As we have already revealed, they are protected by a presidential executive order and seventy-year-old US Supreme Court decision.[16,86]

While we are on the topic of "alarming or embarrassing facts," it's important to note that the Department of Defense and its services require all publications produced by its veterans and employees to be reviewed by the Department of Defense Office of Prepublication and Security Review. Rightfully required to prevent classified material from being published; however, the DoD also abuses this privilege by delaying or halting the publication of embarrassing information.

That is why everything referenced in this book was sourced via FOIA requests, documents freely available to the general public and interviews attained and conducted *after* I was terminated for whistleblowing in 2014. Nothing used in this book is subject to DoD prepublication review because everything is available to the general public and has already been redacted and cleared for release. I even produced the photos in 2020 using my own personal weapons and gear.

Not wanting their dirty secrets revealed, as I have demonstrated, the DoD and government have a history of weaponizing laws and regulations to avoid accountability. They have used conspiracy to conceal their responsibility for decades of poisoning veterans, their civilian employees, and our families. Why did I submit this publication for the Department of Defense and the Navy to review?

Simple, to remove their legal standing in any attempt to stop its publication and strip me of the ability to get this information to those who need to see it.

As stated in Chapter 1, through FOIA requests and diligent review of court transcripts and evidence, I uncovered documents and testimony chronicling how senior Department of Defense personnel falsified official reports, statements, and even testimony during a federal hearing to attack my credibility and conceal the poisoning of veterans and federal employees. The stakes involved in concealing this information are very high for a number of reasons but in no way justified.

Either way, the numbers of female veterans committing suicide is alarming. The over 50 percent difference between men and women (30.5 percent men to 85.2 percent women)[66] is telling. So what changed?

September 11, 2001, we went to war. Veterans have been at war now for over twenty consecutive years. I have. I served in the Cold War from 1986 through 1991. Iran, 1987. Iraq, 1991. Iraq again in 2003. Drug War for six years of my career. Just doing my part.

In PTSD and suicide-related diagnoses, the accepted explanation is that veterans who had not experienced war were suddenly thrust into it and therefore must have suffered some form of mental trauma. Unable to cope with the things they must have done or experienced, veterans turn to suicide as a form of relief. Therefore, veterans who committed suicide obviously suffered from PTSD.

"Poor veterans," says the government. "So loyal to the nation; let's pass new laws to help them."

"They suffer from a mental illness," and they're "never the same when they come back," says President Donald Trump. Trump passes executive orders. Congress passes new laws with all kinds of riders on bills, which have nothing at all to do with helping veterans, and yet here we are, still dying and suffering the same sickness, symptoms, and disease. Nothing has changed. Nothing has been solved.

Taxpayers are spending more money. Nonprofits pop up like weeds after a summer shower. Everybody pats themselves on the back and says, "What a great thing we are doing for our veterans," and "Thank you for your service." The sun is shining, birds are chirping, everybody is happy and content. Friends of bureaucrats and nonprofits are making money, and yet here we are, still here—sick, dying, and committing suicide like never before.

But hold on, wait a minute. What caused this sudden increase in veteran suicide? Women are the key to discovery. So what changed in 2001?

We did not experience a sudden influx of women into the military. Their numbers have remained pretty consistent over the years.

We did not suddenly send more women to war. They worked and trained for years in the same fields and job codes before and during the war. Female foot soldiers were foot soldiers, pilots were pilots, and so on.

Women did not perform more combat missions than men. Veterans going to war was not the only metric that drastically increased with symptoms that mirror PTSD. The number of veterans exposed to lead, firearms, ordnance, dioxins, furans, PCBs, and other poisoning increased as well. Deployments doubled, going from six months to ten, twelve, and more. Time to rest and reset between deployments was cut in half or done away with altogether. Training for war increased.

Both men and women conducted more live-fire training with weapons and ordnance. They were forced to eat, sleep, use, and live with their weapons and were poisoned. They contaminated everything they came into contact with both in training after 2001 and throughout the numerous deployments they endured.

Chronic stress in live-fire training and during deployments across the board for both warfighters and non-warfighting veterans alike increased as well.

Troops were required to deploy more. Forces were spread thin. When deployed, troops work and are on-call seven days per week, twenty-four hours per day. Remember what the 1975 NIOSH report revealed earlier[17]? It identified:

"The physiological stresses associated with the position of range officer should be considered . . . By its very nature the job demands close confinement, constant watchfulness for violations, rote repetition and exposure to high noise levels and to lead dust and fumes."

It then recommends:

"A rotation system should be instituted for the range officer position. It is suggested that a one month of duty be followed by three months of alternate activity. This change is suggested not only to alleviate any possible lead absorption . . . but to prevent undue psychological stresses associated with the position."

The Navy recognized this. Prior to 2001, a deployment rotation was six months deployed followed by an eighteen-month rest, ship refit, and crew-training period. It still is for Navy SEAL teams.[92] This mirrors NIOSH's "one month of duty be followed by three months of alternate activity." But does it really?

A Navy sailor, my niece just returned from such a deployment. Immediately after returning from a six-month deployment, she is at sea again off the coast of San Diego. Training day and night with her crew members, they are readying to deploy on yet another six-month-or-more tour within a year. She has been told it may be as long as nine months to a year. She is a single mom and not by choice.

Her stress is further compounded by having twenty-four-hour duty on that ship every three days when she is based at home. Working seven days per week, eighteen to twenty hours a day while deployed off San Diego's coast, training for war, she has to arrange twenty-four-hour childcare. Both being on duty in port and while deployed takes a serious toll. I haven't scratched the surface yet.

My son, now a disabled Navy veteran, left the Navy recently after five years. During his last two years, he completed three tours overseas in Europe, Africa, the Middle East, and Western Pacific. He served as an Air Force–trained Navy Raven (specially trained security forces personnel) and as a boat driver on his last deployment on a Navy Mk VI patrol boat. He was a weapons instructor and operator for his command as well. He fired weapons at Camp Pendleton ranges and the Naval Special Warfare Desert Warfare Training Facility in California. Some of the same ranges I shot and worked at throughout my career.

Deployed for eighteen months out of twenty-four, while at home for six months, he was constantly on the road or off the coast, training for war. The Navy would not grant him the vacation time he had earned. He had enough. Had he not left the Navy, they were going to immediately send him out on yet another six-month tour. That would have meant being deployed two years out of his last two and a half years of service. The VA still refuses to recognize the symptoms he displays from nonstop deployment and training for war, denying him treatment and benefits.

So not only have we been at war since 2001—due to the military being unable to meet its recruitment goals and failure to meet manning requirements,[46] people fed up with the constant deployments leaving the military, attrition from injuries, and mandatory retirement regulations—the military has increased the burden on those who remain, increasing their workload as well as deployment times and time away from home training for war.

My niece said one ship has been deployed for longer than one year because the ship that was supposed to relieve it keeps breaking down.

Working them harder and longer, they have no time to decompress, rest, and reset. Surely not the "one month of duty be followed by three months of alternate activity to prevent undue psychological stresses associated with the position" recommended by NIOSH in 1975 and practiced by the Navy until 2001.

Daily work requirements and deployment stress is compounded by the threat of being fired for being overweight, high-year tenure layoffs before retirement eligibility, and a stagnant and dated advancement, wage, and promotion system that hasn't kept pace with our allies' modern navies.

In addition, the wages veterans earn while trying to maintain a household and family they rarely see has increased stress levels in our troops. Veterans in other modern navies are paid overtime.

Our veterans work twelve-, sixteen-, and eighteen-hour days seven days per week for the same pay as those who work eight hours a day, five days per week. The Navy band makes the same pay and receives the same benefits and retirement as my niece, who works seven days per week, twelve to eighteen hours per day, as well as those young Navy SEALs or Army and Marine foot soldiers fighting our battles.

THERE IS NO FAIR PAY FOR THOSE WHO PUT IN AND WORK THE HOURS!

Not fair, is it?

There are also the dangers of increased live-fire training, combat, and deployment to countries that want us dead. Veterans are living in the poisoning and stress-induced state of fight or flight twenty-four hours per day, seven days per week, three hundred sixty-five days per year without proper rest and time to reset.

Compounding the above, the metrics that increased with symptoms mirroring PTSD include the added exposures to lead and the other 145 hazardous and toxic compounds that accompany them. Add in dioxins, furans, PCBs from burning oil wells and shit pit and burn pit duties, complications from chronic tinnitus, chronic pain from poisoning and injuries, exposure to all manner of cleaning solvents, and so on and you have a twenty-four-hour-per-day exposure to all manner of toxic substances and medical conditions with symptoms that mirror PTSD.

Comorbidities with the same symptoms that, when ignored, result in misdiagnosis, mistreatment, worsening symptoms, and suicide.

Xenostressors and xenobiotics.

So are women inferior to men in the military, causing them to commit suicide at such a higher rate?

Are men so superior at dealing with stress that it causes such a great disparity in veteran suicide? The VA thinks so.

Are women less able to cope with the loss of so much time away from home and family? Are they committing suicide because of sexual harassment and rape, like the VA would have you believe?

Unwanted pregnancy? Unfair work practices? What is it? Why the increases and huge disparity over male suicide rates? Were all these studies completed by men, with no input from women?

Is there a concerted effort among the government to portray women as inferior to men?

On the surface, it all seems quite misogynistic. Government studies show women must be inferior to men in the military, right?

Whew! Let me assuage the tension that these questions illicit. I'd be angry if I were a woman and read that stuff.

Having a daughter and niece in the military, as well as serving with many hard-core female professionals for almost three decades, I can assure you there is an explanation. If the reason was an easy one, the VA, Department of Defense, and government could trot out to console the families and victims of these suicides, they would have already done so.

The answer is none of the above. The government has the answer but avoids publicizing it, accepting culpability (and financial liability), and taking action to stop it. Instead, they work to conceal it from the public.

If you look in Dr. Cabral's book[50] at the chapter "Toxic Enemy #5 Stress," you will find an easy-to-understand diagram that illustrates the effects of stress on the body. It demonstrates how stress in the fight-or-flight mode activates the sympathetic nervous system of the autonomic nervous system and the effects on the body from the release of many different hormones.

Figure it out yet?

HORMONES!

Earlier, I discussed the many differing effects poisoning has on the body and how it affects systems throughout the whole body, corrupting and interrupting the normal production and regulation of hormones as well as various required chemical compounds. The effects on the brain; nervous, immune, and hemopoietic systems; organs and growth; and women's reproduction and menstrual cycles were also discussed. Now, do you understand?

As pointed out earlier, women experience plenty of natural hormonal activity not experienced by men that is exacerbated by the psychological, neurological, and physiological effects of corrupted hormone production. The fact that females went to war and cannot function under stress as well as a man is, somehow, wrongly but factually correct. The government relying on that unspoken, unjust, dishonest, and immoral conclusion is both appalling and offensive.

Female Suicide Increases

First, let me state:

> Evidence exists documenting women experienced higher levels of veteran suicide over men because of the disruption of normal hormone production and regulation exacerbating the symptoms of menstruation, ovulation, pregnancy, and postpartum directly attributable to increases in the chronic long-term stress and poisoning they have experienced since 2001.

Men experience the same disruptions but not those endured by women. I've pretty much covered the effects of poisoning. What are the effects of years of chronic long-term stress on the body and mind?

The CDC's NIOSH conducted a study on workplace violence for nurses.[76] Its website states:

> *Without therapeutic intervention, being subjected to work-related stress, injury, or abuse over the long term may lead to burnout, a chronic condition manifested by cynicism, anger, resentment, and emotional exhaustion. People suffering from burnout often do not connect their feelings and behavior with the chronic stress they are under.*
>
> *Absorbing responsibility for something over which one has no control can lead to depression. High rates of obesity among nurses have also been associated with daily and insidious job-related stress such as short-staffing and insufficient time for proper nutrition (Han, Trinkoff, Storr, & Geiger-Brown, 2011).*
>
> *It is important to recognize the range of possible responses to stress and trauma as normal. With therapeutic intervention, unhealthy response to chronic stress, and/or acute crisis can be avoided.*

NIOSH also states[79]:

> *Stress sets off an alarm in the brain, which responds by preparing the body for defensive action. The nervous system is aroused and hormones are released to sharpen the senses, quicken the pulse, deepen respiration, and tense the muscles. This response (sometimes called the fight or flight response) is important because it helps us defend against threatening situations. The response is preprogrammed biologically. Everyone responds in much the same way, regardless of whether the stressful situation is at work or home.*
>
> *Short-lived or infrequent episodes of stress pose little risk. But when stressful situations go unresolved, the body is kept in a constant state of activation, which increases the rate of wear and tear to biological systems. Ultimately, fatigue or damage results, and the ability of the body to repair and defend itself can become seriously compromised. As a result, the risk of injury or disease escalates.*

In the past 20 years, many studies have looked at the relationship between job stress and a variety of ailments. Mood and sleep disturbances, upset stomach and headache, and disturbed relationships with family and friends are examples of stress-related problems that are quick to develop and are commonly seen in these studies. These early signs of job stress are usually easy to recognize. But the effects of job stress on chronic diseases are more difficult to see because chronic diseases take a long time to develop and can be influenced by many factors other than stress. Nonetheless, evidence is rapidly accumulating to suggest that stress plays an important role in several types of chronic health problems—especially cardiovascular disease, musculoskeletal disorders, and psychological disorders.

Job Stress and Health: What the Research Tells Us

Cardiovascular Disease—Many studies suggest that psychologically demanding jobs that allow employees little control over the work process increase the risk of cardiovascular disease.

Musculoskeletal Disorders—On the basis of research by NIOSH and many other organizations, it is widely believed that job stress increases the risk for development of back and upper-extremity musculoskeletal disorders.

Psychological Disorders—Several studies suggest that differences in rates of mental health problems (such as depression and burnout) for various occupations are due partly to differences in job stress levels. (Economic and lifestyle differences between occupations may also contribute to some of these problems.)

Workplace Injury—Although more study is needed, there is a growing concern that stressful working conditions interfere with safe work practices and set the stage for injuries at work.

Suicide, Cancer, Ulcers, and Impaired Immune Function— Some studies suggest a relationship between stressful working conditions and these health problems. However, more research is needed before firm conclusions can be drawn.

Published in 1999, over twenty years ago, this study[79] establishes that the government acknowledged the effects of chronic long-term stress. But what makes women so different from men?

During a woman's menstruation, ovulation, pregnancy, and postpartum periods, a female's body endures a number of changes that rely upon the normal, uninterrupted flow of hormones and other chemical compounds to rebuild and replenish it. NIOSH states[80]:

> "Female sex hormones called estrogen and progesterone are produced by the ovaries. These hormones are responsible for sexual development and for preparing the uterine wall every month to hold and nourish a fertilized egg during pregnancy. These hormones also contribute to the health of the heart, bones, liver, brain, and many other tissues. So, a reproductive hazard that alters your estrogen and progesterone production can also reduce your general health."

How about the production of blood during the menstrual cycle? Remember the earlier discussion on how lead poisoning hinders the normal production of and shortens the average life span of red blood cells? A woman's body requires more red blood cells than a man's and can tolerate the interruptions in its production and life span less. This is especially exaggerated during the blood loss of menstruation and the added requirements for more blood during pregnancy.

The body and its autonomic processes are stressed to produce more blood in a poisoned female than one who is not. This means that organs and systems that are already stressed and damaged by poisoning need to produce even more of the hormones and compounds that are already in short supply. The body undergoes an alarmed state of fight or flight due to the lack of available blood, sending signals throughout the body demanding that more be produced. The whole body is basically out of hormonal balance.

How about the stresses placed upon the blood-brain barrier, as discussed earlier? Remember how poisoning alters permeability, allowing chemical compounds to flow into and out of the brain that the blood-brain barrier would normally stop? That creates chemical imbalances, which directly affect the brain and behavior.

Pregnancy? The body relies upon normal hormone and chemical compound production and regulation to keep itself healthy and build a baby. Again, the body and autonomic processes are stressed more in a poisoned female than one who is not.

Postpartum depression and stress? The body—expelling the fetus in normal, premature, or stillborn birth or miscarriage—experiences massive, immediate hormonal changes, trying to compensate for the sudden loss as well as the forced rebuilding processes required for it to return to a normal cycle of ovulation and menstruation.

Having an adult daughter, being married for thirty years, and working with young female sailors has given me the insight, experience, and opportunity to observe and interact with females during all these occasions.

Think about a young female soldier, Marine, or Seabee tasked with erecting a tent in the desert in 110°F heat. What do you think she goes through when suffering headaches, cramps, and a heavy flow during menstruation? She is miserable, angry, depressed, hot, and sticky all at the same time. Not only is she sweating profusely and becoming dehydrated alongside her male counterparts, but her body is also working harder and is subject to anemia and further dehydration from a lack of blood. Consider the consequences to her cardiovascular system. Chief Marley Jones died so quickly in 2001 that the only words she could utter were "Oh my!"

The same is true for the female fighter pilot flying a six-, eight-, or ten-hour mission. Think about how she feels sitting the entire time, not able to move, legs spread apart, feet on the aircraft's rudder pedals. She can't whip out a used water bottle, nonchalantly fill it up, shake it off, tuck it back in, zip up, and carry on like a guy can. Heavy flow while menstruating? Tough. She is miserable but doesn't dare show it. She is too professional.

What about that female soldier or Marine out on patrol? They have to pack tampons, maxi pads, and wet wipes in addition to all the other gear male soldiers do. Try walking around with 95 to 135 pounds of gear on an eight-hour hump in one hundred–plus degree heat and near 100 percent humidity. They can't throw the used tampons and pads away; they have to carry them back with them. Bring Ziploc baggies? Bad flow day? Cramps? Suck it up.

There are no showers or wash facilities to change in. All they can do is a quick wipe in the bushes while fighting flies, cram another one in and slap a new one on, bag up the bloody trash, and carry on. They are miserable but professionally soldier on without complaint.

Then there is the female soldier who stands guard for eight hours with nowhere to go.

Think about the female Sailor or Marine on a ship at sea bobbing up and down, up and down, back and forth twenty-four hours a day, seven days a week.

What about experiencing a bleed-through while on patrol, standing guard in a white uniform or sitting in the pilot's seat? Tough. Many who are deployed don't get a chance to shower for days at a time. Females in the military don't get to call time-out, run to the bathroom, refresh themselves, maybe shower, and change clothes at these times.

What about the other things they face while serving alongside their male counterparts? Pregnancy? Being a single mom and having to leave your child while trying to balance a military career? Breasts leaking milk due to lactation? Am I too fat, and are they going to kick me out of the service because of it? And on and on . . .

Then there are miscarriages, stillborn babies, babies born with birth defects—all symptoms of poisoning. How about postpartum depression? Ever deal with young women going through that? I have.

Females deal with a lot more stress on a daily basis than their male counterparts—females in the military times ten. A good argument can be made that well-rounded female veterans tend to deal with stress better than the men they serve with. I'll support that with decades of experience fighting alongside them.

In addition, both men and women in the military experience stresses that civilians don't.

- Veterans deploy to countries that don't want them, living and working under constant threat of assassination.
- They are on guard, in a heightened state of awareness of fight or flight from the constant high-stress training and deployments they experience year in and year out.
- They are forced to work with foreign soldiers who, at any moment, can turn on and kill them.
- They are forced to work with Saudi pilots right here in the United States, who can shoot them in the classroom right on a military base.
- They fly aircraft older than they are, which may or may not have had the proper maintenance or are just too old and worn out to fly safely.
- They drive or ride in a vehicle, wondering if this is the day they'll hit an improvised explosive device (IED) or land mine.
- They travel in Navy and Coast Guard ships through typhoons or heavy seas, puking their guts out, a thousand miles from the nearest land, wondering if the ship will sink. Up and down, up and down, for days and weeks on end.
- They sleep in a barracks room with twenty-four or more strangers, some of which may be foreign nationals.
- They are required to perform tasks that they know are poisoning them and their families.
- They worry if their ship's officers are competent enough to not run their ship into another in the middle of the ocean, killing them and their shipmates.
- They have to salute the officers let off the hook and not held accountable for murdering their shipmates, even after confessing they were responsible for running their ship into another.

- They have to hide in a bunker as Iranian missiles impact outside around them and then endure the news reports that no one was injured, while they and their fellow soldiers writhe on the ground in agony from concussions and traumatic brain injuries.
- They worry if they will be forced to leave the service because of the extra pounds they packed on from excess cortisol production due to years of chronic stress.
- They wonder if they will meet the ever-changing advancement requirements to reach retirement before being kicked out of the service for high-year tenure with no benefits, some after fourteen years of honorable service.
- They have to work eighteen-hour days, seven days per week, in a high-stress environment, experiencing all of the above for weeks and months.
- They wonder if they are doing the right thing as politicians bicker, like petulant children, over whether or not they should even be there after being at war for more than twenty years.
- They stress over whether or not to engage the enemy in combat for fear of being jailed upon their return home.
- The list goes on and on. Chronic long-term stress suffered for days, months, and years takes its toll. How about law enforcement and first responders?
- Working in a city or town where people do not want them.
- Sitting in a patrol car, wondering if someone is going to sneak up and execute them while stopped at a red light
- Walking a beat, constantly looking over their shoulder, wondering the same.
- Wondering if their coffee or lunch has been spat in, poisoned, or worse.
- Preparing for that person in the car they approach at a traffic stop wondering if it is an ambush.
- Wondering if that bucket full of liquid a citizen threw on them contains an acid or a poison that will hurt or kill them or poison their family.

- Being prepared for the bodily fluids a person may try to throw at them.
- Relaxing in the station before being called into immediate action, forced to wear seventy pounds or more of protective gear to fight a fire for hours on a hot, humid summer day.
- Wondering if the mayor, district attorney, or the city they work for will support the decisions they make on the job following the laws the city made in the first place or executing their duties in accordance with their training and policies.
- Wondering time and again why they even bother as politicians bicker over whether they should even be there or not . . .

All the while carrying a lead-contaminated weapon in contaminated gear in a lead-contaminated vehicle, knowing they are poisoning themselves, their families, and homes.

First responders and more all experience the same chronic long-term stress as military veterans and law enforcement. Firefighters are exposed to the same dioxins, furans, and PCBs mentioned earlier in every burning building they encounter.

As you can see, stress is real, and in the last twenty years, chronic long-term stress has increased for veterans, law enforcement, and first responders alike.

What we can conclude from existing research documented by the government is that *everyone* who serves in the military, law enforcement, fire department, etc., and who is exposed to these poisons and chronic long-term stress will forever have their bodies, minds, behavior, and mental capacity irrevocably altered by their service.

Reading "Toxic Enemy #5 Stress" in Dr. Cabral's book resulted in discoveries and an epiphany that changed me and my family's life. Researching his conclusions led to an understanding that I have been poisoned. The symptoms I suffer are not because of a mental illness. I have been poisoned; my body and mind have been conditioned and forever changed through years of service to a government that was well aware of what it was doing to me and my loved ones.

I now understand that without an explanation, the depression, anxiety, irritability, and so on that I suffered from were the result of doubting and questioning myself. I doubted myself after relying on the VA and government to provide an honest diagnosis for the cause of my symptoms. An honest diagnosis and treatment that they failed to provide.

Instead, I uncovered how they misdiagnosed my symptoms because they blatantly ignored the cause and took the easy way out with a diagnosis of PTSD. Rather than a diagnosis with a real cause, backed up by years of symptoms documented in my medical records and evidence of exposure, they labeled me as mentally deficient, suffering a mental illness, a disorder.

To those of you who have experienced this poisoning, chronic long-term stress, and have been misdiagnosed with PTSD or have thoughts of suicide because you can't cope with the symptoms identified here, you are not crazy, going nuts, mentally deficient, or less of a person than you were before:

WE HAVE BEEN POISONED!

Many of us are suffering the tangible effects of poisoning, years of chronic long-term stress, and complications from tinnitus and pain from our injuries. Our symptoms are explainable. It is not because of mental issues caused by events that we observed or participated in. We have been misled. We did the best we could for the time, place, and circumstances we experienced.

We reacted the way we were trained and conditioned to—actions we were once rewarded for. Our medals and performance evaluations document that fact. It was not our fault. Whatever happened, happened. As the government has said, PTSD is not responsible for the symptoms we suffered years and decades after a traumatic event.

The depression, anxiety, forgetfulness, irritability, and behavioral changes we suffer are caused by poisoning, chronic long-term stress, traumatic brain injury, multiple sclerosis, complications from chronic tinnitus, pain, years of military training and conditioning, and any number of other comorbidities and causes. Not PTSD!

The same goes for the decisions we made, actions we took, and behaviors we displayed. They were all undertaken and executed *under the influence* of the poisoning and stress we endured. We were not given the chance to make those decisions with a clear head. It was not our fault. It is the government's fault.

Knowing this has allowed me some peace and the ability to move on. It has placed my wife, kids, and friends at ease. I hope this knowledge brings you and your loved ones the same peace of mind as well.

CHAPTER 10
Consequences

I began this book identifying the veterans I served with who lost their lives to heart failure at an early age. I think I've clearly established they were victims of the chronic poisoning, long-term chronic stress, and other causes identified here. We are all victims of a Navy and government that refuse to protect us from the poisoning they knowingly subject us to, poisoning they continue subjecting new generations of veterans and their families to today.

The photos in Chapter 4 provide a visual picture identifying how these poisons spread throughout the community, to our families, and to those who have never even fired a gun.

Through the references I have presented, I have established the sickness, symptoms, and disease this poisoning is responsible for.

I revealed the government's gross negligence, willful poisoning, and mistreatment of its veterans, law enforcement, and first responder personnel.

I documented the plight of female veterans and their children into the future.

Along with the above, I identified the cause for the increases in suicide.

I disclosed the same poisons, sicknesses, and diseases were caused by Agent Orange, Gulf War Syndrome, burn pits, and firearms poisoning. I verified that the firefighters, police, first responders, and demolition crews of the 9/11 World Trade Center terrorist attack suffer from the same poisoning as well.

I learned that despite the government recognizing the same cancer-causing and highly toxic poisons in all the above, they continue to deny treatment and benefits to us for it.

I examined how extreme conditioning, long-term chronic stress, pain, and tinnitus affect the body and mind in the same way as poisoning.

Disgustingly, despite decades of research conducted by multiple government agencies, I confirmed that the VA recognizes the symptoms of this poisoning, misdiagnoses them as PTSD and other illnesses, and mistreats those who suffer from it. Malpractice on a grand scale.

Most of all, I've clearly made the case that the US government is culpable, having known of these toxic compounds for fifty years on more[3] and of their responsibility to protect us. I've made the case that our government has known the result of chronic long-term stress for forty-five years[17] and has failed to protect us from it while willingly subjecting us to it and the poisoning that continues to cause our sickness, disease, and death.

I also divulged that the government willfully falsified documents, reports, and testimony under oath to conceal it while taking advantage of laws it passed to protect them from accountability.

So who are the victims in all this and what does this cost them? Sickness and death aren't the only cost in all this. There is the crushing burden of the financial cost to the victims, their families, and the taxpayer as well.

The loss of a job and the income of a breadwinner isn't the largest loss to those suffering from this poisoning; instead, it is the inability to pay for needed long-term medical care. Not just the immediate symptoms and long-term disabilities but also the cost of medical care required through the coming years. Symptoms and disease that appear and worsen as these poisons continue leaching out of our bones and fatty tissues for forty years or more after leaving our jobs and the source of our poisoning.

Veterans and their families are denied medical care and benefits, and they are forced to pay out of pocket because those affected are misdiagnosed. They are misdiagnosed because the cause of the sickness is unknown, not recognized, or worse, concealed from them and their families.

Those affected and their families are forced to rely on welfare, Medicaid, and Medicare, and they know that it is not enough to cover their medical bills. Deductibles are quickly exceeded. Families are forced into poverty. They lose their homes, fortune, future, and dignity. To add insult to injury, veterans are forced to find and fund health care on their own for themselves and their families.

That's right: veterans and their families have to pay for their medical expenses after leaving the service. Birth defects, sickness, disease, and death willingly thrust upon us by the military and government have to be paid for by veterans and their families. Even veterans who are granted "free" health care by the VA for injuries sustained in war are forced to pay for Medicare when they turn sixty-five. If we do not pay, the VA refuses care and ejects us into our welfare system. This system will eat away and drain all our resources and property.

Veterans' families affected by this poisoning have to pay as well. Gone is the famous "medical care for life." It doesn't exist. Families are forced to pay for medical care in the form of TRICARE. At sixty-five, it will be canceled and can only be retained by paying not only for TRICARE Insurance but also Medicare as well. Let's not forget that the deductibles still apply.

But the deductibles do not cover the sickness, disease, and death caused by a military and government that concealed this poisoning from those it willfully poisoned. When deductibles are exceeded, the family is forced to pay more, forcing them into further poverty.

Think about that a moment. The Department of Defense and government ignores its own reports recognizing that it is poisoning its veterans and their families,[2,18,24] ignores the findings and recommendations of our country and the world's top subject matter experts,[24,26–28] hides behind a presidential executive order,[16] 1950 US Supreme Court decision,[86] the Federal Tort Claims Act of 1942, and Federal Sovereign Immunity.

Sovereign Immunity is a term derived from British common law doctrine based on the idea that the King could do no wrong. That's right, the federal government can decide whether or not to allow you to file suit against them if they so choose.

The principle was not mentioned in the original United States Constitution, however the courts have recognized it both as a principle that was inherited from English common law and as a practical, logical inference (that the government cannot be compelled by the courts because it is the power of the government that creates the courts in the first place).[96]

The Federal Tort Claims Act, passed August 2, 1946, is a federal statute permitting private parties to sue the United States in a federal court for most torts committed by persons acting on behalf of the United States. It contains a two-year statute of limitations meaning that you have two years to file in court from the date of injury. Did not know you were injured? Government concealing information or refusing to provide information via FOIA requests? Can't afford an attorney? Government officials ignoring your attempts to hold those responsible accountable? Writing a book whistleblowing their activities is your only recourse.

The *Feres Doctrine* is the result of a 1950 US Supreme Court decision. In 1946, a lawsuit was filed under the 1946 Federal Tort Claims Act on behalf of a soldier killed when his barracks caught fire. In *Feres v. United* States, 340 U.S. 135, 71 S. Ct. 153, 95 L. Ed. 152, the US Supreme Court ruled the military and government cannot be held liable for claims under the Federal Tort Claims Act for injuries incurred from activities incident to military service. This was presumably done to prevent soldiers and their families from suing the government for the negligent orders given or acts committed during war.

Agent Orange, burn pits, lead poisoning victim? Too bad, can't sue. How about that civilian spouse or military member suffering from the loss of a child due to the incompetence of the staff of a military hospital? Can't sue either. Military member suffering death or permanent disability because of the Covid shot they were required to get? Nope. Poisoned by the lead the military knew was poisoning you and your family?[18] Tough, suck it up, can't sue.

Presidential Executive Order 12196, as I pointed out earlier, *signed by President Ronald Reagan on February 26, 1980, it requires all of government to comply with OSHA regulations with one notable exception. It states in section 1-101: This order applies to all agencies of the Executive Branch except military personnel and uniquely military equipment, systems, and operations.*

Do you understand now? Military members, military contractors, and their families cannot hold the military and government accountable or seek compensation for damages suffered at the hands of our crooked, negligent, incompetent officers and Department of Defense officials. This requires veterans and their families to pay for medical care for the sickness, injuries, disease, and losses the government's actions have bestowed on them.

The government is free from accountability, allowing them to continue poisoning future generations of our nation's heroes, their spouses, and their children. And, as we have shown here, they do.

Family members, both sickened or not, lose pensions, disability payments, and benefits when the veteran dies from their injuries, sickness, and disease. Suddenly, after losing a spouse or parent, families endure the financial loss of the breadwinner's retirement, medical and disability pay, and benefits. They are then forced to prove their loved one's death was caused by a service-connected illness.

Dependency Indemnity Compensation (DIC) is a VA benefit for eligible survivors of military service members who died in the line of duty or eligible survivors of veterans whose death resulted from a service-related injury or disease. The basic monthly tax-free DIC benefit is $1,357.56 for 2021. That is a small percentage of the retirement and disability benefits and pay a veteran's spouse and family loses upon their death. It won't even cover the funeral, mortgage and bills.

To add insult to injury, to receive DIC, surviving spouses and their children must prove their loved one's death was caused by their military service. If they fail to service-connect the cause of death, they get nothing. No records, no access to records, did not know the cause of death related to things like those we have reviewed here, can't afford an attorney, no money.

Spouses who raised their children alone, at home, while veterans fought the wars Congress and our government thrust them into, that dead veteran's family is plunged into poverty and debt. They are forced to enter welfare lines hoping various nonprofits and donations will assist them. All because of the fraud and gross willful negligence of a government that forced this poisoning upon them. A government that offered no assistance to the veteran upon their leaving the service.

That's right, upon leaving the service, it is up to the veteran to recognize their symptoms, sickness, and disease; translate the records they have gathered; and prove their sickness was caused as a result of military service. When I say "translate," I mean the VA does not use the same codes and information as military doctors and facilities. In fact, the VA does not even use the same codes, information, research, and studies produced by other government agencies such as the EPA, NTP, CDC, or the Department of Health and Human Services either.

Despite the Department of Defense and VA having direct access to the largest database of affected personnel on the planet and multiple departments dealing with research, mental health, neurology, toxicology, cardiology, and so on, for reasons unknown, the military does not communicate with the VA. How ineffective is the current system?

Upon leaving the service, all military medical and occupational health clinic records must be gathered by the veteran, from every doctor and medical facility around the world where they were treated over their entire career. From enlistment to separation or retirement. If they do not have the records, treatment and benefits will be denied by the VA. Military hospitals, clinics, and medical facilities that have closed or no longer exist? No records! No treatment, no benefits.

After leaving the military, it is up to the veteran to provide print-ed copies and a disc containing those records to the VA. The veteran is then responsible for translating the information within those re-cords into a claim to receive treatment and disability benefits. Can't read records that are thirty years old or understand or interpret a doc-tor's scribble? Never knew you were being poisoned? Not mentally or physically capable of doing the necessary work? No treatment and no benefits. It is a tragedy.

The VA does not do any of this for the veteran nor do they even provide treatment until a service connection is made. *VA doctors pro-vide no assistance to veterans for the claim process.*

The same goes for the veteran's family members. Didn't know they were being poisoned? Can't prove their injuries were caused by military service? They are on their own and have to pay for their med-ical care. Even if it can be proved, you cannot file suit to hold anyone accountable to cover the medical costs.[86]

So other than the above, what are the consequences to the rest of our country? How about that police officer or shooting range em-ployee? The employee who sorted and hung contaminated uniforms at the local military surplus store or handled used guns in a gun store? How many employees become sick and cannot file for workers' com-pensation to cover their medical expenses because they have been de-nied the critical information necessary to attain it? What about their families? They have no idea what is causing their sickness, disease, or birth defects.

And what about the homeless who are wearing those contaminat-ed surplus uniforms and using surplus cots and blankets at the local homeless shelters? Remember the photos in Chapter 4? How many people suffer from this poisoning? What about the surrounding com-munity?

The community we lived in throughout my Navy career is be-ing poisoned as well. Remember the 1999 Navy engineering[18] or the CDC and NIOSH reports[4,19] documenting the spread of these poi-sons into the community, homes, and lives of those around us?

Have you ever seen a military service member in an airport, grocery store, rental car, or restaurant wearing a camouflaged uniform, coveralls, or flight suit? How about law enforcement wearing their guns, the hunter, and the gun store or shooting range employee from the place of business down the street? How do you know if they have come from a shooting range or contaminated workplace to poison your community? They are spreading the toxic compounds on their skin, clothing, and footwear. How about those same people going home?

Knowing what you know today, would you let your loved one return home in contaminated clothing? Drive the family vehicle home from work? Track it in the house into the carpeting? Sit on the furniture to enjoy that cold frosty after a hard day of work or lie on the bed without showering (decontaminating) and changing clothes? How about the hugs and kisses passed around to the children and spouse? See the pictures in Chapter 4? It is not just veterans and law enforcement who are poisoned. Remember that sixteen-year-old who had her appendix mistakenly removed?[44]

How about the construction worker or painter who spent the day sanding lead-contaminated paint off that old house or tearing down that old gun range? Do you do your own home improvements? What about the law enforcement officer coming from the shooting range? What about the women and children in the photos in Chapter 4 and viewed online at competitions using three guns?[90] All these people and more are poisoning the communities we live in. How do I know? I am guilty of all the above, since my first visit to a gun range at age six and throughout my entire Navy career.

Do you think you are safe? How old is the house you live in, and where is it located? In San Diego, California, there is a gun range close to our old house that has been closed for many years. It is situated right in the middle of a busy area of town next to restaurants, a hospital, and apartment complexes. That range held military contracts to train Navy sailors.

Boarded up and encircled with an eight-foot-tall chain-link fence covered in green tarps, this prime real estate will likely sit there until the owner dies and the city forgets who owned it, or it will be torn down or repurposed "in the dead of night" so as not to be noticed and replaced with something else. The problem is you can't just tear it down, the lead dust within will permeate the entire neighborhood and even the roadway as the debris is carried away.

If it suddenly "burns down," the lead dust will be spread by the flames and debris just like the burn pits of Afghanistan and Iraq or New York City after 9/11. The problem facing the owners and the city is that every bit of that building is now hazardous waste to be demolished per OSHA regulations, classified and containerized per RCRA regulations, transported per RCRA and DOT regulations, and disposed of per RCRA and EPCRA regulations. Do you think the owner, city, and state planned and budgeted for that when it was allowed to open? No. Who do you think gets stuck paying the bill? If you answered, "The taxpayer," you'd be right.

It's not just gun ranges. How about the neighborhood you live in? There are yellow and brown warning signs all over our old neighborhood in San Diego. One sign sits on a playground, in a park, next to an elementary school.

These signs, posted all around the community, notify residents that they live on a former military artillery and gun firing range— Camp Elliott. These signs say that if you see bullets and explosive shells on the ground, don't pick them up; call the authorities. In addition, established swimming pool companies in the area refuse to install pools in this community for fear of digging up explosives! So how much lead and other hazardous and toxic compounds are buried in the soil there?

Do you live around an outdoor range? That park, elementary school, and the surrounding homes lie to the south of the Marine Corps Miramar Air Station gun ranges. Ever see the old Tom Cruise movie about the Navy's top gun school? That's the place. You can hear the gunfire from those ranges daily. Because it is a dry, dusty desert environment, the wind blows contaminated dust from decades of use into our old neighborhood. To the north of this range is the Miramar Reservoir, which provides drinking water to the city of San Diego. Where do you get your drinking water from?

Do you know what a Superfund Site is? Of course not. They have been forgotten by all except those who live near or on one.

"The EPA's Superfund program is responsible for cleaning up some of the nation's most contaminated land and responding to environmental emergencies, oil spills, and natural disasters."[81]

My sister told me of one where she lives on the south side of Houston, Texas—the Brio Superfund site.[82] How does she know about it? It is in the news occasionally when flooding occurs, releasing toxic compounds into the surrounding city.

> *The Brio Superfund site is a former industrial location in Harris County, Texas . . . It is a federal Superfund site, although it was deleted from the National Priorities List in December 2006. A neighboring residential subdivision called South Bend, now abandoned, was located along and north of the northern boundary of Brio North. The former South Bend neighborhood consisted of about 670 homes, an elementary school, and a Little League baseball field . . .*
>
> *The 58-acre Brio Refinery site was home to several chemical companies between 1957 and 1982, when the owner, Brio Refinery Inc., declared bankruptcy and ceased operations. During that period, the site had been used for copper recovery and petroleum re-refining, typically the processing of tar, sludge, and other residue from oil tanks and other sources, as also occurred at the adjacent Dixie Oil Processors site. Throughout the years, at both sites, unprocessed petroleum and waste materials were stored in 12 large earthen pits, ranging from 14 to 32 feet deep and extending into porous soil and, thus, groundwater. Leaks from these pits also spilled into a local drainage ditch, Mud Gulley, and subsequently, via the adjoining Clear Creek,*

*into Galveston Bay. By the late 1980s, the EPA had detected **copper,*** ***vinyl chloride, 1,1,2-trichloroethane, fluorene, styrene, ethyl-*** ***benzene, toluene, benzene, and other toxic chemicals,*** *including numerous chlorinated volatile organic compounds (VOCs), in the air and groundwater.*

The EPA placed the Brio site on the National Priorities List in 1984. Beginning in 1989, the EPA began remediation by demolishing buildings, digging out contaminated soils for processing or disposal, containing groundwater by use of a physical barrier, and capping the site. The site was removed from the National Priorities List in 2006...

Women in the area had reported an above average rate of miscarriages and there was an increase in upper respiratory ailments, central nervous system disorders, and birth defects (particularly reproductive and heart problems). Some of the residents moved out, fearing for their health and for that of their children. Former residents have since reported various illnesses which include cancer, vasculitis, and autoimmune disease.

Recognize the chemical compounds "copper, vinyl chloride, 1,1,2-trichloroethane, fluorene, styrene, ethylbenzene, toluene, benzene, and other toxic chemicals, including numerous chlorinated volatile organic compounds (VOCs)"? They are also listed in Tables 2.1 and 5.1. They are all found in firearms and ordnance poisoning, military burn pits, and the air, water, and on the ground of the Gulf War.

How about the symptoms? Recognize "miscarriages, upper respiratory ailments, central nervous system disorders, birth defects (particularly reproductive and heart problems), various illnesses which include cancer, vasculitis, and autoimmune disease"?

They are the lead, Agent Orange, Gulf War, and burn pit poisoning symptoms that we reviewed earlier. Look back at Table 6.1 in Chapter 6. They are there as well. Do you live near a Superfund Site? How do you know? Who picked up the tab for all this after the "owner, Brio

Refinery Inc., declared bankruptcy and ceased operations"? If you answered, "The taxpayer," you'd be correct.

Take a look at the "Fish Consumption Bans and Advisories" of my home state.[83] Dioxins, mercury, and PCBs are responsible for poisoning fish throughout the state and Gulf of Mexico. The same chemical compounds found in firearms poisoning, Vietnam, and the Gulf Wars of the past twenty years. It's not just in my home state—every state has similar bans and advisories.

How about the cities of Detroit and Flint, Michigan? Are you familiar with the stories in the news reporting on the lead in the drinking water there? Do you have lead pipes in your city or home? We lived in military housing that did.

What do slumlords and the US military have in common? They both abuse the law, allowing tenants to live in lead-contaminated housing. Ever hear of a process called *encapsulation*?

Encapsulation is the process where lead dust that is detected on surfaces is painted over to "encapsulate" it into the paint. Testing that surface after encapsulation will result in little to no lead detection. Why do you think that the federal government's Department of Housing and Urban Development (HUD) and city and state governments have multiple lead clearance standards (laws)?

A lead clearance standard is the maximum allowable amount of lead dust detectable on a surface requiring immediate removal. Revised in 2017, the HUD standards[84] were lowered to:

Interior floors: < 10 μg/ft2
Porch floors: < 40 μg/ft2
Windowsills: < 100 μg/ft2
Window troughs: < 100 μg/ft2

What does this mean? < 10 μg/ft2 means less than 10 micrograms of lead dust per square foot. Why the different levels?

HUD, the government, recognizes encapsulated lead dust in painted surfaces wears and chips off painted porch floors, old painted windows, and the window troughs they slide up and down in. Those paint chips and that dust settle onto the floors under the window to be tracked in and around the house from the painted porch. So instead of requiring homes to have the lead contamination removed, slumlords and the military simply paint over it again so that the lead cannot be detected. It's all legal, but who suffers? Does it really matter what level we allow on those floors and windowsills? Remember, the CDC says, "There is no known lower threshold limit for lead exposure and harmful health effects."[88]

How about that toddler who eats the paint chips, or the unsuspecting homeowner renovating that old house, sanding walls full of encapsulated lead? The slumlord just keeps on renting, and the military continues to require its personnel to keep on living in old, contaminated housing to be *ambushed at Home.*[32]

Before I proceed any further, I should give credit where credit is due. In 2018, I came across an October 17, 2014, *Seattle Times* article, "Loaded with Lead."[85] As part of this multipart series, authors and reporters Christine Willmsen, Lewis Kamb, and Justin Mayo really opened my eyes to the world of lead poisoning throughout our communities and the country. Still a good read, their research identified the true extent of the problem giving me the perspective I needed to pursue my research.

Their series revealed and provided documented proof of lead poisoning spreading throughout the community—schools and schoolchildren, range workers, police officers, their families, homes, vehicles, and so on. "Loaded with Lead" covered areas of the community poisoned with lead that I had never even considered.

Reading it, I realized I was guilty of contaminating the community I live in too. Just look at the pictures in Chapter 4. Soldiers and sailors like me, over our entire careers, wore contaminated uniforms and clothing home and out to breakfast, lunch, and dinner at restaurants in the communities that surrounded the bases where we served. We also contaminated the hotels we stayed in and the personal, rental, and government vehicles we drove. We did it at home just like we did overseas in war.

As a civilian, I used to shoot at a local Indian reservation gun range and then eat lunch across the street at the casino buffet. They had an eight-hundred-yard rifle range and several pistol and steel target ranges.

I would back my truck up to the rifle firing line and shoot long-range, pistol, and steels all morning. They had a Porta Potty for a bathroom and little else. When I finished, I would wash my hands with soap and water using a gallon jug I'd brought along. Then I would drive across the street and enjoy a nice lunch at their buffet before going home. I took my wife and kids there too.

I now realize that I was contaminating everything I touched at that casino. I was poisoning patrons who had never even touched a gun. Furthermore, depending on which way the wind was blowing, my pickup truck would get inundated with toxic lead and compounds blown onto and inside it from the shooters at the range. That includes the occasional dust devil that stirred up the toxic compounds to poison us all. I was poisoning innocent bystanders within the community, my family, and my friends, even after I left the range.

How can that Indian casino, the restaurants, coffee shops, hotels, rental car companies, and the surrounding communities in general stop the poisoning of their facilities and equipment? Simple: ban military in camouflaged uniforms, coveralls, and flight suits from the premises and use of their facilities and vehicles. That goes for anyone who works in and uses firing ranges. Ban them too. It is the only way to stop the spread of these hazardous and toxic compounds into the community.

The home is next to be poisoned. In 2014, I could not get the level of lead in my blood to go down. Despite twenty-nine years in the Navy as a top weapons expert and instructor training America's elite, I had not yet seen the 1999 Department of the Navy report,[18] a report that documented how I was spreading that poisoning into the community, my home, and vehicles. I panicked. I forced myself to think it through. I had stopped working at a firing range, so that wasn't it. I hit the internet and started reading articles. Secondhand exposure popped up. Everything that I had touched after leaving the range was obviously contaminated.

I got rid of my entire wardrobe. *Everything.* Shoes, boots, socks, underwear, old Navy uniforms, everything—all my clothing, jackets, motorcycle gear, hats, helmets, even the clothes hangers in the closet. We got rid of my wife's and autistic son's as well. I was forced to replace the carpeting, furniture, and anything else I came into contact with after arriving home before dropping my clothes into the laundry on the way to the shower.

I bought lead decontamination products and decontaminated my garage and closet. I replaced the chest of drawers, bed, and nightstands in the bedroom. I painted the walls in my house. After getting rid of my vehicles and cleansing my life of every possible contamination point, I waited for the next month's test. My efforts were rewarded with a blood lead level that continues to decline today.

That was over six years ago. Now, it is a waiting game for it to completely leach out of my bones over the next thirty-four years or more. I will be ninety-two, if it doesn't kill me first. That includes the dioxins in my fatty tissues and anything else that poisoned my body during my career.

What are the consequences to the community, the taxpayer, and those who have never even picked up a gun? Sickness, disease, death, and the crushing weight of trillions of dollars spent with no progress in sight to mitigate or stop it. But that's not all. As you will see, it gets much worse.

CHAPTER 11

Crimes, Murder, and Criminal Negligence

Earlier in the book, I identified the 1999 US Marine Corps Department of the Navy engineering study "Reducing Lead Contamination and Exposure on Military Firing Ranges through the Practical Application of Ballistic Containment Systems."[18] I disclosed that the Department of the Navy and Department of Defense *recognized*, over twenty years ago, that they were poisoning us and our families. They *recognized* and identified actions that they failed to take to stop it.

I related the actions taken by senior Naval Special Warfare Command and Navy personnel to conceal that they were poisoning us. These were not just my supervisors—there were at least four admirals, the secretaries of the Navy and defense, and even President Donald Trump. Not just me—all Navy SWCCs, SEALs, others, and our families too. So what are the consequences for us and the public?

Corporal Ian David Long killed twelve people on November 7, 2018, in Thousand Oaks, California, before committing suicide. Corporal Long was reported to have enlisted in the Marine Corps in 2008 at age eighteen. Prior to enlisting, information surfaced that he was just another typical high school kid.

When Long decided to join the Marine Corps, he reported for basic training to begin his training firing rifles and then machine guns at one of two Marine Corps bases. On the East Coast, marine recruits report for basic training to Parris Island in South Carolina.

Parris Island has its own rifle and gun ranges. Parris Island and its ranges were established in 1915. On the West Coast, in California, recruits use the ranges at Camp Pendleton. Camp Pendleton was established in 1942.

In 2008, at the age of eighteen and while his young brain was still growing and developing, Recruit Long was startled awake by a metal trash can bouncing across the floor that had been thrown by a drill instructor to begin his first day of basic training. Immediately driven into a state of adrenaline-induced fight or flight, his body would begin its decline serving in this state for the majority of his short Marine Corps career.

Later, in basic training, he would initially be exposed to the lead and sixty-one other toxic compounds that the Marine Corps, Department of Defense, and government had known for over eight years would poison him,[2,6,18] resulting in the behavioral issues that ended ten years later with thirteen dead at the Borderline Bar and Grill in Thousand Oaks, California.

The US Marine Corps and Department of Defense were aware of his poisoning and the symptoms he would begin to experience, which they had recognized as being caused by chronic long-term stress and poisoning.[Table 6.1] They knew that as he kneeled and lay on the ground at the firing line while learning to fire a weapon, up to 105 years of accumulated lead and sixty-one other toxic compounds would be ground into his uniform, boots, hands, and skin. Toxic dust so small, it was being absorbed directly through his skin and into his bloodstream to immediately begin his poisoning. Poisoning they knew would continue a minimum of forty years or more after he left the Marine Corps.

They knew that as he fired his weapon, he was producing over sixty-two different toxic compounds as gun smoke, gases, and particulate matter that wafted and washed over his person and uniform to be absorbed directly through his skin, lungs, eyes, and mucous membranes.

They knew that the sweat rolling down from his hair carried it into his mouth and eyes. They knew that even when he was done firing, he was still further contaminating his hands and poisoning himself by picking up empty bullet casings, putting them into his hat, and carrying and cleaning his guns and equipment.

They knew that the place where he would clean his guns was contaminated with decades of lead and toxic compounds deposited by previous Marines. They knew that as he cleaned his gun and equipment, the solvents he used dried out his skin, allowing the lead to be more easily absorbed and poisoning him further.

They knew that lead would be distributed throughout his body, directly into his bones, where it would accumulate to poison him over the next forty years or more. The dioxins would be deposited in his fatty tissues and brain.

They knew the uniform and boots he wore into the chow hall to eat were spreading the contamination from the firing point at the range. They had known for two years, since 2005,[4] that soap and water did not remove the lead from his hands and face and that it contaminated the food he ate, further poisoning him. The government and Department of Defense had developed special cleansers that could remove almost 100 percent of the lead and other toxic compounds from his skin but failed to provide and require its use.

When he marched to his barracks, they knew it, too, was horribly contaminated by him and those who came before. They knew that their uniforms and boots contaminated their homes and barracks. They knew that when Corporal Long showered, it did no good because soap and water did not remove the lead from his hair and body. They knew that lead from his hair and body contaminated the clothes he wore and the bed and bedding he slept on. They knew the laundry from all his fellow Marines shared and spread that contamination farther.

When Corporal Long became a machine gunner, they knew the ranges he lay down to train on were horribly contaminated with tens of millions of rounds worth of toxic dust and particulate matter deposited all around him for up to ninety-three years or more. Toxic dust down to less than 2.5 microns in size, consisting of up to 146 hazardous and toxic compounds. Toxic dust smaller than the diameter of a human hair, his red blood cells, or even bacteria would waft up into the air when disturbed to continue poisoning every young Marine long after he was gone.

When he deployed to Afghanistan in 2010, they knew that he lived with his guns for seven months, day in and day out, firing and cleaning them. They knew he was poisoning himself twenty-four hours out of every day that he was deployed. Carrying his gun, he poisoned himself even while eating and sleeping with the toxic compounds and carcinogens that were on his person, uniforms, gear, and boots. These same toxic compounds spread through the air from the burning feces, urine, medical waste, and debris of war from the camp's military burn pits.

Whether deployed or at home, the Department of Defense and government knew that Corporal Long would wear his uniforms home from work, contaminating his personal vehicle, home, wife, their carpeting, and the family laundry, just like the Marine Corps and Navy had identified back in 1999.[18]

They knew that the poisoning would cause the sickness, disease, and symptoms he displayed. They knew exactly what those symptoms were. The neurobehavioral effects of this poisoning included adrenal burnout, anxiety, apprehension, cognitive dysfunction, confusion, decrease in sex drive, depression, distraction, forgetfulness, hyperactivity, hypertension, insomnia, irritability, impaired judgment, loss of concentration, memory loss, mood disorders, panic attacks, paranoia, and racing mind and restlessness. The symptoms and neurobehavioral effects of chronic, long-term stress caused the same.

They knew his wife could suffer from these symptoms, as she was being poisoned too. They knew the military housing they lived in was poisoned as well. They knew that the lead deposited in their bodies would continue to poison them for at least the next forty years. They knew—as with many military families—miscarriage, stillborn babies, birth defects in children, and even domestic violence and divorce would result from this poisoning, and yet they did nothing to stop it. Reports revealed a failed marriage in 2011.

After Corporal Long left the Marine Corps in 2013 and through the night of November 7, 2018, many reports of behaviors identified as firearms and burn pit poisoning and chronic long-term stress symptoms have surfaced. These behaviors and symptoms were directly attributable to his service as a United States Marine. Corporal Long was poisoned and suffered the effects.

These neurophysiological effects did not allow his young eighteen-year-old brain to develop normally before his twenty-first birthday. The Marine Corps had prevented young Corporal Long from drinking alcohol and smoking cigarettes and yet, for reasons unknown, poisoned his young brain and body anyway. Poisoning that would result in severe neurobehavioral effects and symptoms ignored by the DoD and VA to be conveniently chalked up to PTSD and mental illness later by the president after his death.

President Donald Trump, the commander in chief of all US forces, blamed young Corporal Long for his problems on a mental deficiency. He would say, "He's a very sick puppy," and "A very, very mentally ill person." He stated Long was "never the same" when he came back from war: "A lot of people said he had the PTSD . . . People come back . . . they come back, they're never the same."

The man who sat as the head of every department in government—who knew Corporal Ian David Long was being poisoned daily while in the Marine Corps; knew that his condition would continue to worsen from poisoning that would last for forty years or more after he left the service; and knew the symptoms, sickness, and disease he would suffer, that they were directly responsible for it and had done nothing to stop it—was pawning it off as that mysterious catchall, "the PTSD."

The news reported on Corporal Long's run-ins with police who were called to his home because he was acting erratically. There were reports of him acting irate and irrationally; neighbors calling the police for allegedly getting into a fight with his mother; volatile arguments with his mother at all hours of the night; holes in the walls of his home, likely from being kicked or punched in. Reports of a mother frustrated that her son wasn't seeking help for his condition.

Reports that Long was loud and appeared to be threatening violence, that he was a "weird" loner who could be aggressively antisocial. Often locking himself in his room, he was purposefully stand-offish. Some attempted to paint him as a disturbed high school kid, seeking in vain for some explanation for his actions.

Reports in the media that ignored that he had passed every screening and test the military performs on all recruits before being allowed to enter into the service. He was an elite, comprising less than 0.5 percent of the entire population of the United States of America.

Critics described Corporal Long's behavior and conveniently stated that he suffered from mental illness and PTSD. They blamed it on the unspeakable things he must have seen or participated in during war; things that obviously mentally scarred him, preventing him from returning and reintegrating into a "normal society" after leaving military service. They used to call those like him "Baby Killers" during the Vietnam War.

They said he suffered from a mental illness, a disorder, instead of the neurobehavioral effects of years of chronic long-term stress, living in a constant state of fight or flight while suffering from firearms and military burn-pit poisoning.

The military and government Corporal Long so faithfully served had known and recognized that they were poisoning him for his entire career. As early as 1975, they knew of the chronic stress he would be placed under during his service.[17]

In 1999, they knew the source, route, and extent contamination would spread, poisoning him and his loved ones, and they failed to institute the actions they identified would stop it.[18]

In 2000, they knew exactly which toxic compounds would poison him.[2,6]

In 2005, they knew that soap and water would not remove it from his skin and failed to require him to use the cleanser they had developed to remove it.[4,19]

In 2005 and 2006, they knew that regardless of what he did to remove the poisons from his skin, it would be absorbed into his bloodstream anyway.[19]

In 2012, reports were issued by our nation's top subject matter experts ignoring the other 145 toxic compounds they knew poisoned all military members using ordnance and guns focusing only on lead.[24-28] They, and Congress, knew the standards in use by the Department of Defense, OSHA, and the VA to protect its military and civilian employees from lead poisoning were not sufficient.[18,24-28] The same VA that continues to ignore the lead and other toxic compounds that have poisoned our veterans in every war. The Marines who came before him and who will follow afterward.

They knew in great detail the sickness and disease that would result from his poisoning. The same symptoms and sickness documented in the news reports across the nation about Ian David Long.

They had violated his human rights, granted under the Constitution to every American, and ignored the rule of law requiring them to:

> "Furnish to each of his employees employment and a place of employment which are free from recognized hazards that are causing or are likely to cause death or serious physical harm to his employees."[8]

A president had signed an executive order exempting the military from the above law, allowing Long's poisoning.[16]

They hide from the consequences of their actions by abusing a presidential executive order and 1950 US Supreme Court decision.[16,86]

They engage in deceit and cover-up to conceal his poisoning.

They knew and yet did nothing to stop it, allowing it to continue today, poisoning new generations of young Marines, service members, employees, and their families.

While his mother, the victims of his violence, and the country grieved and mourned, searching in vain for an explanation, the Marine Corps, Navy, Department of Defense, and government continue to stand by quietly, hoping no one will notice their responsibility and the role they played in the deaths of twelve innocent people and one poisoned Marine, on the night of November 7, 2018, in Thousand Oaks, California.

Not just Ian Long. How about Adam Lanza, the Sandy Hook Elementary School shooter? His mother bought him the guns he used, and he toyed with his contaminated weapons and gear all day in his room while playing video games.

Stephen Paddock, the Las Vegas mass murderer? He was a gun fanatic who lived with guns throughout both his homes. He reportedly bought thirty-three guns in the year prior to his attack. Twenty-four were found in the hotel room he fired from, eighteen in one home, and seven in another. Think these men properly cleaned, maintained, and decontaminated their weapons and homes? See a pattern of contamination and poisoning here?

So what came first: the chicken or the egg? Mass murder? Destructive behaviors? Chronic long-term stress? Poisoning? How many other veterans can you find who are responsible for other mass shootings and violent behaviors?

Corporal Long, like so many other veterans, was a typical American, who experienced a gradual onset of symptoms that were ignored by the Marine Corps, military, and Veterans Affairs. I am sure his mother didn't know about it either. Symptoms caused by poisons leaching out of his body. The continuous, systematic deterioration of his endocrine (hormone) and nervous system within his brain that brought about the changes in his behavior and eventual suicide.

Symptoms the military knew he would experience identified in Table 6.1 above that include anxiety, apprehension, attention deficit, brain fog, premature cognitive aging, cognitive dysfunction, confusion, developmental delay, distraction, fatigue, forgetfulness, headache, hyperactivity, hyperesthesia hypertension (increase in the sensitivity of any of your senses, such as sight, sound, touch, and smell), insomnia, impaired judgment, impaired short-term memory, irritability, learning difficulties, loss of coordination, lower IQ memory, mood disorders, narcosis, nervous irritability, panic attacks, paranoia, PTSD, racing mind, restlessness, and schizophrenia. How many symptoms can you spot that account for the behaviors reported in the press a few pages above?

As of today, there is still no official explanation as to why Ian David Long committed this atrocity other than he was "mentally unstable" and "likely suffered from PTSD." As President Trump said, "He's a very sick puppy . . . A very, very mentally ill person."

Listed below are a few more recent atrocities committed by those under the influence of the poisoning, chronic long-term stress, extreme training and conditioning, and other comorbidities I have reviewed here. These are men I worked with during my naval career:

- 2016: Navy SEAL Theo Andrew Krah beat and stabbed a man to death in Santa Monica, California.
- 2017: Navy SEAL Team (Redacted[101]   ) members tied up, suffocated, and killed Staff Sergeant Logan J. Melgar in Bamako, Mali.
- 2017: Navy SEAL Stephen Varanko kidnapped and raped a fellow sailor in Fort Knox, Kentucky.
- 2018: Navy SEAL Brit Slabinski was in the news for mutilating dead bodies and reportedly ordering the killing of civilian males prior to conducting raids in battle during his career.
- 2019: Four naval special warfare sailors were arrested in Okinawa, Japan, for destroying a police car and being drunk and disorderly.
- 2019: An entire Navy SEAL platoon was sent home from Iraq for sexual misconduct and drinking while deployed.

- 2019: Navy SEAL Eddie Gallagher was wrongly accused of stabbing a man to death. As it turned out, Naval Special Warfare Command and the Navy were caught falsifying and concealing testimony and evidence. One of the SEALs testifying against Gallagher admitted to the killing after being granted immunity. Did they make bad decisions in the field that were revealed during this case? Yes.

In June 2020, former Navy SEAL Commander Jocko Willink was recorded on the cable news show *Fox & Friends* saying[92]:

> "So, in the SEAL teams, we would spend eighteen months . . . preparing for a six-month deployment overseas . . . When I ran SEAL training and the SEAL training I ran was not carrying logs around and carrying boats on your head—but I ran the tactical training for the SEAL teams. And what we would do is we would put these guys in highly stressful situations over and over and over again . . . and the reason for that was we wanted to teach them how to control their emotions . . ."

Even when safe at home, away from war, the military continues to drive veterans into a constant state of fight or flight in training with insufficient time to rest and reset. Missing from Willink's statement is the constant exposure to the poisons identified here while his SEALs conducted this high stress training at horribly contaminated ranges like the one I worked in. How do I know? You will find out in the next book, *Conspiracy and Cover-up*.

How about using the same uniforms and gear year-round? Eating, sleeping, and living in them both during deployment in war and the eighteen months spent training for the next. How about the tens of millions of rounds that have contaminated every army, Marine, and Navy SWCC and SEAL–training venue here in the states?

Not just one deployment. How about the eighteen consecutive years I spent deploying every year during the seven tours and hundreds of deployments, high risk and special operations that veterans like me have endured? I know vets who have been deployed more times than me and in much worse conditions. Whether deployed or at home, there was constant exposure to chronic stress and poisoning, year in and year out.

The above examples of Willink's Navy SEALs' activities are but a few. There are many more; most have been concealed and are unknown to the public. Things I can't reveal in this book without the Navy stopping its publication. Things I will reveal in the next.

Ian David Long, every one of those Navy SEALs, all the above were acting under the influence of years of chronic poisoning, chronic long-term stress, extreme training and conditioning, and living in a constant state of fight or flight without sufficient rest and reset. Xenostressors and xenobiotics. All exhibited the neurobehavioral effects documented here and in the numerous government reports that I have provided.

The recent 2020 news article "Ethics Slips Involving Navy SEALs, Army Green Berets Stem from Combat Culture, Review Finds"[93] reveals that both Naval Special Warfare Command and Special Operations Command attempted to shift the blame away from the science the Department of Defense and government has recognized for fifty years or more yet continues to cover up.

Science that clearly identifies the direct cause of the behavioral issues, poor decision-making, violent actions, and the majority of illness and disease suffered by our veterans, their family members, and others from poisoning and other stressors.

Poisoning by the United States Navy and Naval Special Warfare Command that I have documented here, consisting of 146 listed hazardous and toxic compounds the DoD and government have recognized since 2000 and failed to stop or mitigate.

Lead and dioxin poisoning known since the Vietnam War and the 1970s.

Poisoning that is allowed to continue through to this day.

Poisoning that affects us all in one way or another.
Poisoning we can stop.

Cleatus Doyle (left) and I enjoying a cold frostie
with black boats beached behind us in South America, 1995.
Photo 1.1

Waiting for dark before beginning operations.
Northern Pacific, 1997.
Photo 1.2

Sixty-eight-foot Sea Spectre. Central America, 1995.
Photo 1.3

Five thousand horsepower roaring through the night on mission. Eighty-two-foot Mk V Special Operations Craft. Western Pacific, 1999.

Photo 1.4

Typical bullets and shells used by civilians and the military today.

Photo 2.2

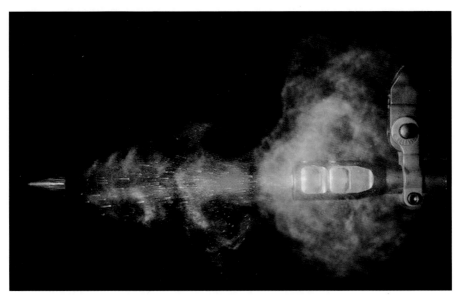

AR15 bullet debris, combustion particles, lead,
and fifty other toxic and hazardous compounds.
Photo 2.3

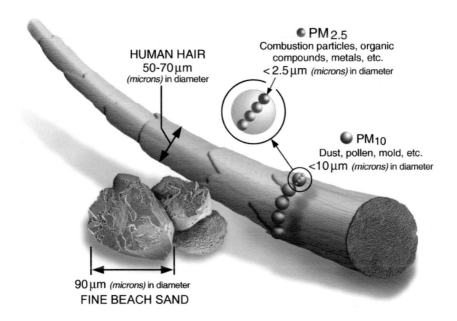

HUMAN HAIR
50-70 μm
(microns) in diameter

● PM$_{2.5}$
Combustion particles, organic
compounds, metals, etc.
< 2.5 μm *(microns)* in diameter

● PM$_{10}$
Dust, pollen, mold, etc.
<10 μm *(microns)* in diameter

90 μm *(microns)* in diameter
FINE BEACH SAND

Comparison of lead and other particles smaller than 2.5 microns.
Photo 2.4

My civilian AR15 (M4 M16 circa 1991).
Photo 4.1

Yellow marks where gas and poisons exit the weapon into the face at 68,000 PSI.
Note how the poison dust grinds into the uniform and skin of the shooter.
Photo 4.2

Shiny tube at the top illustrates how gas pressure is removed from the gun barrel
and directed back into the face of the shooter.
Photo 4.3

M1A (civilian version of the M1 Garand/M14) dating back to 1933.
Photo 4.4

Sig Virtus, a modern AR replacement.
Gases exit at the front of the barrel instead of in the face of the shooter.
Photo 4.5

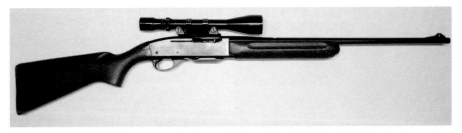

Typical hunting rifle in use today circa 1957.
Photo 4.6

Poison dust spreads to the hands and head of the shooter.
Photo 4.7, Photo 4.8

Poisons spreading further onto and into the shooter as well as the environment.
Photo 4.9, Photo 4.10

Poisons spreading to the vehicle, home, and family.
Photo 4.11, Photo 4.12, Photo 4.13, Photo 4.14, Photo 4.15, Photo 4.16

Poisons spreading into stores and restaurants and throughout the community.
Photo 4.17, Photo 4.18

CHAPTER 12
Where Do We Go from Here?

I am forced to close this book despite having so much more to say. I could easily double its size. The first of a number of books that I intend to write, as a new author revealing such important discoveries, I knew I had to get this out as quickly as possible.

Continuing my research, every time I thought the book was done, new information I would uncover required it to grow. What began as simply whistleblowing the actions of my supervisors and Naval Special Warfare Command in poisoning us grew into revealing the dark truth and science behind a massive government conspiracy. Not just gross willful negligence, as you will see in the next book, a combined effort by multiple government agencies to ignore and cover it up.

My research has revealed numerous official government reports and documents chronicling the military, Department of Defense, VA, and Department of Labor (OSHA) being at odds with the EPA, FDA, Department of Health and Human Services, Housing and Urban Development, and other government subject matter experts. That includes the National Academy of Sciences, Engineering, and Medicine and multiple highly regarded universities and medical institutions across the country and around the world. The battle cry of "Follow the Science" we hear today in fighting COVID-19 is entirely ignored by our government and its leaders when it comes to our veterans' and their families' poisoning.

Official reports and documents produced to downplay and ignore the significance of and allow the continued poisoning of our military, law enforcement, and first responder veterans. Information cherry-picked to support false, predetermined conclusions and storylines to justify gross willful—if not criminal—negligence and cover-up. Actions contrary to the tenets we, as Americans, require of our government, its employees, and our elected leaders to protect us from "recognized hazards that are causing or are likely to cause death or serious physical harm."

The Commander in Chief and Chief Executive Officer of the United States, Justice Department, Department of Defense, Department of Labor (OSHA), and Veterans Affairs have failed us, establishing a willingness to ignore the will of the people and the laws and regulations that exist to protect us.

Only a few brave souls, medical and research subject matter experts, within the Department of Health and Human Services, Food and Drug Administration, Environmental Protection Agency, and Housing and Urban Development have addressed their findings within their own organizations and published the content necessary for us to demand change.

So what have I done? From 2014 to 2020, I have been whistleblowing my findings to every person in the chain of command, from Naval Special Warfare Command's Admiral Brian Losey through to President Donald Trump. The documentation I provided to them chronicles my discovery and actions to address my findings since 2005 as an Active-Duty Navy Chief. It has provided them the necessary evidence to stop our poisoning and hold accountable those who have broken the law, poisoned us, and are killing us. What have they done in response? Nothing. It's business as usual.

Naval Special Warfare Command, the Department of the Navy, the Department of Defense, the Department of Labor, and Veterans Affairs have established a willingness to ignore evidence of illegal activity and current research. Instead, they work to conceal[93] and ignore their responsibility while cutting benefits and health care for veterans and our families.[94,95] As I have discovered, they do so willingly while recognizing the hazards that are causing or are likely to cause death or serious physical harm to our veterans, their families, and other affected employees across the nation.

Exhibiting not just gross willful negligence, they have willfully failed to comply with federal and military laws and regulations. Senior government officials have conspired and engaged in lies and deceit to conceal the sickness, disease, and death caused by our poisoning to maintain their pay and position.

For fact checkers, evidence to corroborate the discoveries I have made and the allegations I have leveled here are available via a Freedom of Information Act request to Commander Naval Special Warfare Command, the Secretary of the Navy, Departments of Defense and Labor, as well as the White House and President Donald Trump. You will find a list of these in the next volume, *Conspiracy and Cover-up*, online and in bookstores soon.

I am also in the process of having my findings validated by accredited subject matter experts and working with them to submit these findings to the Department of Health and Human Services' National Toxicology Program for research and validation.

Submitting the information I have revealed here to multiple nonprofits to include Burn Pits 360, Wounded Warriors, Gary Senise Foundation, etc., I hope to generate the coordinated effort needed to get this information recognized and changes made to assist our veterans into the future and alleviate the suicide so many resort to.

I will continue doing everything in my power to ensure every person affected has the tools necessary to deal with this poisoning, remove it from their lives, and gain the medical care and benefits owed to us by a government that has forgotten its role in furnishing "his employees employment and a place of employment which are free from recognized hazards that are causing or are likely to cause death or serious physical harm to his employees."[8] All employees, our families, our communities, and the environment as well. You can follow my efforts at www.johnplyons.com and on social media.

What Can You Do?

First, if you are serving in the military, especially if you are female, in any kind of role involving weapons, weapons maintenance, or range facilities,

GET OUT!

If you want to have children within the next 40 years, evidence presented here infers that you and your children will have your lives irrevocably changed. All veterans serving in these roles as well.

If you are contemplating joining the military,

**DO NOT ENLIST IN THE MILITARY!
THE MINUTE YOU SIGN THAT CONTRACT,
YOU RELINQUISH YOUR AND YOUR FUTURE
FAMILY'S RIGHTS, ALLOWING OUR GOVERNMENT
TO POISON YOU BOTH
WHENEVER THEY WISH.
YOU CAN DO NOTHING ABOUT IT!**

Had I known then what I know now, I never would have gone into the Navy! I would not have subjected my wife to this poisoning or allowed my children or niece to join. Especially my daughter and niece!

If your spouse or family member works in any job in the military involving weapons, weapons maintenance, or range facilities,

**PUT YOUR FOOT DOWN!
EDUCATE THEM AND WORK TO DISTANCE
YOURSELF AND YOUR CHILDREN FROM THE
POISONING REVEALED HERE.**

In short,

OUR LEADERS IN THE MILITARY AND GOVERNMENT HAVE BECOME BUREAUCRATS INCAPABLE OF FOLLOWING ORDERS, REGULATIONS, AND THE LAW. THEY ARE UNWORTHY OF THE SACRIFICE THEY DEMAND OF OUR VETERANS.

Until the Department of Defense and Labor, VA, and government enforce and abide by existing laws and regulations and take action to recognize this poisoning and the other comorbidities identified here, granting full medical care and benefits to our veterans and their families,

OUR COUNTRY DOES NOT DESERVE OUR SACRIFICE!

Until our citizens demand Congress nullify the Supreme Court's Feres Decision and Reagan's Presidential Executive Order and removes the restrictions placed upon the EPA to allow those responsible to be held accountable,

WE SHOULD NOT SERVE!

As you will learn in the next volume, it gets much worse.

Next, get educated, and let's end this together. Had the government taken the actions it has recognized necessary to stop, slow, or mitigate this poisoning, we would not be where we are today. Spread the word educating those around you! Stop the spread of these poisons into our homes, lives, and surrounding communities! Assist them in learning how to remove it from their lives!

Last, get involved with your local politicians. Force them to listen and take action. Vote! What this book and the next reveal is a government and military incapable of policing itself without direct voter involvement.

Congress needs to pass new laws forcing the military to comply with the OSHA regulations that exist to protect all employees and their families. They need to allow veterans and their families to file suit to hold those accountable for their negligence, not protect them from prosecution for the crimes they commit. They need to ensure our veterans and their families get free health care and compensation for life for the birth defects, sickness, disease, and death that service to our nation has bestowed upon us. Not just our veterans, their entire families that were poisoned, just like the DoD, Navy, and CDC have identified since 1999.[2,4,6,18]

In addition:

ALL FEMALES SHOULD BE BANNED FROM MILITARY SERVICE IN ANY ACTIVITY EXPOSING THEM TO WEAPONS AND THIS POISONING!

As the increase in female veteran suicide demonstrates, female veterans, family members, and their unborn children suffer the brunt of this poisoning and will do so for forty years after last exposure. If this doesn't happen, then our leaders are unworthy of our trust and sacrifice.

In conclusion, there needs to be one organization responsible for establishing the standards within all government and policing compliance to ensure our veterans and all other employees "a place of employment which are free from recognized hazards that are causing or are likely to cause death or serious physical harm to his employee."[8]

That organization should consist of the brightest medical minds within the CDC and Department of Health and Human Services. Not the bureaucrats and politicians within the military, OSHA, and VA. As I have shown you here, they have failed, continuing to use standards adopted back in 1978! Research over the past forty-two years now results in the CDC stating;

"There is no known lower threshold limit for lead exposure and harmful health effects."[81]

There should also be one organization that establishes the standards within all government and that polices compliance to ensure our communities and environment are safe. That organization should consist of the best and brightest scientific minds within the Environmental Protection Agency. Again, as I have demonstrated, the military, OSHA, and VA have failed to protect us. All of us!

Don't forget, Congress needs to act to free those organizations to do their jobs, not shackle them by installing enforcement restrictions like the one-liner within good legislation. Remember the TSCA's Section 3, (2), (B), (v)? It bans the EPA from enforcement of any regulations over "shot shells, cartridges and components of shot shells and cartridges." How is that benefiting the health and safety of our nation?

How am I doing?

Recently, my good friend Joker called to inform me that yet another coworker I am acquainted with suffered a heart attack. A retired Navy SEAL I'll call Bryan is employed as a civilian at, once again, Naval Special Warfare Command. We believe Bryan to be 57 years old. Me?

I have now been prescribed medication for congestive heart failure. When the doctor sent me the medication, I looked up the symptoms. The first thing that pops up on the ole internet is transthyretin amyloid cardiomyopathy (ATTR-CM).

One type is hereditary (which I have no family history of) and the other is wild-type associated with aging. This type most commonly affects men over sixty.

What are the symptoms? They include fatigue, pain or numbness in the lower back and legs, bilateral carpal tunnel syndrome, gastrointestinal issues, hip and/or knee replacement, peripheral neuropathy, chest pain, and more. I have suffered all these symptoms and more for years! What drives my VA doctors nuts is that I don't suffer from shortness of breath, swelling in the arms or lower legs, irregular heartbeat, and some of the other symptoms common to those suffering from heart disease. Again, it's not rocket science.

Recognize the lead poisoning symptoms? How about symptoms of dioxin poisoning, chronic long-term stress, pain, or tinnitus? As I have demonstrated, it doesn't matter. They are all the same anyway.

Doctor Thomas Gibson, a retired, forty-year clinical psychologist and former Director of Psychology at multiple well-known hospitals, whom I have been discussing my findings with, asked me one day, "John, have you given any thought to just forgetting all of this and enjoying your retirement and what time you have left?" He said, "You could go fishing, travel with your wife; there is so much more to life than spending all of your time doing this research, working day and night."

I told him:

> "It's a responsibility, Doc. This isn't about me anymore. This is about those who I served with and their families. Those I poisoned. It's about the ones who aren't here anymore because of it.
>
> "It's about the kids coming into the military blind and naïve, believing their superiors care and will take care of them and their families. This is about restoring honor in service to our nation and exposing those who lack and betray it.
>
> "It is about redemption and apologizing to those whom my actions have poisoned during all my years of service—my wife, my children, my good friends. Those who trusted me to bring them home safe and sound in one piece.
>
> "To them I would say, 'I didn't fail you—our leaders and government failed us. I am sorry. I didn't know; they never told me.'"

References

1.   Theodore Roosevelt, *A Book-Lover's Holidays in the Open*, January 1, 1916.

2.   US Army Environmental Center (USAEC) Contract No. GS-10F-0131K, Order No. DAKF11-01-F-0072, https://www3.epa.gov/ttn/chief/ap42/ch15/bgdocs/b15_fp3.pdf.

3.   Occupational Safety and Health Act of 1970.

4.   Esswein, E., Boeniger, M. F., *Preventing the Toxic Hand-Off*, September 2005, https://www.researchgate.net/publication/311667267_Preventing_the_Toxic_Hand_Off.

5.   National Shooting Sports Foundation, *Sport Shooting Participation in the United States in 2014*, http://www.armalot.com/wp-content/uploads/2016/08/NSSF-Sport-Shooting-Participation-Report-1.pdf.

6.   Environmental Protection Agency's AP 42 Chapter 15, https://www3.epa.gov/ttn/chief/ap42/ch15/index.html.

7.   Diez-Silva, M., Dao, M., Han, Lim, C. T., and Suresh, S., *Shape and Biomechanical Characteristics of Human Red Blood Cells in Health and Disease*, May 2010, https://www.ncbi.nlm.nih.gov/pmc/articles/PMC2998922/.

8.   OSHA General Duty Clause 29 U.S.C. § 654, 5(a)1,2.

9.   Clean Air Act of 1971.

10.   Lead-Based Paint Poisoning Prevention Act (LBPPPA) of 1971.

11.   Clean Water Act (CWA) of 1972.

12.   Emergency Planning and Community Right-to-Know Act (EPCRA) of 1986.

13.   EPA, *Particulate Matter (PM) Pollution, Particulate Matter (PM) Basics*, https://www.epa.gov/pm-pollution/particulate-matter-pm-basics.

14.   Toxic Substances Control Act (TSCA) of 1976.

15.   Resource and Recovery Act (RCRA) of 1976.

16.   Presidential Executive Order 12196, https://www.archives.gov/federal-register/codification/executive-order/12196.html.

17.   Anania, T. L., Seta, J. A. NIOSH, *Lead Exposure and Design Consideration for Indoor Firing Ranges*, December 1975, https://www.cdc.gov/niosh/docs/76-130/default.html.

18.   US Marine Corps Department of the Navy Engineering Study, B. L. Jones, *Reducing Lead Contamination and Exposure on Military Firing Ranges through the Practical Application of Ballistic Containment Systems*, Fourth Edition, 1999, http://supertrap.com/ST_Downloads_files/Pb5-stdy.pdf.

19.   Esswein, E., Boeniger, M. F., Ashley, K., *Handwipe Method for Removing Lead from Skin*, 2005, https://www.cdc.gov/niosh/nioshtic-2/20040187.html.

20.   Filon, F. L., Boeniger, M., Maina, G., Adami, G., Spinelli, P., Damian, P., *Skin Absorption of Inorganic Lead (PbO) and the Effect of Skin Cleansers*, 2006, https://pubmed.ncbi.nlm.nih.gov/16832226/.

21.   CDC, NIOSH, *Information for Workers, Health Problems Caused by Lead*, June 18, 2018, https://www.cdc.gov/niosh/topics/lead/health.html.

22.   VA, *Veterans Administration War Related Illness and Injury Study Center*, September 2019, https://www.warrelatedillness.va.gov/education/exposures/lead.asp.

23.   OSHA, "Health Effects of Lead." https://www.osha.gov/SLTC/lead/healtheffects.html.

24.   National Academy of Sciences Department of Defense Contract W81K04-11-D-0017, *Potential Health Risks to DOD Firing-Range Personnel from Recurrent Lead Exposure*, Dec 2012, https://www.nap.edu/read/18249/chapter/1.

25. National Academy of Sciences, University of Washington Research, https://www.washington.edu/research/or/honors-and-awards/national-academy-of-sciences/.

26. National Academy of Sciences Congressional Briefing Department of Defense Contract W81K04-11-D-0017, https://www.nationalacademies.org/OCGA/Briefings/OCGA_150023.

27. NTP, *NTP Monograph on Health Effects of Low-Level Lead*, June 13, 2012, https://ntp.niehs.nih.gov/ntp/ohat/lead/final/leadappendixd_final_508.pdf

28. EPA, *Integrated Science Assessment for Lead*, February 2012, http://cfpub.epa.gov/ncea/isa/recordisplay.cfm?deid=235331.

29. CDC, "Childhood Lead Poisoning Prevention: Pregnant Women." https://www.cdc.gov/nceh/lead/prevention/pregnant.htm.

30. NIOSH, "Lead: Information for Workers—Health Problems Caused by Lead." https://www.cdc.gov/niosh/topics/lead/health.html.

31. VA, *Facts about Suicide among Women Veterans*, August 2017, https://www.mentalhealth.va.gov/docs/VA-Women-Veterans-Fact-Sheet.pdf.

32. Schneyer, J., Januta, A. "Ambushed at Home—Children Poisoned by Lead on U.S. Army Bases as Hazards Go Ignored." Reuters. August 16, 2018. https://www.reuters.com/investigates/special-report/usa-military-housing

33. ATDSR, *Lead Toxicity: What Is the Biological Fate of Lead in the Body?*, June 12, 2017, https://www.atsdr.cdc.gov/csem/csem.asp?csem=34&po=9.

34. Mason, L. H., Harp, J. P., Han, D. Y. "Pb Neurotoxicity: Neuropsychological Effects of Lead Toxicity." *BioMed Research International.* January 2, 2014. https://www.ncbi.nlm.nih.gov/pmc/articles/PMC3909981/.

35. Biology Dictionary. "Autonomic Nervous System." 2019. https://biologydictionary.net/autonomic-nervous-system/.

36. Sanders, T., Liu, Y., Buchner, V., Tchounwou, P. B., *Neurotoxic Effects and Biomarkers of Lead Exposure: A Review*, 2009, https://www.ncbi.nlm.nih.gov/pmc/articles/PMC2858639/.

37. WebMD, *What Is White Matter Disease?*, 2019, https://www.webmd.com/brain/white-matter-disease#1.

38. Strain, J., Didehbani, N., Cullum, C. M., Mansinghani, S., Conover, H., Kraut, M. A., Hart, J. Jr., Womack, K. B., *Depressive Symptoms and White Matter Dysfunction in Retired NFL Players with Concussion History*, July 2, 2013, https://www.ncbi.nlm.nih.gov/pmc/articles/PMC3770203/.

39. Flora, G., Gupta, D., Tiwari, A., *Toxicity of Lead: A Review with Recent Updates*, 2012, https://www.ncbi.nlm.nih.gov/pmc/articles/PMC3485653/.

40. Andrade, V. L., Mateus, M. L., Batoreu, M. C., Aschner, M., Marreilha dos santos, A. P., *Lead, Arsenic and Manganese Metal Mixture Exposures: Focus on Biomarkers of Effect*, 2015, https://www.ncbi.nlm.nih.gov/pmc/articles/PMC4470849/.

41. CDC, NIOSH, *Information for Workers, Health Problems Caused by Lead*, 2018, https://www.cdc.gov/niosh/topics/lead/health.html.

42. EPA, "ACE: Health-Neurodevelopmental Disorders," 2019, https://www.epa.gov/americaschildrenenvironment/ace-health-neurodevelopmental-disorders.

43. NIH, *Lead in Kids' Blood Linked with Behavioral and Emotional Problems*, June 2014, https://www.nih.gov/news-events/news-releases/lead-kids-blood-linked-behavioral-emotional-problems.

44. Marginean, C. O., Melit, L. E., Moldovan, H., Lupu, V. V., Marginean, M. O., *Lead Poisoning in a 16-Year-Old Girl: A Case Report and a Review of the Literature (CARE Compliant)* 2016, https://www.ncbi.nlm.nih.gov/pmc/articles/PMC5044910/.

45. VA, *Traumatic Brain Injury*, https://www.research.va.gov/topics/tbi.cfm.

46. Grady, J., US Naval Institute News, *Panel: Pentagon Facing Future Recruiting Challenge Due to Lack of Candidates*, October 12, 2017, https://news.usni.org/2017/10/12/panel-pentagon-facing-future-recruiting-challenge-due-lack-candidates.

47. NINDS, *Multiple Sclerosis Information Page*, https://www.ninds.nih.gov/Disorders/All-Disorders/Multiple-Sclerosis-Information-Page.

48. NIMH, *Post-Traumatic Stress Disorder: What Is Post-Traumatic Stress Disorder, or PTSD?*, https://www.nimh.nih.gov/health/publications/post-traumatic-stress-disorder-ptsd/index.shtml.

49. Navy OPNAVINST 3500.39 (Series), *Operational Risk Management (ORM)*, https://www.cnic.navy.mil/regions/cnrma/om/safety/operational_risk_management.html.

50. Cabral, S., *The Rain Barrel Effect*," 2018.

51. Birnbaum, L. S., *The Mechanism of Dioxin Toxicity: Relationship to Risk Assessment*, November 1994, https://www.ncbi.nlm.nih.gov/pmc/articles/PMC1566802/.

52. EPA, *Dioxins and Furans*, https://archive.epa.gov/epawaste/hazard/wastemin/web/pdf/dioxfura.pdf.

53. EPA, *Health Assessment Document for 2,3,7,8-Tetrachlorodibenzo-p-Dioxin (TCDD) and Related Compounds*," 1994, https://nepis.epa.gov/Exe/ZyPDF.cgi/300021WU.PDF?Dockey=300021WU.PDF.

54. EPA, *Learn about Dioxin*, https://www.epa.gov/dioxin/learn-about-dioxin.

55. Lorber, M., Gibb, H., Grant, L. D., Pinto, J. P., Pleil, J., Cleverly, D., *Assessment of Inhalation Exposures and Potential Health Risks to the General Population That Resulted from the Collapse of the World Trade Center Towers*, 2007, https://cfpub.epa.gov/si/si_public_record_report.cfm?Lab=NCEA&dirEntryId=127846.

56. US Navy, *What Is Dioxin?*, https://www.med.navy.mil/sites/nmcphc/Documents/environmental-programs/risk-communication/posters/Dioxsml.pdf.

57. VA, *Diseases Related to Agent Orange*, https://www.va.gov/disability/eligibility/hazardous-materials-exposure/agent-orange/related-diseases/.

58. VA, *Gulf War Veterans' Medically Unexplained Illnesses*, https://www.publichealth.va.gov/exposures/gulfwar/medically-unexplained-illness.asp.

59. US Navy, *Navy Guidance for Conducting Human Health Risk Assessments—Dioxin*, 2001, https://www.med.navy.mil/sites/nmcphc/Documents/environmental-programs/risk-assessment/PTC_DIOXINS_IP.pdf.

60. VA, *Burn Pits (Trash and Feces Fires)*, https://www.warrelatedillness.va.gov/education/exposures/burn-pits.asp.

61. Pirkle, J. L., Wolfe, W. H., Patterson, D. G., Needham, L. L., Michalek, J. E., Miner, J. C., Peterson, M. R., Phillips, D. L., *Estimates of the Half-Life of 2,3,7,8-Tetrachlorodibenzo-p-Dioxin in Vietnam Veterans of Operation Ranch Hand*," UT Health San Antonio, 1989, https://scholars.uthscsa.edu/en/publications/estimates-of-the-half-life-of-2378-tetrachlorodibenzo-p-dioxin-in.

62. NIMH, *5 Things You Should Know about Stress*, https://www.nimh.nih.gov/health/publications/stress/index.shtml.

63. NIOSH, *Job Stress*, https://www.cdc.gov/niosh/topics/aircrew/job-stress.html.

64. NIOSH, *Traumatic Incident Stress*, https://www.cdc.gov/niosh/topics/traumaticincident/default.html#stress.

65. NICHD, *Stress System Malfunction Could Lead to Serious, Life-Threatening Disease*, 2002, https://www.nichd.nih.gov/newsroom/releases/stress.

66. NIH, National Heart, Lung, and Blood Institute https://www.nhlbi.nih.gov/health-topics/sleep-apnea.

67. VA, Sleep Apnea Fact Sheet, https://www.veterantraining.va.gov/apps/checkup/resources/documents/fact-sheet-sleep-apnea.pdf

68. Operation Military Kids, Does Sleep Apnea Qualify as a VA Disability? Rob, V., 2 December 2020.

69. VA, M21-1, Part III, Subpart iv, Chapter 4, Section F - Respiratory Conditions Topic 5. Sleep Apnea and Related Disabilities.

70. Sleep Foundation, The Connection Between Sleep Apnea and PTSD, Logan Foley & Dr. Anis Rehman, February 2021.

71. VA, PTSD: National Center for PTSD, Sleep Problems in Veterans with PTSD, Philip German, PhD, https://www.ptsd.va.gov/professional/treat/cooccurring/sleep_problems_vets.asp.

72. VA National Center for PTSD, PTSD Research Quarterly Volume 27/No.4, PTSD and Sleep, Philip Gehrman, PhD; Gerlinde Harb, PhD; Richard Ross, MD PhD.

73. Bray, R. M., Camlin, C. S., Fairbank, J. A., Dunteman, G. H., Wheeless, S. C. "The Effects of Stress on Job Functioning of Military Men and Women." June 2010. https://www.ncbi.nlm.nih.gov/pmc/articles/PMC2883251/.

74. NIMH, *Post-Traumatic Stress Disorder*, https://www.nimh.nih.gov/health/topics/post-traumatic-stress-disorder-ptsd/index.shtml.

75. VA, *PTSD: National Center for PTSD—How Common Is PTSD in Women?*, https://www.ptsd.va.gov/understand/common/common_women.asp.

76. VA, *Facts about Veteran Suicide*, July 2016, https://www.va.gov/opa/publications/factsheets/Suicide_Prevention_FactSheet_New_VA_Stats_070616_1400.pdf.

77. VA, *Facts about Suicide among Women Veterans*, August 2017, https://www.mentalhealth.va.gov/docs/VA-Women-Veterans-Fact-Sheet.pdf.

78. NIOSH, *Workplace Violence Prevention for Nurses*, https://wwwn.cdc.gov/wpvhc/Course.aspx/Slide/Unit2_9.

79. NIOSH, *Stress at Work*, 1999, https://www.cdc.gov/niosh/docs/99-101/default.html.

80. NIOSH, *The Female Reproductive System*, https://www.cdc.gov/niosh/topics/repro/femalereproductivesystem.html.

81. EPA. "Superfund." https://www.cpa.gov/superfund.

82. Wikipedia. "Brio Superfund Site." https://en.wikipedia.org/wiki/Brio_Superfund_site.

83. Texas Parks and Wildlife. "Fish Consumption Bans and Advisories." https://tpwd.texas.gov/regulations/outdoor-annual/fishing/general-rules-regulations/fish-consumption-bans-and-advisories.

84. HUD. "Revised Dust-Lead Action Levels for Risk Assessment and Clearance; Clearance of Porch Floors." Revised. 2017. https://www.hud.gov/sites/documents/LEADDUSTCLEARANCE.PDF.

85. Willmsen, C., Kamb, L., Mayo, J. "Loaded with Lead." *Seattle Times*. October 17, 2014. http://projects.seattletimes.com/2014/loaded-with-lead/1/.

86. *Feres v. United States*, US Supreme Court 340 U.S. 135 (1950)

87. American Heart Association. "What is Transthyretin Amyloid Cardiomyopathy (ATTR-CM)?" https://www.heart.org/-/media/files/health-topics/answers-by-heart/abh_what-is-attrcm_v2_a.pdf?la=en&hash=FD4B12B23CF6CD8BF-3691373CA29B869840A483D.

88. CDC Office of Science. "Combatting the Dangers of Heavy Metal Contamination: The CDC Can Lead the Way!" https://www.cdc.gov/os/technology/techtransfer/successstories/leadwipes.htm.

89. Navy Seal M4 Rifle Images, https://www.bing.com/images/search?q=navy+seal+m4+rifle+wikimedia&form=HDRSC2&-first=1&scenario=ImageBasicHover.

90. "Competition Using Three Guns" Images, https://www.bing.com/images/search?q=competition+using+3+guns&form=HDRSC2&-first=1&scenario=ImageHoverTitle.

91.   ASTM STP1533, *Handwipe Method for Removing Lead from Skin,* *American Society for Testing and Materials,* https://www.astm.org/ DIGITAL_LIBRARY/STP/PAGES/STP49744S.htm.

92.   Fox News, *Retired Navy SEAL Jocko Willink: Why Police Officers* *Need Far More Training,* 23 June 2020, https://www.foxnews.com/ media/jocko-willink-why-police-officers-need-far-more-training.

93.   Associated Press, Fox News, *Ethics Slips Involving Navy Seals, Army* *Green Berets Stem From Combat Culture, Review Finds,* 28 January 2020, https://www.foxnews.com/us/ethics-navy-seals-army-green-berets-combat-culture.

94.   Corey Dickstein, Stars and Stripes, *Trump Rejects Reported $2.2* *Billion In Cuts to Military Health Care That Pentagon Proposed,* August 18, 2020, https://www.stripes.com/news/us/trump-rejects-report-ed-2-2-billion-in-cuts-to-military-health-care-that-pentagon-pro-posed-1.641734.

95.   Leo Shane III, Military Times, This Proposed VA Health Care Change Could Save You Time—And Save VA Billions, March 21, 2019, https://www.militarytimes.com/news/pentagon-con-gress/2019/03/21/va-eyes-saving-billions-by-cutting-back-on-unneeded-medical-exams/.

96.   Lobato, John; Theodore, Jeffrey (May 14, 2006). "Federal Sovereign Immunity." Harvard Law School.

97.   EPA, "What You Need to Know About Lead Poisoning," 2014, https://www.epa.gov/sites/default/files/2014-05/documents/what_you_need_to_know_about_lead_poisoning.pdf.

98.   High speed ballistics photography by Herra Kuulapaa, www.kuu-lapaa.com/home/highspeed.html.

99.   Naval Health Research Center Technical Report 00-48, "A Survey of Self-Reported Injuries Among Special Boat Operators," https://www.ullmandynamics.com/wp-content/uploads/2010/10/US_Navy_HSPC_boat_injuries.pdf.

100. Eagle, Nagai, Morgan, Hendershot, Sell (October 20, 2017), "Naval Special Warfare (NSW) Crewmen Demonstrate Diminished Cervical Strength and Range of Motion Compared to NSW Students," https://pubmed.ncbi.nlm.nih.gov/29036862/.

101. Department of Defense Office of Prepublication Review, reference document 22-SB-0023, February 14, 2022.

Photo Credits

About the Author

John Patrick Lyons was born in Houston, Texas. At the age of fifteen, he took a job at the Port of Houston and later worked in the oilfields of South Texas. In 1985, John enlisted in the United States Navy and became one of the first Navy Special Operations Special Warfare Combatant-Craft Crewmen (Navy SWCC). Chief Lyons went on to become a Navy and Special Operations accredited weapons, ordnance, LASER, and firing range expert and instructor. After retiring from the Navy in 2009, John continued working for the Naval Special Warfare Command, instructing, training, and qualifying West Coast Navy SEALs, SWCCs, and other Special Operations personnel in weapons proficiency and gun and LASER firing range safety.

In 2014, John learned that he had been massively poisoned with lead. After being fired for whistleblowing, he went to work to find out how he'd been poisoned. Suffering from congestive heart failure and other degenerative poisoning symptoms, John continued whistleblowing in an effort to help his fellow veterans, their families, and the nation overcome the disdain shown by the Navy and government toward those they had poisoned.

An avid outdoorsman and conservationist, retired Navy Chief John P. Lyons resides in his home state of Texas with his wife of thirty years, his autistic son, and his loyal dogs Shelby and Diesel.

Parting Shot: Navy SWCC

Earlier this year, you may have heard that the first female Navy SWCC was welcomed into the fold. Reflecting upon her achievement and the dangers I knew she would face got me thinking of yet another cover-up I have known about for some time that needed to be addressed. In the spirit of *Treason and Betrayal*, I did some further digging.

In 2001, while walking through Naval Special Boat Squadron ONE in Coronado, California, I was approached by their Navy SEAL Chief Corpsman. A good guy I have known and worked with off and on for sixteen years, a man I will call Rob, handed me a report and said I should read it.

Rob knew that I had been battling knee and back problems for some time. In fact, he had overseen my recovery from ACL replacements in both knees just two years earlier. I had returned home from yet another deployment in July 1998, had two quick surgeries, and headed out the door again in January 1999 to conduct counter drug ops down South. A normally cheerful, good-natured guy, Rob's tone of voice and the serious look on his face stopped me dead in my tracks. I sat down in his office to read the report.

The investigative report was completed by Naval and Special Operations Command's (Redacted[101]   ). It was conducted to research the effect of the shock and g loads experienced by the crews of high-speed boats Navy SEALs and SWCCs like me served on.

In short, when a boat launches off of a wave at high speed, it can reach heights of twenty feet or more. When the boat lands and hits the water, the boat, its equipment, and its crew experience phenomenal g loads upon impact.

The g load we are concerned with is not just the force of gravity an object experiences at rest on earth. It is the force compounded by the speed at which it impacts the earth from a fall. While reading this book, you and the chair you are sitting on are experiencing 1 g, or 1 times the force of gravity. Jump up and down and you are experiencing around 2 g the moment you hit the ground. The higher you go, the faster you fall, and the more g you experience. Jump off of the roof of your house and land flat footed on the concrete driveway below, and you are experiencing over 20 g. How do I know this?

The (Redacted[101]) report chronicled bringing a NASA physiologist on a one-hour high-speed boat ride. Although I am sure the physiologist had a great time roaring across the waves, the report identified that the NASA equipment strapped to the boat to measure g forces broke. You see, the g loads experienced by the pilots and astronauts the NASA physiologist was accustomed to measuring differ greatly from those we experience on high-speed boats.

Pilots and astronauts experience a gradual onset of gravitational changes as the craft they ride accelerates at a slower rate than the instant deceleration we experience on high-speed boats. While a fighter pilot may experience up to 9 g and an astronaut 3 g, the events they experience are controlled and measured. SWCCs commonly experience these g-load changes without warning in the dark of night.

The report explained that the NASA physiologist then went home, built better equipment, and returned for another boat ride. The results?

The report identified the number and types of g loads SWCCS experience throughout one hour while riding a boat at high speed. Although the information I am reporting here is burned into memory, don't quote me on the exact numbers. During that one-hour boat ride, the crewmembers experienced:

- greater than 200 events over 4 g,
- greater than 65 events over 7 g,
- greater than 24 events over 15 g,
- greater than 8 events over 20 g, and
- greater than 3 events over 23 g.

Get it? A 240 lb. special operator, and the gear we wear, experiencing 1 g at rest exerts 240 lb. on every joint in his/her body. If that person jumps up and down and experiences 2 g, that person's joints and musculoskeletal system experience the jolt of being hit with 480 lb. of force. 10 g? 2400 lb. of force. 20 g? 4800 lb., and so on. Pretty basic and not scientifically correct, I know, but you get the basic idea, right? (Redacted[101]) and the Navy did.

The reason for the serious look on Rob's face as I read the report was revealed in the last paragraph. It stated that "if the Navy chooses to recognize the results of this report, high-speed boat operations must cease until sufficient mitigation of these forces are put in place to reduce the hazard to Navy personnel." What did (Redacted[101]) and the Navy do? They buried it. I cannot find it anywhere.

Rob said, "John, that is your copy. With your injuries, you are going to need it in the future to establish service connection for VA benefits." Because I have been institutionalized to obey orders and maintained a security clearance my entire career, I replied, "Rob, I don't think I am authorized to keep this report. Thanks for thinking of me, but no." If you are reading this and have a copy, send it to me at johnplyons.com. It is time for it to see the light of day.

Years after being poisoned and fired for whistleblowing, while conducting research into the Navy's malfeasance, I spoke with fellow SWCCs who continually identified that the Navy was covering up their injuries as well. To validate those allegations, I found additional Navy investigations were conducted around the same time but failed to identify or address the issues the Navy's (Redacted[101]) had documented in its reports.

The first, Naval Health Research Center Technical Report 00-48, *A Survey of Self-Reported Injuries Among Special Boat Operators,*[99] contains the statement:

> *Report No. 00-48, supported by the Office of Naval Research, Arlington, VA under work unit 62233NMM33P30.6801. The views expressed in this paper are those of the authors and do not*

reflect the official policy or position of the Department of the Navy, the Department of Defense, or the U.S. Government. Approved for public release; distribution unlimited.

The second, *Naval Special Warfare (NSW) Crewmen Demonstrate Diminished Cervical Strength and Range of Motion Compared to NSW Students,[100]* contains the statement:

This study was funded by the Office of Naval Research, grant number #N00014-11-1-0929. The opinions or assertions contained herein are the private views of the authors and are not to be construed as official or reflecting the views of the NSCA, Department of the Navy, Department of Defense, nor the U.S. government.

Missing from these reports is the raw data and direct acknowledgement of the danger we are subjected to that is identified in the (Redacted[101]   ) report mentioned above. Get it?

All three of these reports substantiate the dangers and long-term consequences to Navy SWCC personnel. All were funded and conducted by the Navy. After burying the (Redacted[101]   ) report, the other two were conducted in a manner to relieve the Navy of its responsibility to officially recognize the hazard and accept responsibility for willfully subjecting our veterans to the major debilitating injuries indicated in these reports. Injuries that would affect us and our families for the remainder of our lives. Remember the federal law quoted repeatedly throughout *Treason and Betrayal?* The Occupational Safety and Health Act of 1970 states:

Duties;
(a) Each employer --
(1) 29 USC 654 shall furnish to each of his employees employment and a place of employment which are free from recognized hazards that are causing or are likely to cause death or serious physical harm to his employees.

What do the above reports identify? SWCCs who serve seven years or longer will experience one or more major debilitating injuries. Me? Since first becoming a boat guy (SWCC) in 1994, I have experienced injuries to my feet, ankles, knees, hips, lower back, and neck.

Compressed discs; bone injuries to my lower spine; ACL, knee, and hip replacement surgeries; carpal tunnel and ulnar neuropathy surgeries; bunions; and massive arthritis throughout my body. Twelve surgeries in total, with at least five more in the near future.

Tramadol (synthetic opiates) for pain and baclofen and naproxen for inflammation and muscle spasms taken every day since 2002. Twenty pills a day. I still have a photo of my desk while deployed to the Western Pacific in 1997 and the three 1000 pill bottles of Motrin, Glucosamine, Chondroitin, and Ambien sitting atop it.

How about the white and gray matter changes in my brain that pro football players experience from high g impacts? I know guys who are far worse off than I.

One Navy SWCC I knew had damage so severe in his lower spine that he is now wheelchair bound, wearing a diaper and shitting in a bag hanging alongside it. Bone chips had worked their way into the horse's tail of nerves at the base of his spine. An inoperable area. The Navy kicked him out with a medical discharge in his twenties, after an eight-year career. He and his wife had a newborn, and she was saddled with having to become the breadwinner while wheelchair-bound dad stayed at home changing diapers. As I will explain in my next book, *Conspiracy and Cover-up*, it gets worse.

So why do I disagree with the path taken in general for all SWCCs and SEALs today?

Before the late 1990s, SEALs and SWCCs were required to serve as regular Navy sailors first. After about five years, petty officers were selected from five basic source ratings: weapons, engineering, communications, navigation, and medical. Proficiency and experience in these fields brought experience to the teams. Time in service brought maturity and self-discipline. We also had enough time in the Navy that by the time debilitating injuries occurred, we could reach full retirement and the financial benefits it brought with it.

Today, kids are not afforded the chance for a normal retirement as they are recruited right out of high school. Injuries earlier in a career mean being kicked out without the pay and benefits afforded by a normal career. It gets worse.

Sitting around talking to Joker, Wilson, and other SWCCs and SEALs about today's teams spotlights the lack of experience, maturity, and discipline. SWCCs and SEALs can't maintain and repair their own boats and gear like we had to before. Joker describes today's SWCCs as NASCAR drivers with their own pit crews. A boat breaks on deployment overseas, and a specialist has to be flown in from the states to fix it. Operations cease until repairs are made. Hell, I remember one cold, dark, stormy February night off Alaska.

One of our boat's outdrives had broken in the middle of a mission. Our guys towed the boat to a nearby, remote uninhabited island. My good friend Bossman performed repairs standing in thirty-four-degree water, in the freezing rain and snow, by the light of a small, green flashlight held in his teeth. We then finished the mission.

Gone are the days a two-boat SWCC detachment and SEAL platoon could fly into a country, complete a mission, and leave before it was known that we were there. Today, it requires millions of dollars and a marching band announcing our presence to all. As I will reveal in the next book, that was the plan.

SWCCs experiencing high g loads on missions subject their musculoskeletal system and internal organs to tremendous stresses. Older, experienced SWCCs recount the number of times we have urinated blood after a particularly hairy ride. You won't find experienced SWCCs wearing boxers on high-speed missions. It's briefs or a jock strap. Got to have that support. How bad can it get?

A good friend I was discussing this with recently recounted a mission to San Clemente Island about seventy-five miles off San Diego, California—normally an hour boat ride. The flat-bottomed

Mk V Special Operations Craft^{Photo 1.4} he was riding leapt off of a wave and dropped about twenty feet into the trough.

An SWCC crewmember immediately dropped to the deck, paralyzed from the neck down. The boat was brought to an abrupt halt, the crewmember was stabilized, and the boat returned to San Diego. It took hours traveling at three to four knots, about five miles per hour. They had to go slowly to prevent further injury.

Investigation revealed that he had simply turned to speak to another SWCC when the sudden impact of the g forces he experienced shocked his spine in such a way as to numb everything below the neck. He had to wear a plastic turtle shell to keep his spine straight for about six weeks before a full recovery.

SWCCs have multiple stories like this spanning a career that highlight the dangers of the profession, but our leaders are unconcerned. Why should they be? They cannot be held accountable. Again, I will make the statement:

OUR LEADERS IN THE MILITARY AND GOVERNMENT HAVE BECOME BUREAUCRATS INCAPABLE OF FOLLOWING ORDERS, REGULATIONS, AND THE LAW. THEY ARE UNWORTHY OF THE SACRIFICE THEY DEMAND OF OUR VETERANS.

To my fellow SWCCs I would say, as veterans, we tend to sacrifice the best years of our youth and health in service to our country. Riding fast boats is cool, but the majority of your life will be lived **after** you retire. Read those reports, take care of yourselves, and . . .

God, Country, Fast Boats!

Bull Shark out . . .